International Models of Changemaker Education

International Models of Changemaker Education

Programs, Methods, and Design

Edited by
Viviana Alexandrowicz and Paul M. Rogers

ROWMAN & LITTLEFIELD
Lanham • Boulder • New York • London

Published by Rowman & Littlefield
An imprint of The Rowman & Littlefield Publishing Group, Inc.
4501 Forbes Boulevard, Suite 200, Lanham, Maryland 20706
www.rowman.com

86-90 Paul Street, London EC2A 4NE, United Kingdom

Copyright © 2022 by Viviana Alexandrowicz and Paul M. Rogers

All rights reserved. No part of this book may be reproduced in any form or by any electronic or mechanical means, including information storage and retrieval systems, without written permission from the publisher, except by a reviewer who may quote passages in a review.

British Library Cataloguing in Publication Information Available

Library of Congress Cataloging-in-Publication Data Available

ISBN 9781475861464 (cloth) | ISBN 9781475861471 (pbk.) | ISBN 9781475861488 (epub)

This book is dedicated to the teachers and teacher educators around the world who are working courageously every day to inspire the next generation of changemakers.

Contents

Foreword   ix
Ross Hall

Acknowledgments   xiii

Introduction   xv
Paul Rogers and Viviana Alexandrowicz

1. Empowering Students through Integration of Supports across Sectors   1
   Mary E. Walsh, Amy Heberle, and Kirsten Rene

2. Education as a Force to Unite: The United World Colleges (UWC) Model of Education   21
   Lodewijk van Oord

3. Community Connected Learning: Social Innovation in Education   35
   Laura Hay

4. Practice What You Teach: A Case for Emotionally Intelligent Educators   63
   Amy McConnell Franklin and Kei Franklin

5. Preparing Student-Teachers as Changemakers: The Case of the School of Education Universidad del Desarollo—Chile   97
   Josefina Santa Cruz, Kiomi Matsumoto, Josefina Valdivia, Trinidad Ríos, and Paulina Guzmán

Contents

6 Born to Live: The Transformative Journey of Colombian Youth as Changemakers through Peace Education   107
Catalina Cock Duque and Ariel Safdie

7 Passion Projects: A Case Study of Changemaker Education in Action   123
Kate Dickinson-Villaseñor

8 Innovating across Multiple Dimensions in Education   137
Carmen Pellicer Iborra, Martín Varela Dávila, Rosa López Oliván, Marta Monserrat Salcedo, and Miguel Ignacio Garcia Morell

9 Changemaker Education Is for Everybody: The Sky School Model   149
Polly Akhurst, Stuart MacAlpine, and Mia Eskelund Pedersen

10 A Learner-Centered Approach to Changemaker Education   159
Maria Isabel Valente-Pires and Luiza Nora

11 Design for Change: A Methodology for Young People to Change the World   175
Asma Hussain, Beatriz Alonso, and Elena Bretón

12 The Ecosystemic Pedagogy of Vila Schools: A Brazilian Educational Proposal for Social and Environmental Transformation   189
Patricia Limaverde

13 Educators as Changemakers: A Model for Infusing Social-Emotional Learning during Educational Transitions to Increase Readiness and Address Intergenerational Poverty   203
Seth Sampson, Nancy Lewin, and Paul Rogers

14 Changemaking in Teacher Education: A Journey from Inspiration to Action   223
Viviana Alexandrowicz

Afterword: Schooling and the Development of Changemakers: An Interview with Ashoka Young Changemaker Victor Ye   247
Viviana Alexandrowicz and Paul Rogers

About the Contributors   257

About the Editors   267

Foreword

Ross Hall

United Kingdom

This book is an important source of inspiration and insight for anyone interested in the burgeoning field of changemaker education: a field of educators, policy makers, researchers, and many others who are working to fundamentally transform the purpose and practice of education.

The contributors of this book exemplify the kind of people who are pioneering in the field and their approaches to education, while differing in context and content bring to life many of the core values and principles that define the field.

THRIVING IN A WORLD OF CHANGE, COMPLEXITY, AND CRISIS

Within the field, there is a shared understanding that the world today is defined by increasing volatility and complexity and that humanity and many other species are faced with intensifying existential crises. On one hand, an awareness of the enormous difficulty and suffering in the world propels many people in the field. On the other hand, there is also a driving optimism that we can solve our problems and create a better world for all. Throughout this book, you will sense a deep devotion to justice, equity, peace, love, flourishing, and universal well-being. Aspirations and values are encapsulated within the term "thriving." This is not to say that the field is defined by a utopian ideal but rather by the conviction that we can determine the direction of our evolution and that we can choose to move in the direction of a thriving future.

INTERCONNECTEDNESS

Another core idea that is implicit in changemaker education is that everyone and everything are at some level interconnected. Thriving is a dynamic process that involves the continuous development and well-being of the whole person (physical, psychological, emotional, relational, and spiritual well-being), of the whole societies (social, political, cultural, and economic well-being), and of our entire planet (soil, water, air, other species, and the biosphere).

LEARNING TO THRIVE TOGETHER

A belief in interconnectedness also implies that it is through our every action, from moment to moment, that we determine the extent to which we thrive together. The field of changemaker education recognizes that the future begins now and with each one of us. Young people are respected as active contributors in the world today. Throughout this book, you will hear about young people learning to care, choose, and act for themselves and each other and the planet together. The development of agency is emphasized. So too is awareness: awareness of what is happening in the world; awareness of my influence on the world; and awareness of my potential to make positive change. There is also recognition that to choose and act optimally—to live for universal well-being—a person needs to develop a wide range of knowledge, skills, attitudes, values, and ways of being in the world. Changemaker education usually incorporates the development of what is variously called the twenty-first-century skills, social and emotional skills, prosocial skills, citizenship, character, and so on. Many people working in the field are focused on the development of the whole human being.

THRIVING LEARNING EXPERIENCES

With a focus on developing a wide range of capacities, it is logical that changemaker education usually involves a wide range of learning environments and experiences. The examples included in this book illustrate the kinds of experiences that are often facilitated by practitioners in the field. There is an emphasis on projects that are rooted in the real world. Learning in the community and in nature is common. Projects are often interdisciplinary and explicitly aimed at helping students solve complex problems. Learning is often student-led and peer-supported. Teachers work as guides, mentors, and researchers. Young people are given responsibility early and trusted to make their own decisions. Learners are encouraged to challenge the status quo, to experiment, and fail. Art, play, making, moving, and meditating are often involved. Learning experiences are frequently adapted to the specific learning needs and preferences of the individual student. While some may be concerned that this kind of experience might detract from academic learning, practitioners in the field show that both academic and changemaking skills can be developed simultaneously and even symbiotically.

THRIVING LEARNING ECOSYSTEMS

The provision of such a wide range of learning experiences, inside and outside of school, inevitably and perhaps necessarily involves a wide range of actors. Throughout this book, you will hear an explicit reference to the role of teachers and non-formal educators. But school leaders, administrators, families, community members, culture makers, policy makers, teacher trainers, researchers, funders, and many others are all implicitly involved in the field of changemaker education. To spread practices like those contained within this book, we need new policies, incentives, assessments, technologies, and other systemic mechanisms. We also need to generate and apply evidence that shows what works and what doesn't. And, at the deepest level, we need new mind-sets. We need to shift what we pay attention to. We need to nurture cultures that put changemaking and thriving at the heart of what it means to grow up and be successful. We need to weave ourselves together into thriving learning ecosystems that are defined by trustful relationships, open collaboration, and collective learning.

It's difficult to think of anything more important than helping young people learn to make positive change and to thrive. My hope is that this book will inspire you—whether you are familiar with or new to the field of changemaker education—to reflect deeply, start new conversations, and make the change.

Acknowledgments

VIVIANA ALEXANDROWICZ

I want to express my gratitude to Vipin Thekk of Ashoka for his encouragement and guidance in beginning my journey as a pioneer and changemaking leader. I truly appreciate my colleague Paul Rogers for his mentorship and invaluable collaboration and dedication in editing and writing this book. Many thanks to my colleagues Reyes Quezada for his continuous support on all changemaking projects and Bobbi Hansen for her endless friendship and support. A special thanks to my graduate PhD student, Dianne Torres, who helped formatting the book. Finally, I would like to acknowledge my wonderful spouse Dave Buster who helped to edit my writing and provided loving moments when I needed them the most.

PAUL ROGERS

My thanks to Ross Hall for his friendship and pioneering leadership in transforming educational systems around the world; to my friends and colleagues Reyes Quezada, James O'Meara, Greg Van Kirk, John Gasko, and the inimitable Bill Drayton for their encouragement and partnership over the years in understanding the role schools of education play in transforming education; to Viviana for her persistence in bringing this project to fruition. Finally, a very special thank you to my incredible life partner Karyn Kessler whose love and support make all the difference.

Introduction

Paul Rogers and Viviana Alexandrowicz

CHANGEMAKER EDUCATION: REFRAMING LEARNING AND TEACHING FOR A WORLD OF CHANGE

All around us we see evidence that we are living in a world of accelerating change, volatility, and hyperconnectivity. The magnitude and reach of these shifts have brought humanity to an unprecedented moment in history, as changes in patterns of urbanization, technological innovation, demographics, and global connectivity bump into each other, triggering even more change across our social and environmental systems. We live in an age of transformation with no end in sight.

For educators, in particular, the implications of these changes are vast and give rise to a number of critical questions. What knowledge, skills, and competencies are most important for young people to learn now and in the future? In what ways and to what degree do teachers and others responsible for curriculum, assessment, and educational policy need to adapt their work to account for a world of rapid, exponential, and constant change? How do we design educational programs and experiences that increase access, success, and mobility for the neediest among us?

Pioneering educators in many countries are responding to these changes by curating learning experiences that support the empowerment of young people to thrive in this new world—and to create a better world for all. A person who is empowered in this way is what we call a *changemaker*—an empathetic person who has the will and the skill to take action, to lead, and to collaborate with others to solve real-world problems in their own lives, in their communities, and across the globe. A changemaker lives for a better world.

The educators who are advancing such empowering learning experiences are pioneering innovative approaches that break radically from the classic industrial model of education. While these approaches do not always employ the same language or methods, what they do share is a recognition that, collectively, we need to redefine the experience of education and the very notion of success for young people growing up in the modern world.

The editors of this volume believe that the time is ripe to bring together voices from around the world who are responding to the challenge of removing the barriers that exist to every young person becoming a changemaker. To this end, we sought to bring forward a group of practitioner-based case studies that highlight the *why*, *what*, and *how* of changemaker education.

CHANGEMAKER EDUCATION: WHAT IT IS AND WHAT IT'S NOT?

Changemaker education is a reality-based approach to learning, teaching, and human development. It is reality-based in that it is a response to our collective awareness of the rapidity, constancy, and ubiquitous nature of change across virtually every social and environmental system on earth. Thus, while changemaker education is framed around a set of values, including empathy, inclusion, equity, and social and environmental justice, at its core, changemaker education is extremely pragmatic. In other words, if we as a species do not adapt our educational systems to prepare the next generation to be the creative and complex problem solvers the world needs, we will be failing our children and potentially dooming our planet and humanity's long-term chances for survival. There exists an imperative around changemaker education that goes beyond transmitting the values of love and respect, even though these core values are deep in the DNA of changemakers.

These words are not meant to be alarmist, but we should be alarmed. Today, millions of children do not have access to basic education, let alone *changemaker education.* These basic issues of equity (as outlined in the United Nations' Sustainable Development Goal #4 whose stated mission is to "Ensure inclusive and equitable quality education and promote lifelong learning opportunities for all") must become the concern of everyone involved in education from classroom teachers, to educational researchers, to policy makers, and to curriculum designers. We simply cannot afford to waste the creativity and spirit of millions of young people around the world, especially young girls.

In addition to dealing with basic issues of educational equity, we also must address the issues of outdated teacher preparation practices, the lack of diversity in the teaching profession, especially a lack of BIPOC teachers, and the global teacher shortage. Although the teacher shortage is different in different regions and countries, the status of the teaching profession and teachers as professionals must also rise to the surface of mainstream educational conversations and stay visible until real change occurs.

The basic equation of education is the simple triangle of a learner, a teacher, and a curriculum. In the case of changemaker education, what we know is that changemaking is not simply a curriculum. A disempowered teacher struggling to find her own voice is not in a position to transmit what it truly means to be a changemaker. Teachers too are on a changemaker journey. In this sense, changemaking is better caught than taught and indeed can be done so regardless of whether a teacher is teaching math, science, language arts, or physical education. Teaching is the mother of all professions and elevating the teaching profession is a critical lever to moving forward with a vision of every young person realizing their own power as a changemaker.

Of course, the curriculum is also an important factor, but given the explosion in knowledge across content areas, fields, and disciplines, the larger challenge is finding a way to keep the curriculum relevant when the future is a moving target. Creating textbooks, tests, and assignments is easy in comparison with creating transformational educational experiences that launch someone on the path to be a changemaker for life. In this regard, involving community members and leaders in the process of education is essential, as role models matter, especially when they arise from within the local context that children and families relate to and understand. The main point here regarding curriculum is that beyond the content and subject matter knowledge (which is rapidly changing), we need a sustainable process, a collaborative and co-creative model of learning, teaching, and knowledge creation where each member of the learning ecosystem sees themselves as a learner and comes to recognize that we need everyone to be a contributor to creating knowledge, solving problems, and moving the world toward a more just and sane future. We're in this together.

There are many bright spots on the curricular landscape that are providing outstanding support for models of changemaker education. These include the widespread adoption of social-emotional learning, project-based learning, environmental and nature-based learning programs, and pedagogical movements like the universal design for learning. These movements have made their way into the mainstream of education and are clearly a part of a shift toward more holistic views of learning and teaching. But, we believe more is needed.

Specifically, what is needed is the call to take action. Indeed, in our view, the most distinctive element of changemaker education is cultivating a bias toward taking action. It's not enough to be well or be emotionally self-regulated or to have grit and resilience. It's not enough to know how to solve problems or to collaborate on a team. It's not enough to understand biodiversity and ecosystem services. What we need is for people to give themselves the permission to tackle really big problems and to find ways to collaborate and lead in service of a better world.

Our goal in this volume is to present to educators (at all levels and from around the globe) a series of high-quality, data-informed, experience-based, practical pedagogical models that can be adopted, adapted, and scaled in other contexts around the world. This volume is not exhaustive in any way, but it is designed to point toward the trend of powerful, innovative, and impactful educational models that share a common endpoint: the opportunity for each person to step into their power as a changemaker.

This book includes the work and voices of colleagues around the globe who are making an impact on the education of children, youth, teachers, administrators, families, and communities. Each chapter presents inspiring stories of changemakers acting to improve the ecosystems, the culture, the mind-sets, the curriculum, and the leadership of their organizations and the communities they serve. In their own unique ways, all of the models described in this publication improve young people's lives and educational opportunities in order to inspire them to change *their* world.

Synopsis of the Chapters

Chapter 1 by Mary E. Walsh, Amy Heberle, and Kirsten Rene at Boston College's Lynch School of Education presents their intervention program focused on addressing students' basic (i.e., nonacademic) needs outside school. This systemic, structured, tailored, and replicable approach supports children in high-poverty, urban schools in reducing educational inequities. City Connects currently serves 30,000 students and focuses on tailoring an individual plan for individual students through identifying their strengths and needs in social-emotional, physical health, family, and academic domains.

The model allows students to access a customized set of services through collaboration with families, teachers, school staff, and community agencies. Through poignant student vignettes, the authors illustrate the project's research findings that point to the intervention's significant impact on achievement and other critical areas of students' lives. Research findings show that students in this program outperform comparison peers on measures of academic achievement. In addition, in City Connects elementary schools, students achieve significantly higher report card scores in reading, writing, and math than students in non-City Connects schools by the end of fifth grade. This impact endures through Grade 12, long after students have left an intervention school. This chapter provides key insights into how educators and communities work as a team to change systems for the benefit of high-risk student groups, including first-generation immigrants.

Chapter 2 features the United World Colleges (UWC) model by Lodewijk van Oord from UWC Maastricht. This chapter provides the historical roots, guiding principles, and philosophies for UWC's global education movement. One goal that permeates UWC's work is realizing their mission "of making education a force that unites people, nations, and cultures for peace and a sustainable future." This model presents a deliberate, diverse, engaged, and motivated community in pursuit of the UWC mission. Students selected for these colleges and pre-Kindergarten schools come from various ethnic, religious, and social backgrounds. van Oord describes a model where students represent the "crew, not passengers" as active participants in the experiential pedagogical approaches used.

Schools that follow this model incorporate approaches such as ongoing community service, outdoor education, project-based learning, and discussions of international affairs. One theory that grounds this model is Allport's contact hypothesis, which stresses the importance of high acquaintance for students to coexist, share, live, and learn together. This theory leads to "getting to know others in profound and meaningful ways" and explains what resources are needed, as well as the challenges, the lessons learned, and the contexts in which the model works best. This chapter presents a compelling example of why educators should consider the nature of the contexts where students live and learn, and the type of real-world experiences they want and need. It reminds educators that educational models must be adaptable to be effective in different parts of the world.

Chapter 3 introduces a qualitative case study by Laura Hay on the Native American Community Academy (NACA) based in New Mexico. This study explores how NACA has helped their students succeed by providing a curriculum and instructional framework that includes: (a) a commitment to community and service that focuses on providing extracurricular programs and internships, (b) a wellness philosophy that offers student support services such as free, high-quality mental health services and which supports families with healthcare, nutrition, and social services on the school site, (c) an integrated curriculum that promotes a culturally and community-based education and rigorous college preparation, and (d) a culture and language context that uses native literature, language, and culture for college preparation and specific coursework that includes storytelling, oral traditions, cultural history, and community presentation.

Hay's study reveals a collective process of reimagining education, aligning practices to community values, and the importance of a schoolwide support system approach to serving students, families, and teachers. The

NACA model shows the importance of incorporating what Hay calls "relational components of culture" that focus on positive relationships, integrated social-emotional learning, restorative justice, belonging and agency, and an enabling physical and symbolic environment. This chapter demonstrates that unlike traditional school systems, which often frame Native American youth in terms of deficits, NACA frames young people in terms of their strengths, as assets to their community, and as the next generation of leaders.

Chapter 4 by Amy and Kei Franklin presents a case for developing emotionally intelligent (EI) educators who are able to guide their students effectively in the development of socio-emotional skills. The authors showcase models for EI training in two schools. They argue that the most effective and efficient way to develop socio-emotional skills in students in order to help them "become effective and ethical changemakers" is to surround them with teachers who embody these attributes and skills. Goals for adult training include the development of EI concepts, skills, and shared language with the teachers, individually and collectively, so they can model and instruct these skills in the classroom.

One school initiative describes intensive coaching of introspection. This initiative promotes the development of instruction that incorporates themes of equity, empathy, inclusion, justice, respect for diverse perspectives and needs, collaborative problem solving, self-awareness, and choice. The second school initiative focuses on how social and emotional skills can be mobilized to engage complex topics with skillful respect, compassion, courage, transparency, and impact on student engagement. This chapter demonstrates how teachers may be prepared to address and facilitate dialogues about issues like racism, marginalization, and sexual identity. The author's transparent description of challenges and successes invites reflection about the feasibility of engaging teachers and students in creating classroom pedagogy and structures that nurture empathy, curiosity, agency, respect, and ethical principles as key qualities for the development of changemaker citizens.

Chapter 5 by Santa Cruz et al. spotlights the University of El Desarrollo's (UDD) teacher education program, an Ashoka Changemaker-designated university in Chile committed to social responsibility and entrepreneurship. In their chapter, they describe a program that offers teacher candidates innovative, nontraditional courses designed to prepare them in "Personal Leadership and Teamwork" and "Forming Citizens for the Twenty-First Century." The authors focus on one of seven internship options consisting of workshops and field experiences geared to prepare early childhood teacher candidates. In the internship, candidates apply design thinking to identify problematic issues at a care center and develop solutions to benefit the children they serve. Example implementation projects include renovating the playground and creating a mobile library that serves children in the community.

The chapter presents data obtained from student reflection papers on the takeaways from the experiences. Findings suggest teacher candidates involved in the internship saw themselves as changemakers. They also showed high levels of incorporation of changemaking values and abilities, including collaborative and empathetic skills, in their practices. A key challenge identified was excluding the educational communities from the changemaking process facilitated by the teacher education program, for example, not inviting the feedback of the care centers' teachers in addressing the teachers' needs. This chapter stresses the importance of two-way community engagement and the value of working in non-school settings as part of teacher training.

Chapter 6 by Catalina Cock Duque and Ariel Safdie from Fundacion Mi Sangre tells the story of the organizations' work with Colombian youth for peacebuilding. For these youth, hope is scarce. They have grown up in a country and communities devastated by guerrilla violence and organized crime rings. The authors present the PAZALOBIEN, which is an educational model that seeks to strengthen young people's curiosity and life skills through art, play, and social entrepreneurship. The intent is to form "changemakers or peacebuilders, free and responsible human beings, capable of living at peace with themselves and their environment, conscientious of their rights." The educational initiative has developed tools that support the youth's development of hope by (a) strengthening and weaving together protective ecosystems of parents, decision makers, and community leaders and (b) developing the youth's twenty-first-century skills, such as self-awareness, positive relationships, the capacity to make healthy decisions, and the ability to transform ideas into concrete actions.

The PAZALOBIEN approach uses simple tools to shift the balance of power between educators and participants. The model is based on three pillars: (a) breaking rigid vertical education structures, (b) flexibility to adapt curricular activities depending on the context, age, and groups to support children's learning by doing, and (c) incorporating socio-emotional support such as educators connecting with and listening to students. This chapter reinforces the importance of establishing human connections as essential to supporting youth. It stresses the importance of helping the development of young leaders who inspire and empower each other through shared lived experiences for the greater good.

Chapter 7 by Kate Dickinson-Villaseñor dives into the heart of changemaking education in action by describing students' engagement in passion projects. These projects promote student-led extended inquiry experiences of their choosing that use students' passion to teach and inspire others through celebration and sharing. This pedagogy promotes academic skills, research, literacy, numeracy, scientific and social inquiry, writing, speaking, and visual and performing arts. Dickinson-Villaseñor presents ideas for the process of motivating students to select topics they deeply care about. She depicts a variety of societal issues students have focused on over the years such as being biracial, service animals, transgender rights, and lighthearted issues, especially in the early grades, such as cooking and magic. She also provides ideas for products including fundraising, murals, and campaigns, resulting from engaging in empathy, teamwork, problem solving, and leadership.

Passion projects honor children as the owners of knowledge, experience, and wonder and offer children an opportunity to lead. The chapter includes templates for developing passion projects and suggestions for connecting with families and community partners. Dickinson-Villaseñor provides insights on challenges, such as measuring learning growth, and stresses that teachers must take a developmental approach to help students become changemakers. This approach means letting students take ownership in choosing and tackling problems they deeply care about and allowing them to grow into addressing larger societal issues.

Chapter 8 by Carmen Pellicer et al. provides a close look at their Fundacion Trilema's educational model based on Rubik's approach to instruction. The school model simultaneously integrates six fundamental areas for effective instruction: curriculum, methodology, assessment, organization, leadership, and personalization. The authors compare the implementation of these areas to a Rubik's cube where all the sides must be moved in a systematic way to achieve the greatest impact on students' transformation. One important aspect that characterizes Trilema schools is their use of "vertical projects" that students develop across the different grade levels. These projects provide opportunities for in-depth learning that fosters curiosity and creative thinking.

Trilema's distinctive instructional approach uses a "four drawers" metaphor that includes four fundamental questions guiding planning and instruction that must ask themselves: (a) What actions do I need to take to encourage students to actively collaborate and interact with each other around course content? (b) What activities will best encourage students to think? (c) What should I do in order for students to show what they know and what they have been learning? and (d) What should I do to maintain ethical tension, to help them be better people and changemakers? Trilema schools prioritize self-assessment and metacognition, integrate them throughout the learning process, and allow for a more personalized and continuous follow-up of students' academic and social progress. This chapter helps explain how collaboration, real-world experiences, and engagement with local community networks "bring the real world into the classroom and the classroom into the real world in order to prepare students for the future real-life situations that they will face."

Chapter 9 by Polly Akhurst et al. tells the story of the Sky School (now Amala School), an organization working with refugee youth in seven countries to provide them with access to quality secondary education. The model addresses critical areas, including social innovation, peacebuilding, people and societies, literacies, arts and cultures, STEM, and innovation. The programs can be accessed in person and online. Part of the programming is designed to meet the needs of students to acquire technology skills, communicate with others outside the classroom, and conduct research on the internet. Akhurst et al. present ideas for partnership with community organizations in low resource environments located in the contexts where refugee youth live. A critical element of the Sky programs is the capacity-building aspect where community members, former refugees, and alumni become facilitators. The authors cite examples of impact, including a youth becoming an entrepreneur and peace builder in Kenya and a community president in Greece. They share the concept of a "context proof" curriculum that can be used with refugee youth groups worldwide. Sky School is a replicable model that offers displaced youth an opportunity for a high-school diploma and helps develop transformative competencies including: learning to create new value, taking responsibility, and managing complexity. Akhurst explains how, after experiencing the approaches used by the Sky School, students can "develop as active, responsible, and compassionate problem solvers and innovators who are able to embrace uncertainty and complexity" in our present world.

Chapter 10 by Maria Isabel Valente-Pires and Luiza Nora focuses on a learner-centered approach to changemaking education with their VOAR model (from the Portuguese language meaning "attachment," "daring/entrepreneurship," "autonomy," and "responsibility"). In this model, educators create environments where students develop autonomy, responsibility, initiative, critical spirit, and ownership to understand the impact of their actions in their communities. To accomplish this goal, the school promotes "attachments" via a tutoring system that provides small group and individual support to help children develop their personalities and academic life. Educational approaches incorporate a collaborative project-based methodology that centers around "doing projects" instead of "studying" topics.

In addition, the authors describe their "teaching is researching" philosophy for engaging students as assets in the learning process. This approach uses three levels of knowledge: (a) what is already known, (b) what people want to know, and (c) structuring knowledge. At the first level, students identify what they already know about a topic and what they don't know. The second level triggers planning, researching, setting up, and presenting a product. The third level confirms the acquired knowledge, presented in a variety of ways. In addition to enriching the students' academic lives, this model helps develop conscious citizens. By using students' councils and school assemblies, "children and teenagers can debate about their needs and problems, make important decisions, regulate the school's life and make respected and supported intervention initiatives," such as solving pollution or addressing the needs of people experiencing homelessness. This chapter validates the fact that through pedagogical models such as VOAR, schools are able to contribute to the development of free and strong personalities in youth, capable of connecting with others and keeping a positive outlook in life.

Chapter 11 by Asma Hussain, Beatriz Alonso, and Elena Bretón presents the methodology and process of the Design for Change (DFC), an organization that engages children and youth in developing changemaking projects. The chapter introduces the DFC's Feel, Imagine, Do, and Share (FIDS) step-by-step framework that has impacted 2 million children and youth across 65 countries. Children use this simple design thinking model to plan and "act on the problems and challenges they face through a lens of empathy, driving them to be active citizens of society." According to the young changemakers interviewed for the chapter, they have felt empowered by this method that facilitates collaboration, brainstorming ideas, and moving from self-doubt to implementing change in the community.

The authors present educational impact evidence that includes being an inclusive initiative with high participation of rural and urban schools and equal numbers of girls and boys, addressing problems such as alcoholism and disability. Studies in partnership with Harvard and consulting firms have helped DFC collect data on their initiatives and results have shown that children improve their twenty-first-century skills: creativity, motivation, confidence, social consciousness, divergent thinking, planning, and collaboration. The DFC's methodology helps change the mind-set of educators and families that children are not too young or helpless to solve the small and big problems they face as individuals, families, or communities. This chapter confirms that by giving students the responsibility of taking action and by helping guide their transformation process in a structured way, children will rise to the occasion and show adults they can change the world.

Chapter 12 by Patricia Limaverde gives insights into an ecosystemic pedagogy utilized by a Brazilian school for environmental education. The author explains how the nontraditional Vila School offers a space where children learn through coexistence, establish their own goals, and carry out projects such as cultivating plants, building toys out of junk, or holding socio-environmental campaigns. The author describes a pedagogy that organizes content in three interconnected axes: (a) a curricular web of incorporated lessons, discussions, homework, and art projects that promote the relationship of caring for oneself, caring for the environment, and caring for nature; (b) group organization that leads to promoting key "living" skills such as collaboration, appreciation for diverse opinions, and conflict mediation; and (c) learning scenarios in the form of eight "laboratories" to research and learn. The labs include learning how to coexist with fauna, studying an orchard and fruits, and using technology for sustainability purposes. Other learning scenarios that prepare students for a real life include workshops on the visual arts for concrete expression and theater to represent unlived experiences. This chapter stresses how student development must be addressed in a comprehensive way and beyond the traditional curriculum to build a better, more supportive, humane world—a world open to coexistence in diversity.

Chapter 13 by Seth Sampson, Nancy Lewin, and Paul Rogers tells the story of a collaborative project in Laredo, Texas, focused on addressing intergenerational poverty and preparing the next generation of teachers. Based on interviews and participant observation, this chapter shares the work of a wide range of stakeholders and centers who are committed to integrating community-based (and other) resources in ways that amplify and reinforce the local knowledge and wisdom (known as the dichos) and that establish culturally responsive pathways supporting the long-term development of youth in Laredo.

The chapter includes the voices and experiences of young teacher candidates and the "tripwires" or barriers they have had to overcome in order to pursue their dreams of becoming teachers and presents a model of sophisticated collaboration that is focused on solving concrete problems and supporting students and families in the community in culturally responsive ways that lead to greater social mobility. The book also provides details of the practical contributions from local, state, and national organizations which are working together to provide young people in Laredo greater avenues of access, a powerful sense of belonging, and ultimately the tools required to succeed as changemaker educators.

Chapter 14 by Viviana Alexandrowicz at the University of San Diego describes the process followed by a teacher education department in its journey to integrate changemaking (CM) into its teacher preparation programs. The author defines and explains CM in the K-12 educational context and its relationship to preparing teachers who can implement CM pedagogy in their classrooms. The chapter reviews educational theories that support CM in education and shows the alignment of the CM principles to the California Teaching Performance Expectations (TPEs) for teacher preparation.

The author presents seven steps taken for the integration of CM into the philosophy and practice of the learning and teaching department. The steps include (1) engaging faculty in introspection, (2) expanding knowledge about CM, (3) sharing resources, (4) connecting theory and practice, (5) aligning to teacher performance expectation and integrating into coursework, (6) developing a changemaker school partnership, and (7) assessing the impact. Alexandrowicz presents highlights of research findings based on students' perceptions of their preparation in becoming changemaker educators. Outcomes presented for the initiative include identifying CM as one of the department's core values and developing a CM center for K-12 education. This chapter reminds readers of the critical role teacher education plays in preparing educators who can effectively facilitate their students' acquisition of twenty-first-century skills for a world that continuously changes and for one that does not yet exist.

The afterword presents a Young Changemaker's views on how young people can be supported by the educational ecosystems of which they are a part, including teachers, adult mentors, and peers. Victor provides suggestions for adults and youth about how to be resilient and persevere as a change maker. The chapter provides readers with ideas on how they can encourage and guide students' development as conscious citizens who are intentional in noticing what is going around them and learning how to take action.

Chapter 1

Empowering Students through Integration of Supports across Sectors

Mary E. Walsh, Amy Heberle, and Kirsten Rene

United States

In high-poverty urban school districts across America, many children face challenges outside of school that present persistent impediments to their academic success and other life goals. Low-income students have lower grades, are at significantly greater risk of dropping out of school, and are significantly less likely to attend college than higher-income students (Janosz et al., 1997; NCES, 2017, 2018; Reardon, 2011). Schools cannot close the sizable income achievement gap without a systematic approach to addressing out-of-school factors (Bryk et al., 2010; Rothstein, 2004; Walsh & Murphy, 2003).

Inequities in educational outcomes are important to address for a number of reasons but particularly because they result in the disempowerment of young people living in poverty, thereby continuing socioeconomic disadvantage. In this chapter, we report on an intervention for high-poverty urban schools that aim to disrupt the cycle of poor educational outcomes and enhance opportunities for academic and life success. The City Connects intervention aims to meet students' in- and out-of-school needs and support their strengths across multiple developmental domains. It utilizes a systemic approach to leveraging for each student a customized set of services and resources available in their schools and/or communities.

The importance of addressing nonacademic challenges in schools has long been recognized by educators. Starting in the early twentieth century, public schools in the United States have increasingly sought to support students' nonacademic needs through the work of school counselors, nurses, social workers, and psychologists, as well as through federally funded free- and reduced-price lunch programs (Tyack, 1992; Walsh & Murphy, 2003). Schools have built a core function called "student support" aimed at addressing these nonacademic challenges. However, these student support efforts have had limited impact because they typically operate on the margins, often in nonsystemic and uncoordinated ways.

This chapter describes the City Connects intervention, an approach to the practice of student support that guides the implementation of systemic, structured, tailored student support in high-poverty, urban schools. City Connects began in one school in Boston in 2001, and it is currently operating in nearly 100 schools in 5 states. City Connects is premised on the insight that, in order for schools to work against the continuation of educational inequality, student support must be a codified and core function that permeates all the work of a school. Further, the City Connects practice emphasizes tailoring supports, that is, identifying each student's strengths and needs in academic, social-emotional, physical health, and family domains, and leveraging a set of community-based services and enrichment opportunities that are aligned with the student's particular strengths and needs. City Connects is a whole school, whole child approach—every child in a school is assessed, and every child in a school gets a student support plan. We consider each of these aspects of the model to be essential to its success.

The City Connects intervention is a good match for the present-day policy and economic context in the United States. In contrast to other developed countries, public investments in US children (e.g., food, housing, and medical supports) are not sufficient to close the family resource gap between low-income and higher-income families. Federal and state governments do not provide all of the diverse services that would be necessary to create an equal opportunity for all children through addressing risk and supporting strengths. They do, however, provide incentives for individuals and community agencies to make the efforts to do so themselves—for example, in the form of tax relief for nonprofit agencies. As noted by Carter and Reardon (2014), much research has been conducted on the consequences of inequality, but less has focused on determining what can be done to reduce inequality. An intervention that can take advantage of existing resources, such as agency resources in the community and student support structures already present in schools, has a practical advantage in the battle against educational inequality.

We begin this chapter by describing the theory that underlies City Connects. We next describe the details of the practice and share the history of its implementation across districts and states. We close with recommendations for others engaged in this work and reflections on the challenges of implementing the model.

SECTION 1—THEORY

The City Connects approach involves empowering children and educators in order to reduce socioeconomic inequality by promoting educational equity.

This approach draws on two overlapping areas of theory: the nature of poverty's effects on children and their families, neighborhoods, and schools, and child development more broadly. Three key insights from these areas of theory guide the City Connects practice. The first is that development is malleable, that is, it is possible to disrupt the mechanisms by which socioeconomic inequality leads to educational inequality. Developmental outcomes can be altered by bolstering protective factors—both internal to the individual child and external in the family, neighborhood, or school—and mitigating risk factors. The second is that any intervention that aims to reduce poverty and promote educational equity must take into account the complexity of developmental context and systems and therefore must be individualized, adaptable over time, and designed with intentionality to customize responses to both strengths and risks. The third is that the school setting is a system in which it is uniquely possible to both bolster sources of resilience and diminish threats to educational equality that stem from socioeconomic inequality.

Effects of Poverty

Beginning in the 1960s with the Coleman Report, there has been increasing recognition that life outside of school has considerable consequences for achievement in school (Coleman et al., 1966; Dearing, 2008; Harrington, 1962). As the income gap between high- and low-income families has widened, so has the achievement gap among children from these families (Reardon, 2011). Research indicates that poverty impacts child development in many ways that, in turn, affect achievement. Poverty exerts its developmental sequelae on and through various domains in a child's life, including the family's access to resources, the child's health status, academic outcomes, and socio-emotional well-being. The most proximal context through which a child may be affected by poverty is the family. While families living in poverty have been demonstrated to manifest significant strengths (Compton-Lilly, 2000; Grady et al., 2010; McCubbin & McCubbin, 1996; Orthner et al., 2004), poverty can limit a family's ability to invest money, time, and energy in fostering children's growth. The investment perspective posits that income allows families to purchase materials, experiences, and services to invest in their children, including books, educational outings to museums, and tutoring (Garrett et al., 1994). This theory suggests that in families with fewer financial resources, children's academic achievement will suffer because they will not have the same access to resources as children from more financially advantaged families (Yeung et al., 2002). The manifestations of childhood poverty include limited access to health insurance, food insecurity, parent under-employment, and inadequate access to (and quality of) child care (Coley & Baker, 2013). All of these limitations restrict the resources a family can provide to support education.

Another theoretical approach, the family process perspective, holds that poverty has harmful associations with child development because of associated challenges such as parent's state of depression and stress and a lower quality of parent-child interactions (Conger et al., 1994). Through these mechanisms, the disadvantage associated with poverty can limit children's readiness for school, cognitive functioning, and social-emotional growth (Dearing, 2008; Rothstein 2004; Yoshikawa et al., 2012). These challenges are growing even more significant as economic disparity and child poverty rates in the United States are rising (Bertelsmann Foundation, 2011; Blow, 2011; Kahn & Martin, 2011; Noah, 2012).

Neighborhoods are another important context of child development. They have the potential to be both a source of risk and a source of support and resources. Indeed, studies have found negative associations between the neighborhood poverty level and academic achievement (for a review, see Leventhal & Brooks-Gunn, 2000). When examining the mechanisms through which neighborhoods affect development, researchers have posited three main avenues: institutional resources, relationships (both peer and adult), and norms/collective efficacy (Leventhal & Brooks-Gunn, 2000). Empirical work has supported the theory that lower-SES neighborhoods are generally associated with negative effects on academic achievement and noncognitive skills such as behavior regulation. For example, neighborhood socioeconomic distress is associated with higher rates of school dropout (Crowder & South, 2003). In contrast, increased neighborhood social capital and higher-quality physical conditions have been associated with higher math and reading achievement (Woolley et al., 2008).

Health is another factor that may mediate the relationship between poverty and child outcomes. For instance, children from impoverished families tend to have lower birth weights and compromised health status compared to children from more affluent families (Brooks-Gunn & Duncan, 1997). Many studies have shown that children growing up poor have a higher risk of malnutrition, higher rates of illnesses such as influenza, meningitis, and lead poisoning, and an increased likelihood of experiencing vision and hearing difficulties (Guo & Harris, 2000). Child health is also correlated with a higher frequency of school absences and poorer achievement (Crosnoe, 2006; Jackson et al., 2011).

Beyond the home, school is the place where children spend most of their time. Consequently, characteristics of the school context are important to consider when approaching child development from a systems perspective. Because public schools are funded by property taxes in the United States, there is an inherent inequality in the structure of schools; the children living in the most impoverished neighborhoods generally attend the poorest schools. Some of the potential negative impacts of poverty on families—such as limited resources and chronic stressors—can affect participation in school through poor attendance, social-emotional challenges that impede the ability to engage in the classroom, and a lack of school readiness (Dearing, 2008; McLoyd, 1998). High-poverty urban schools often serve large populations of students who experience residential mobility (Alexander et al., 1996; Gruman et al., 2008; Heinlein & Shinn, 2000; Rumberger, 2003) as well as linguistically diverse students (Genesee et al., 2005)—both groups that are at particularly high risk of a disempowering school experience due to lack of resources and skills to meet their needs. Research also indicates that high-poverty schools are often staffed by school personnel with lower qualifications and experience (Clotfelter et al., 2006; Lankford et al., 2002), placing students in these schools at a further disadvantage.

Considering the Whole Child: A Systems Perspective

Poverty can influence multiple domains of a child's development, including family functioning, health, and academic and socio-emotional outcomes. Classic developmental systems theories posit that child development is the result of the interactions between the various contexts in which the child lives, including the school, home, and neighborhood. This theoretical position emphasizes the importance of looking at the whole child and the various contexts that may contribute to his or her development when designing interventions.

Bronfenbrenner's bioecological model (Bronfenbrenner, 1994; Bronfenbrenner & Morris, 1998) is a classic systems theory proposing that development takes place through interactions between the child and the people or objects in his or her most proximal contexts. According to this theory, the child lives at the center of a number of interrelated contexts, each with unique characteristics that influence the child's developmental trajectory. This means that the characteristics of the home, school, and community will have direct and indirect effects on child outcomes.

Developmental-relational systems theory (Ford & Lerner, 1992; Lerner, 1995) was developed out of the bioecological model and also considers children to be embedded in a reciprocal relationship with their environment. This theory assumes that development occurs simultaneously across multiple levels of the individual, including physical (e.g., growth), cognitive (e.g., academic skills), affective (e.g., emotional regulation), and social (e.g., interactions with others) domains. This theory emphasizes the mutually influential and bidirectional relationships between individuals and their contexts that drive development across the lifespan (Lerner, 2011; Overton, 2010).

The developmental-relational systems theory also emphasizes that outcomes are a result of the interactions between risk factors, strengths, and protective factors, but that the presence of a risk factor does not necessarily lead to a negative outcome. This tenet is important because it assumes that outcomes are malleable and that appropriate interventions can make a substantial difference in child outcomes despite the presence of risk factors associated with poverty across the multiple systems in which the child develops. Sources of resilience that serve to counteract or buffer against risk factors may include characteristics of the individual, family, or context such as school (Masten, 2007).

Schools as Sites for Nurturing the Whole Child in Context

Given that the average US student spends nearly 1,300 hours in school during a school year (NCES, 2012), it is logical to consider schools as the site for interventions that can help to reduce inequality. More importantly, schools are the place where the various contexts and systems in a child's life intersect. Schools are nested within neighborhoods whose characteristics, particularly socioeconomic status, greatly influence the quality of the school. Families interact with teachers through informal conversations or parent-teacher conferences and may be present at the school for various events and activities. Children act as messengers between the school and home, carrying communication (such as in the form of newsletters) and homework between the two settings. The home is a setting where the norms and expectations of the classroom may be either reinforced or negated. Services that address family, health, academic, and socio-emotional needs may exist within the school, or school personnel may make referrals within the community to address students' needs in any of these domains. Importantly, children living in poverty generally live in impoverished families, *and* live in impoverished communities, *and* attend impoverished schools. The effects of poverty across these settings may be interactive and cumulative. Clearly, the many systems of a child's development intersect at the school. If we are committed to tackling the poverty and inequality that infiltrates these systems, schools must be considered a critical access point and an effective setting for interventions.

Unfortunately, most high-poverty urban schools in the United States do not have an efficient system for implementing the current policy approach or connecting students to agencies that align with their specific strengths and needs. City Connects was developed in response to this lack of comprehensive, optimized student support, based on existing theory on developmental contexts and poverty.

SECTION 2—THE CITY CONNECTS PRACTICE MODEL: THE CITY CONNECTS APPROACH

The goal of the City Connects intervention is to provide every student in a pre-K to Grade-8 with a customized set of services and supports to promote optimal development and achievement. City Connects also implements a secondary school approach with the same goal, but, because of the different structural setup of the school, it utilizes slightly modified strategies. The core components of the City Connects intervention are as follows:

- *City Connects Coordinator*

  At the core of the intervention is a City Connects Coordinator in each school, trained as a school counselor or school social worker, who connects students to a customized set of services through collaboration with families, teachers, school staff, and community agencies. School counselors and school social workers in the United States have a minimum of a master's degree (generally requiring four undergraduate years and two to three graduate years of study) and are licensed mental health professionals. The City Connects Coordinator follows standardized practices codified in the City Connects Practice Manual, as shown in figure 1.1 and detailed in the components below. In some districts, the City Connects Coordinator is a new position created in the school, and, in others, an existing position (e.g., a school counselor role) is redefined to include responsibility for implementing the City Connects model. Typically, there is one City Connects Coordinator for every 400 students in the school.

- *Whole Class Review*

  The City Connects Coordinator works with each classroom teacher to review each and every student in the class and develop customized support plans that address their individual strengths and needs. There are five

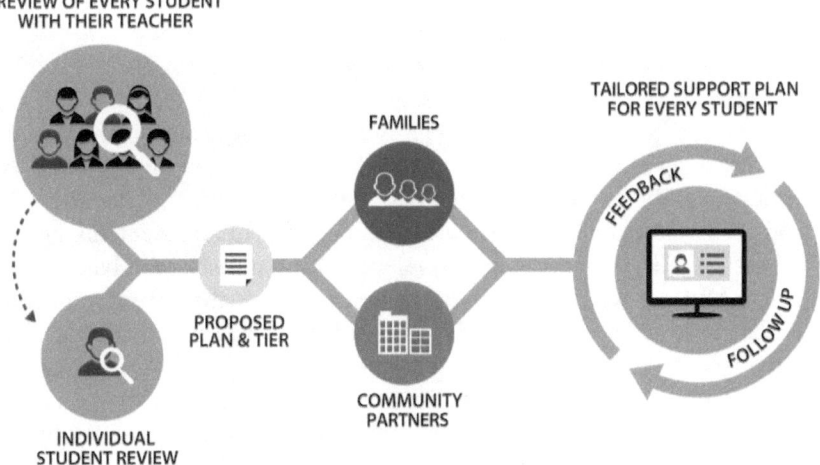

Figure 1.1 The City Connects Core Practice.

aspects of the Whole Class Review (WCR): (1) identifying the strengths and needs of each student across four domains (i.e., academic, social/emotional/behavioral, health, and family), (2) identifying and locating appropriate school-based and/or community-based services and enrichments, (3) establishing the connection between these service providers and individual children and their families, (4) documenting and tracking the delivery of services, and (5) following up to ensure the appropriateness of fit. As they conduct the WCR, the teacher and City Connects Coordinator group students into three tiers: strengths and minimal risk (Tier 1), strengths and mild (Tier 2a) to moderate (Tier 2b) risk, and strengths and severe risk (Tier 3).

- *Individual Student Review*

  Students identified as having intensive needs at any point during the school year receive an Individual Student Review (ISR). The ISR is conducted by the student support team—an existing school structure that can include school psychologists, teachers, principals, nurses, and occasionally community agency staff members; it is typically led by the City Connects Coordinator. The team discusses and develops specific measurable goals and strategies for the student. The City Connects Coordinator communicates with the family before and after the ISR. Typically, 8 percent to 10 percent of the students in a school receive an ISR in a given year.

- *Community Agency Partnerships*

  A critical aspect of the City Connects Coordinator's role is developing and maintaining partnerships with community agencies and institutions. These relationships are vital to providing all students with the support and enrichment they need to thrive. In the 2016–2017 academic year, for example, across 83 City Connects schools, over 212,000 services were delivered by more than 1,100 different community partners.

- *Connecting Students to Services, Tracking, and Follow-Up*

  During and after these conversations with teachers, school staff and leaders, and community agency representatives, City Connects Coordinators, working closely with families, connect each student to the particular enrichment and service programs that will best meet his or her strengths and needs. To aid with the process and to permit streamlined tracking and follow-up, City Connects has developed a proprietary web-based database—MyConnects. MyConnects database allows for secure collection of data on student reviews, individual student plans, service referrals, and providers (both school-based and community agencies) who deliver services. The database systematizes the work of referring students to services, contributing to efficiency, and enabling one City Connects Coordinator to serve 400 students. MyConnects data are used for several purposes, including record-keeping at the individual and school level, monitoring and evaluating the implementation of the intervention throughout the school year, and conducting research on the effectiveness of the intervention. Services can be classified into three broad categories: prevention and enrichment, early intervention, and intensive/crisis intervention. Each category includes services of different types. The tailoring of services is accomplished through different combinations of quantity and type of services from these three broad categories, resulting in a unique set of services for each student.

Growth of the Model

City Connects was developed in the 1990s out of a partnership between researchers and leaders at Boston College, educators and administrators in a Boston Public elementary school, and community agency leaders. This partnership was developed with the purpose of exploring ways to address out-of-school factors that impact students' success and thriving in school. From 1999 to 2001, in an iterative process, members of the partnership repeatedly convened school principals, teachers, other school and district staff, representatives of community agencies, and families to develop a practice that systematized the work traditionally done in schools by school counselors, nurses, psychologists, community partners, and others. The resulting system, designed to permit measurement of outcomes, was initially implemented in Boston schools in the 2001–2002 academic year.

City Connects has proved replicable. It expanded to a new area of Boston in the 2007–2008 school year. Since that time, the expanding evidence base has led more districts and states to seek out City Connects as a comprehensive approach to supporting all students. Over the years, City Connects has been implemented in the public, charter, and Catholic schools in nearly twenty cities across the following seven states: Connecticut, Indiana, Massachusetts, Minnesota, New York, Ohio, and Tennessee. It is currently serving approximately 30,000 students. Anonymous surveys across the network consistently indicate high levels of satisfaction among principals, teachers, and community partners. City Connects is now recognized nationally as a comprehensive approach to student support that can be delivered at a low cost and that yields significant, positive outcomes for children's achievement and well-being.

Empirical Evaluation

The results of City Connects' evaluation demonstrate that the intervention has a significant impact on achievement and other critical areas of students' lives. Due to the intervention's organic growth over time, randomization at the school level has not been possible. However, we have utilized a variety of rigorous quasi-experimental methods to test hypotheses about the intervention, including fixed-effects modeling, multilevel models with propensity score weights, and regression discontinuity approaches. A consistent set of findings demonstrates that being in a City Connects school makes a difference. Beginning in elementary school, and continuing after leaving a City Connects school and moving onto a variety of middle schools, City Connects students outperform comparison peers on measures of academic achievement. Students in City Connects elementary schools achieve significantly higher report card scores in reading, writing, and math than students in non-City Connects schools by the end of fifth grade. The magnitude of these positive effects was as high as the negative effects of poverty. After leaving the intervention schools in Grade 5, City Connects students achieve higher grades and standardized statewide test scores in middle school than comparison students (Walsh et al., 2014). Additionally, students enrolled in City Connects schools have lower rates of chronic absenteeism than children in comparison schools (City Connects, 2014). This effect endures through Grade 12, long after students have left an intervention school. City Connects is beneficial for many high-risk groups of students, including the first-generation immigrants, who tend to have higher standardized test scores when enrolled in City Connects schools compared to their counterparts in nonintervention schools (Dearing et al., 2016). Finally, students enrolled in City Connects elementary schools up to Grade 5 were less likely to drop out of high school (Lee St. John et al., 2018).

City Connects is unique in that it is cost-effective, with a benefit/cost ratio of 3:1 ($3 of benefit for every $1 spent) (Bowden et al., 2015). The intervention places individualized attention on every child instead of just the highest or lowest achievers and tailors support in order to buffer the risk factors and encourage the strengths of every child. These features, along with the systematic use of high-quality data, make City Connects different from any other student support intervention that exists today. Importantly, our proprietary data management system (i.e., MyConnects) allows us to track the progress of thousands of children from school entry to graduation, making it easier to adjust supports and services in unison with the dynamics of each student's development. Existing theoretical and empirical work all point to the importance of a systematized, holistic, school-based intervention that can address needs and bolster strengths in the domains of health, academics, socioemotional functioning, and family. We believe that intervening in the lives of impoverished children during elementary school is critically important, and City Connects has the potential to make a significant impact on reducing educational inequality.

Individual Student Vignettes

In addition to evaluating the large-scale outcomes of the City Connects intervention, it is critical to reflect on how the intervention impacts individual students' developmental trajectories. Regardless of a student's level of risk, a tailored student support plan is generated, and the student is connected with a unique set of support services and enrichment opportunities. Throughout the course of a given school year, it is possible to discern the impact of City Connects by telling students powerful stories. The following vignettes illustrate the array of school- and community-based services a student may receive in order to meet their unique strengths and needs throughout the school year. While the vignettes are based on real data, names and other identifying details have been changed to protect confidentiality.

Harold's Story

Harold is a male student in the fifth grade at a public elementary school located in an urban neighborhood in the eastern United States. Harold moved to the United States from a Caribbean country and currently lives with his father and brothers. In the initial WCR conversation, Harold's teacher and the City Connects Coordinator noted strengths and needs across academic, social-emotional/behavioral, health, and family domains reflecting intensive educational risk (Tier 3). With respect to academics, Harold is below grade level in all subjects. His teacher noted academic strengths in math fluency, enjoyment of school, and a capacity for hard work. Responding well to positive attention was identified as a social-emotional/behavioral strength. In terms of social-emotional/behavioral needs, Harold regularly struggles with transitions, which can lead to impulsive behavior and significant emotional dysregulation. Poor sleep habits are noted as a health-related challenge, and his health strengths include being physically active and practicing good hygiene. In the area of family-related needs, it was noted that Harold is often hungry and that his family has previously experienced financial strains including lack of access to transportation and homelessness. Harold and his family speak their native language at home, and his father does not speak or understand English; this language barrier has presented difficulties related to communication with school staff and access to resources and employment opportunities. Family strengths include being receptive to resources and support.

Over and above the services offered to all students in his school and in his grade (e.g., arts and science programming and health screenings), Harold received numerous individual services to address barriers to learning. Harold received school-based counseling and in-home family therapy with a clinician who spoke his family's native language. He and his brothers were also provided with winter clothing from a community agency (Cradles to Crayons), access to free summer programming, and a connection to local food pantries. Due to his learning challenges and difficulties with behavioral regulation, he was also referred for neuropsychological testing and outpatient occupational therapy.

The City Connects Coordinator noted that Harold responded positively to these supports throughout the school year. Prior to receiving the winter clothing, Harold did not own a coat and would arrive at school in a sweatshirt. Access to appropriate winter gear contributed to Harold's improved attendance, as he was able to safely travel to school during inclement weather using his coat, boots, and uniform-compliant warm shirts and pants. He presented as proud to wear this new clothing in school. Harold's emotional and behavioral needs were appropriately addressed via the counseling services provided in school and at home, which likely contributed to increased engagement during the school day and led to increased positive reinforcement from teachers. Finally, as a result of the neuropsychological evaluation, a formal Individualized Education Plan (IEP) was put in place in response to Harold's academic needs. Participation in these tailored supports served to bolster Harold's existing individual and family strengths and to address his intensive needs across domains.

Micah's Story

Micah is a male student in the fourth grade at a public elementary school located in the same urban neighborhood in the eastern United States. He is the only child who lives with his mother. It is reported that Micah's father managed challenges with substance abuse and has not been present in Micah's life since birth. At the outset of the school year, Micah's classroom teacher and the City Connects Coordinator noted strengths and needs reflecting minimal educational risk (Tier 1). During the WCR conversation, the teacher noted that Micah is performing above grade level in reading, math, and writing and that he has many academic interests. In terms of academic risk factors, Micah has a tendency to rush through his classwork at times. With respect to social-emotional and behavioral functioning, Micah has a positive disposition and has many friends in class; his needs involve a tendency to be overly social and become distracted. Health strengths include good hygiene and a high level of physical activity; no health-related needs are identified. Family strengths include a mother who is involved in Micah's education and regularly communicates with school staff.

Based on the assessment of his strengths and needs, Micah received a variety of services. Some were universal supports offered to all students in the school, including an arts program that aligns with the school literacy curriculum (The Arts Project), a program that offers students in urban school settings experiences with gardening (City Seeds), and a program that builds social-emotional skills through games (Play to Learn). Micah also received services offered to his all fourth-grade students, including a health screening procedure and a field trip to a historical site. Finally, Micah received three individually tailored services: a music program that offers performance opportunities, which was a match for his specific musical interest and offered transportation; an after-school program that provides homework help as well as opportunities to engage in science activities, soccer, basketball, and arts and crafts; and a before-school program that coordinates indoor and outdoor physical activities.

It was observed that participation in these support services and enrichment opportunities optimized Micah's strengths and addressed his identified needs across developmental domains. Micah's story provides an important example of the critical role of prevention and early intervention efforts in the absence of intensive needs.

SECTION 3—LESSONS LEARNED AND RECOMMENDATIONS

Our experience and our research indicate that City Connects is a scalable, evidence-based, data-driven, and practical student support model. In this section, we share lessons and challenges from our experiences as developers and evaluators of the model.

Resources, Collaborations, and Contexts

City Connects operates on the assumption that individualized integration of resources from across sectors (i.e., healthcare, housing, extracurricular programming, etc.) will lead to increased access to appropriate services among children in a City Connects school. This assumption hinges on resources actually being available in a community. As we have implemented the model primarily in densely populated urban settings within the United States, it has been the case that needed resources are in fact available (though they may not be accessed without the model). In addition, the network of relationships that is developed through the implementation of the model can be leveraged to develop new services and resources when an unmet area of need is identified. However, the model has not been tested in geographic areas in which many resources to support basic needs may be unavailable or located at a great distance from the families being served (as in some rural areas of the United States and internationally).

City Connects is highly dependent on effective collaboration—for example, between City Connects Coordinators, teachers, and school administrators; between City Connects Coordinators, students, and families; and between City Connects Coordinators, families, and community partners. Implementation tends to be most successful in districts in which stakeholder buy-in is moderately high. In addition, we have found that a planning and needs assessment process with the district is essential to develop buy-in. Further, City Connects Coordinators must be aware of and capable of serving the cultural and linguistic populations in their schools. In schools with a diverse, multilingual student body, effective interpretation services are essential.

Time Frames

As we have noted, the work of City Connects is dependent on the development of a strong, collaborative network of community partners as well as on trusting relationships between teachers, administrators, and the City Connects Coordinator. Our experience is that most City Connects Coordinators require at least one full school year to develop these relationships effectively. Thus, the full implementation does not occur until the second year of implementation, and our data suggests that measurable benefits to students are detectable beginning in the third year of implementation. City Connects changes the system of practice within a school with respect to student support. We recommend that districts and schools with an interest in City Connects or similar models are prepared to commit to implementation for the long term.

Empowerment through Optimized Student Support

City Connects serves to empower students in high-poverty schools, bolstering their strengths and attending to their needs across domains so that they can approach their academic pursuits with a similar system of support to their more economically advantaged peers. Students receive the message that adults in their school view them as whole people, with complex strengths and needs. We also view the model as empowering teachers. In addition to high rates of satisfaction with the approach, teachers have reported greater empathy for their students as a result of City Connects. We believe this outcome stems from the fact that City Connects reduces teachers' hopelessness regarding their most marginalized students. In a school with no structured student support program, teachers are often aware of students' out-of-school needs but lack the resources to address them effectively. In contrast, in a City Connects school, teachers have a trusted and knowledgeable colleague, the City Connects Coordinator, who is able to connect students with complex behavioral and family needs to the available resources in the community by drawing on the network they have developed. Further, because each student is assessed every Fall, many concerns can be addressed proactively rather than waiting for a crisis to develop. In a City Connects school, teachers are empowered to approach their students with optimism and to form deep relationships with them, knowing that supports are available if challenging circumstances emerge.

RECOMMENDATIONS

As illustrated through our review of current theory and empirical findings in the literature on childhood poverty and child development, out-of-school factors significantly impact children's ability to thrive in and out of school. For that reason, it is essential that schools be prepared to identify and address students' out-of-school needs and strengths. Our experience reinforces this data- and theory-informed premise, showing that City Connects promotes students' thriving and empowers educators in their work with the most marginalized students. Our recommendation is that all schools—but particularly schools that serve a large number of marginalized students, such as high-poverty urban schools—implement a structured, systemic, whole school, whole child student support practice. This need not be City Connects, but neither should we accept the past norm of unsystematic, reactive, and non-data-driven student support practices.

REFERENCES

Alexander, K. L., Entwisle, D. R., & Dauber, S. L. (1996). Children in motion: School transfers and elementary school performance. *Journal of Educational Research*, *90*(1), 3–12. doi: 10.1080/00220671.1996.9944438.

Bertelsmann Foundation. (2011). *Social justice in the OECD—How do the member states compare? Sustainable governance indicators 2011*. Gütersloh, Germany: Bertelsmann Stiftung.

Blow, C. M. (2011). America's exploding pipe dream. *The New York Times*. Retrieved from www.nytimes.com/2011/10/29/opinion/blow-americasexploding-pipe-dream.html?_r=2&hp.

Bowden, A. B., Belfield, C. R., Levin, H. M., Shand, R., Wang, A., & Morales, M. (2015). *A benefit-cost analysis of City Connects*. Center for Benefit-Cost Studies of Education, Teachers College, Columbia University.

Bronfenbrenner, U. (1994). *Ecological models of human development*. In T. Husten & T. N. Postlethwaite (Eds), *International encyclopedia of education* (2nd ed., Vol. 3, pp. 1643–1647). New York: Elsevier Science.

Bronfenbrenner, U., & Morris, P. A. (1998). The ecology of developmental processes. In W. Damon & R. M. Lerner (Eds), *Handbook of child psychology, vol.*

1: Theoretical models of human development (5th ed., pp. 993–1023). New York: John Wiley and Sons, Inc.

Brooks-Gunn, J., & Duncan, G. J. (1997). The effects of poverty on children. *The Future of Children, 7*(2), 55–71.

Bryk, A. S., Sebring, P. B., Allensworth, E., Luppescu, S., & Easton, J. Q. (2010). *Organizing schools for improvement: Lessons from Chicago.* Chicago, IL: University of Chicago Press.

Carter, P. L., & Reardon, S. F. (2014). *Inequality matters.* New York: William T. Grant Foundation.

City Connects. (2014). *The impact of City Connects: Progress report 2014.* Retrieved from http://www.bc.edu/schools/lsoe/cityconnects/results/reports.html.

Clotfelter, C., Ladd, H. F., Vigdor, J., & Wheeler, J. (2006). High-poverty schools and the distribution of teachers and principals. *NCL Review, 85,* 1345.

Coleman, J. S., Campbell, E. Q., Hobson, C. J., McPartland, J., Mood, A. M., Weinfeld, F. D., & York, R. L. (1966). *Equality of educational opportunity.* Washington, DC: US Department of Health, Education, and Welfare, Office of Education.

Coley, R. J., & Baker, B. (2013). *Poverty and education: Finding the way forward.* Princeton, NJ: The ETS Center for Research on Human Capital and Education.

Compton-Lilly, C. (2000). "Staying on Children": Challenging stereotypes about urban parents. *Language Arts, 77*(5), 420–427.

Conger, R. D., Ge, X., Elder, G. H., Lorenz, F. O., & Simons, R. L. (1994). Economic stress, coercive family process, and developmental problems of adolescents. *Child Development, 65*(2), 541–561. doi: 10.2307/1131401.

Crosnoe, R. (2006). Health and the education of children from racial/ethnic minority and immigrant families. *Journal of Health and Social Behavior, 47*(1), 77–93. doi: 10.1177/002214650604700106.

Crowder, K., & South, S. J. (2003). Neighborhood distress and school dropout: The variable significance of community context. *Social Science Research, 32,* 659–698. doi: 10.1016/S0049-089X(03)00035-8.

Dearing, E. (2008). The psychological costs of growing up poor. *Annals of the New York Science Academy of Sciences, 1136,* 324–332. doi: 10.1196/annals.1425.006.

Dearing, E., Walsh, M. E., Sibley, E., Lee-St John, T., Foley, C., & Raczek, A. E. (2016). Can community and school-based supports improve the achievement of first-generation immigrant children attending high-poverty schools? *Child Development, 87*(3), 883–897.

Ford, D. H., & Lerner, R. M. (1992). *Developmental systems theory: An integrative approach.* Newbury Park, CA: Sage.

Garrett, P., Ng'andu, N., & Ferron, J. (1994). Poverty experience of young children and the quality of their home environments. *Child Development, 65*(2), 331–345.

Genesee, F., Lindholm-Leary, K., Saunders, W., & Christian, D. (2005). English language learners in US schools: An overview of research findings. *Journal of Education for Students Placed at Risk, 10*(4), 363–385.

Grady, S., Bielick, S., & Aud, S. (2010). *Trends in the use of school choice: 1993 to 2007*. Statistical Analysis Report. NCES 2010-004. National Center for Education Statistics.

Gruman, D. H., Harachi, T. W., Abbott, R. D., Catalano, R. F., & Fleming, C. B. (2008). Longitudinal effects of student mobility on three dimensions of elementary school engagement. *Child Development, 79*(6), 1833–1852. doi: 10.1111/j.1467-8624.2008.01229.

Guo, G., & Harris, K. M. (2000). The mechanisms medicating the effects of poverty on children's intellectual development. *Demography, 37*(4), 431–447. doi: 10.1353/dem.2000.0005.

Harrington, M. (1962). *The other America: Poverty in the United States*. New York, NY: Simon & Schuster.

Heinlein, L. M., & Shinn, M. (2000). School mobility and student achievement in an urban setting. *Psychology in the Schools, 37*(4), 349–357. doi: 10.1002/1520-6807(200007)37:4<359: AID-PITS6>3.0.CO;2-1.

Jackson, S. L., Vann, W. F., Kotch, J. B., Pahlel, B. T., & Lee, J. Y. (2011). Impact of poor oral health on children's school attendance and performance. *American Journal of Public Health, 101*(10), 1900–1906. doi: 10.2105/AJPH.2010.200915.

Janosz, M., LeBlanc, M., Boulerice, B., & Tremblay, R. E. (1997). Disentangling the weight of school dropout predictors: A test on two longitudinal samples. *Journal of Youth and Adolescence, 26*, 733–762.

Kahn, C. B., & Martin, J. K. (2011). *The measure of poverty: A Boston indicators project special report*. Boston: The Boston Foundation. Retrieved from http://www.tbf.org/uploadedFiles/tbforg/Utility_Navigation/Multimedia_Library/Reports/Final%20Poverty%20report.pdf.

Lankford, H., Loeb, S., & Wyckoff, J. (2002). Teacher sorting and the plight of urban schools: A descriptive analysis. *Educational Evaluation and Policy Analysis, 24*(1), 37–62. doi: 10.3102/01623737024001037.

Lee-St. John, T., Walsh, M., Raczek, A., Vuilleumier, C., Foley, C., Heberle, A., & Dearing, E. (In press). The long-term impact of systemic student support in elementary school: Reducing high school dropout. *AERA Open*.

Lerner, R. M. (1995). Developing individuals within changing contexts: Implications of developmental contextualism for human development research, policy, and programs. In T. A. Kindermann & J. Valsiner (Eds), *Development of person-context relations*. Hillsdale, NJ: Lawrence Erlbaum.

Lerner, R. M. (2011). Structure and process in relational, developmental systems theories: A commentary on contemporary changes in the understanding of developmental change across the life span. *Human Development, 54*, 34–43. doi: 10.1159/000324866.

Leventhal, T., & Brooks-Gunn, J. (2000). The neighborhoods they live in: The effects of neighborhood residence on child and adolescent outcomes. *Psychological Bulletin, 126*(2), 309–337. doi: 10.1037/0033-2909.126.2.309.

Masten, A. S. (2007). Resilience in developing systems: Progress and promise as the fourth wave rises. *Development and Psychopathology, 19*(3), 921–930.

McCubbin, M. A., & McCubbin, H. I. (1996). Resiliency in families: A conceptual model of family adjustment and adaptation in response to stress and crises. In *Family assessment: Resiliency, coping and adaptation: Inventories for research and practice* (pp. 1–64). Madison: University of Wisconsin System.

McLoyd, V. C. (1998). Socioeconomic disadvantage and child development. *American Psychologist, 53*(2), 185–204. doi: 10.1037/0003-066X.53.2.185.

National Center for Education Statistics. (2012). *Number and percentage distribution of kindergarten-terminal private schools, kindergarten students, and full-time equivalent (FTE) kindergarten teachers, by selected characteristics: United States, 2011–12.* Washington, DC: U.S. Department of Education.

National Center for Education Statistics. (2017). *Percentage of recent high school completers enrolled in college, by income level: 1974 through 2017.* Washington, DC: U.S. Department of Education.

National Center for Education Statistics. (2018). *Trends in high school dropout and completion rates in the United States: 2014.* Washington, DC: U.S. Department of Education.

Noah, T. (2012). *The great divergence: America's growing inequality crisis and what we can do about it.* New York, NY: Bloomsbury Press.

Orthner, D. K., Jones-Sanpei, H., & Williamson, S. (2004). The resilience and strengths of low-income families. *Family Relations, 53*(2), 159–167.

Overton, W. F. (2010). Life-span development: Concepts and issues. In R. M. Lerner (Ed-in-chief) and W. F. Overton (Vol. Ed.), *The handbook of life-span development: Vol. 1. Cognition, biology, and methods* (pp. 1–29). Hoboken, NJ: Wiley.

Reardon, S. F. (2011). The widening academic achievement gap between the rich and the poor: New evidence and possible explanations. In G. Duncan & R. Murnane (Eds), *Whither opportunity? Rising inequality, schools, and children's life chances* (pp. 91–115). New York, NY: Russell Sage Foundation Press.

Rothstein, R. (2004). *Class and schools: Using social, economic, and educational reform to close the black-white achievement gap.* Washington, DC: Economic Policy Institute.

Rumberger, R. W. (2003). The causes and consequences of student mobility. *The Journal of Negro Education, 72*(1), 6–21. doi: 10.2307/3211287.

Tyack, D. (1992). Health and social services in public schools: Historical perspectives. *The Future of Children, 2*, 19–31.

Walsh, M. E., Madaus, G. F., Raczek, A. E., Dearing, E., Foley, C., An, C., ... Beaton, A. (2014). A new model for student support in high-poverty urban elementary schools: Effects on elementary and middle school academic outcomes. *American Educational Research Journal, 51*(4), 704–737.

Walsh, M. E., & Murphy, J. (2003). *Children, health, and learning.* San Francisco, CA: Jossey-Bass.

Woolley, M. E., Grogan-Kaylor, A., Gilster, M. E., Karb, R. A., Gant, L. M., Reischl, T., & Alaimo, K. (2008). Neighborhood social capital, poor physical conditions, and school achievement. *Children & Schools, 30*(3), 133–145. doi: 10.1093/cs/30.3.133.

Yeung, W. J., Linver, M. R., & Brooks–Gunn, J. (2002). How money matters for young children's development: Parental investment and family processes. *Child Development, 73*(6), 1861–1879.

Yoshikawa, H., Aber, J. L., & Beardslee, W. R. (2012). The effects of poverty on the mental, emotional, and behavioral health of children and youth: Implications for prevention. *American Psychologist, 67*(4), 272. doi: 10.1037/a0028015.

Chapter 2

Education as a Force to Unite

The United World Colleges (UWC) Model of Education

Lodewijk van Oord

Netherland

United World Colleges, more commonly known as UWC, is a global education movement united by its mission "to make education a force to unite people, nations and cultures for peace and a sustainable future" (UWC, 2019). To this end, UWC provides challenging and transformative educational programs infused by a set of nine values: international and intercultural understanding, celebration of difference, personal responsibility and integrity, mutual responsibility and respect, compassion and service, respect for the environment, a sense of idealism, personal challenge, action and personal example. Over the course of its fifty-five-year history, UWC has established itself as a pioneer for values-based pedagogy and is increasingly recognized as a best-practice example in the field of global education (Chung, 2018).

UWC students are rigorously selected on their promise and potential to become agents for positive change. Students are sought and selected by national committees operating in 160 countries and territories and a large majority receive means-tested financial aid, allowing them to attend regardless of their family's ability to pay. As a result, UWC brings together students from an incredible variety of national, ethnic, religious, and social-economic backgrounds. Following John Dewey's credo that school is not a preparation for life but life itself (Dewey, 1897), UWC aims to create deliberately diverse communities where young people learn to develop and execute a wide range of initiatives in the pursuit of a more peaceful and sustainable planet. Although the different UWC schools and colleges run a variety of academic programs and courses, each UWC curriculum is always designed with the specific purpose to foster the UWC mission and values.

The UWC model of education is rooted in an experiential approach to learning. The notion that students are the crew and not the passengers of the ship, in the words of UWC's founding pedagogue Kurt Hahn (1886–1974), is deeply ingrained in the UWC model of education (Röhrs & Tunstall-Behrens, 1970; UWC, 2019). Students are unusually given high degrees of trust, authentic responsibility, and autonomy. They are challenged to pursue their ideals and ambitions, develop their own service projects and social enterprises, and in the process learn how to reflect, analyze, and recover from failure. The combination of a rigorous academic program and a wide range of values-driven activities and projects allow students to develop the knowledge, skills, and dispositions needed to challenge the status quo and create positive change in the world.

TARGET POPULATION

The UWC movement distinguishes between UWC schools and UWC colleges. Some of the schools enroll students as early as the age of four and offer full kindergarten, primary, and/or secondary programs. The UWC colleges typically enroll students from the age of sixteen for a two-year pre-university program. Approximately 11,000 students currently attend one of the eighteen UWC schools and colleges around the world. The UWC national selection committees usually target students aged fifteen to sixteen, selecting meritorious students for the two-year pre-university residential program. The UWC model of education has at its heart the idea that a UWC education takes place within a "deliberately diverse" community. Bringing together students from very different walks of life is an expensive ambition, and the scholarship offerings to selected students are a very important aspect of the distinctiveness of UWC. "UWC has an aspiration to become fully needs blind, with scholarship provision for all those who need it," explains Jens Waltermann, the UWC International Executive Director:

> The UWC schools and colleges are independent schools that are not built on economic privilege. We want students from very privileged backgrounds, students from underprivileged backgrounds and everything in-between. This diversity is the source of our strength and is central to generating the changemaking mindset that we're here to nurture. (In Hall, 2016)

There is a growing realization within the movement that the real divisions of our time are not primarily between young people from different national or ethnic backgrounds. The real divide is between those who have a passport and those who don't. Between those who have every opportunity and those who don't see any. UWC has become more vocal about its desire to bridge this growing disparity, for instance, by seeking partnerships and scholarships for refugees and students from other challenged and disadvantaged backgrounds.

BEGINNINGS OF UWC

UWC results from the vision of pioneering educators, who believed that education can be a powerful vehicle to foster societal change. In times of political tension, they created schools that served as evidence to the argument that human differences can be overcome and that people, despite their political and cultural differences, can learn to live together peacefully and meaningfully. This idealism led to the establishment of UWC Atlantic College in Wales in 1962. At the height of the Cold War, German educator Kurt Hahn, who fled Nazi-Germany in 1933 and settled in the United Kingdom, created a school where students from Western and Eastern Europe could live and learn together in the pursuit of peace and international understanding. At the same time in Apartheid South Africa, headmaster Michael Stern created Waterford School on a hilltop in Swaziland and provocatively called it a multiracial South African school in exile. "We are trying to prove nothing except that there is nothing to prove," said Stern. "At the worst we shall find it as difficult as starting any new school anywhere; at the best we shall have made our small contribution to better human understanding in southern Africa" (In Smith, 2013).

This, in a nutshell, is why the UWC model of education was created: to develop small but powerful centers of educational innovation where young people learn to overcome the barriers and social divides created by their parents and grandparents, thus proving that there is, indeed, nothing to prove. New UWC schools and colleges have typically been set up in regions with social and political challenges, allowing the UWC institution to make a significant societal impact. For instance, UWC Adriatic was established in 1982 in the multiethnic border region of Italy and Former Yugoslavia, allowing Western and Eastern European students to come to school together. Likewise, the UWC College in Bosnia and Herzegovina was established in the city of Mostar after the Balkan Wars and features as a model for integrated education across the ethnic divides.

GUIDING PRINCIPLES AND PHILOSOPHIES

In general terms, the notion of learning as a process of personal transformation to enable societal change goes back to theorists such as John Dewey,

Lev Vygotsky, and Paulo Freire. In their constructivist views, learning takes place when the individual learner interacts with the wider world. Just as the rubbing of one's hands creates friction, the interaction of an individual with the social environment creates learning (van Oord, 2013). It is the task of the educator to offer students diverse opportunities to interact with, and act *in*, the social world. More specifically, the UWC model of education is inspired by the work and writings of Kurt Hahn. Hahn's educational ideas were derived from a very critical view of Western culture and society. "The scientific and technical progress we have witnessed [. . .] has been immense," he wrote shortly after World War II. "But it has been accompanied by deterioration in human worth" (Hahn, 1947). He believed young people, in particular, suffered from a disease that he termed "spectatoritis"(Hahn, 1959). A new education was needed to help students discover their place in the world and trigger them to dedicate their lives to the common good. Although Hahn's analysis of society at times appears to be dated, very few will challenge the notion that in our digitalized and device-driven world today, many young people suffer from spectatoritis. In this sense, his analysis and proposed remedy for the ills of society come across as remarkably topical and accurate.

The UWC model of education can perhaps best be understood as the application of the contact hypothesis in an educational setting. In his groundbreaking *The Nature of Prejudice* (1954), the social psychologist Gordon Allport developed a set of principles for prejudice reduction. This approach is commonly known as the "contact hypothesis," according to which prejudice may be reduced by equal status contact between majority and minority groups in the pursuit of common goals (Allport, 1954, p. 281).

Since the launch of the contact hypothesis, a vast number of scholars have conducted experiments and studies in which they tried to validate Allport's predictive claim. This process of fine-tuning led to a fair level of consensus among scholars that the following four essential conditions are necessary for the reduction of prejudice (Brown, 1995): First, the contact should take place in a context with *social and institutional support*. It is vital to create a framework that unambiguously endorses the goals of the integrative process. The most important reason for this institutional support is that it creates a new social climate in which improved contact can emerge and people's meaning perspectives can indeed transform. Second, successful contact should have a *high acquaintance potential*. In other words, contact between groups will only reduce prejudice if it permits the development of close relationships between individual members of the different groups. This condition allows individuals to discover similarities between themselves and out-group members, which has turned out to be an effective cause of attitude change. The third necessary condition is *equal status contact*, which means that existing inequalities between the different groups should be removed as far as possible. Prejudice often consists of the belief that out-group members are of inferior status. Any situation without equal status contact is therefore more likely to reinforce the prejudice than counter it. The fourth essential condition for prejudice reduction is the pursuit of common goals or *co-operation*, allowing group members to build confidence and mutual trust across the group divides.

Kurt Hahn was particularly interested in this last feature, and his educational programs evolved around the pursuit of common goals. Students were compelled to challenge themselves at sea and in the mountains and through service to the community. When at Gordonstoun, his first school in the United Kingdom, a potential sponsor asked him what a sailing expedition could do for international understanding and co-operation, Hahn replied:

> I said we had at the moment the application before us for a future king of an Arab country to enter Gordonstoun. I happened to have at the school some Jews [as well]. If the Arab and one of these Jews were to go out sailing on our Schooner, the Prince Louis, perhaps in a North-easterly gale, and if they were to become thoroughly seasick together, I would have done something for international education. (Hahn, 1954)

Although Hahn may not have been familiar with Allport's contact hypothesis, he clearly understood that if he could create a situation in which "an Arab" and "a Jew" became thoroughly seasick together (stretching equal status contact to the limit) in an attempt to cope with a north-easterly gale (the pursuit of a common goal), he would have done something to overcome intergroup tensions that no doubt would have existed between these two students in the early 1950s.

HOW DOES THE MODEL WORK?

In 2013, UWC published the model shown in figure 2.1 as a visualization of its educational model. The deliberately diverse community, unified by the nine UWC values, can be seen in the center of the circles. Teachers use these values to inform their teaching practice, and the UWC schools and colleges design programs that offer a wide variety of educational experiences to nurture the UWC values.

Individual schools and colleges have the autonomy to design their own courses, programs, and activities and take maximum advantage of local opportunities. Elements that feature at all UWC schools and colleges are ongoing community service, outdoor education, various forms of

Figure 2.1 The UWC Model of Education.

project-based learning, and dialogue and discussions on international affairs. In more recent years, various schools and colleges have also adopted programs in the area of complexity thinking, social entrepreneurship, and critical engagement in conflict. UWC Costa Rica, for instance, has developed an innovative *Agentes de Cambio* (Agents of Change) program, allowing students to develop the practical skills and critical attitudes to seek change in society through entrepreneurship and STEM-related initiatives (UWCCR, 2019).

Despite the wealth of programs and activities available at UWC schools and colleges, it is probably the ongoing community service component that sets UWC schools and colleges most notably apart from other mission-driven educational institutions. It is common for UWC students to engage in service projects on a weekly basis, which means that they can give back to the local community on a regular basis and develop ongoing relationships with people in need. This allows students to develop and demonstrate much needed attitudes and attributes, such as empathy, courageous action, personal example, and selfless leadership. Looking back at their UWC experience, many graduates identify their service commitments as the most transformative part of their UWC education.

THE IMPORTANCE OF TIME

In order for students to experiment with the UWC values and develop their own initiatives in the pursuit of a more peaceful and sustainable world, it is important to give ample time to the process. In line with the second "essential condition" of Allport's contact hypothesis, which stresses the importance of high acquaintance potential, the key to a UWC model of education is the fact that students spend at least two years living and learning together and as a result get to know each other in profound and meaningful ways. It is the sustained depth of the experience which allows for the personal transformation that UWC hopes to trigger in its students.

In addition to the eighteen UWC schools and colleges, the movement also organizes a range of short courses and summer programs. During these programs, the facilitators—often UWC staff or graduates themselves—create meaningful experiences and conversations for the participants with the aim to condense the UWC experience into a period of one or two weeks. The lasting impact of a short course may be less significant and measurable than the impact of a "full" UWC education, yet the short courses are seen to be a very valuable way to pursue the UWC mission. The movement's strategic plan has identified a desire to offer significantly more short courses in different locations around the world over the next years (UWC, 2017). As demand on UWC schools and colleges is high, the short courses allow a wider audience to be impacted by the UWC model of education as well as the flexibility to tailor-make programs to a specific context or skill set.

RESOURCES REQUIRED FOR IMPLEMENTATION

UWC schools and colleges are resourced in a variety of ways. UWC Maastricht is currently the only UWC school operating within a government system of state-funded schools, allowing the schools fees to remain relatively modest. Other schools and colleges are funded through a combination of parental contributions and support from donors such as graduates, private individuals, companies, and foundations. All UWC schools and colleges are responsible for their own financial well-being, and most have fundraising and advancement staff working to this end. In addition, UWC International runs an increasingly successful fundraising campaign, to raise scholarships for the various UWC schools and colleges. As the number of UWC graduates grows, there is an expectation that the alumni network will increasingly carry the cost of scholarships for current students through the establishment of a generational commitment. As the UWC strategy puts it, this generational commitment will ensure that each student receives as much scholarship funding as needed to attend UWC and then seeks to "return" over the course of his or her lifetime as much as possible to support a new UWC student (UWC, 2017).

EVIDENCE OF IMPACT

Besides a wealth of anecdotal evidence and personal testimonies of UWC alumni reflecting on the impact their UWC education has had on their personal development and life choices, various academic studies have also investigated the impact of a UWC education (e.g., Skidelsky, 1969; Branson, 1997, Mahlstedt, 2003; van Oord, 2008a; Malkamäki, 2017). The outcome of these studies is positive and indicates that the UWC model of education has a significant impact on those who experience a UWC education. In recent years, UWC has embarked on a more substantial and full-scale impact study in partnership with Project Zero at the Harvard Graduate School of Education. Under the leadership of Howard Gardner, the research team will carry out a four-year longitudinal study with a cohort of current students at all eighteen UWC schools and colleges and with selected groups of alumni. The goal of the research is to capture the ways in which UWC has affected these students and alumni. "The results will not only inform UWC's practices,' write the researchers, 'but also contribute to knowledge about diverse international schools and their degree of mission effectiveness" (Project Zero, 2018). The UWC community awaits the publication of the results of this study in 2022.

THE ROLE OF COLLABORATION AND PARTNERSHIP

UWC has established a wide range of partnerships with like-minded organizations and foundations. These partnerships either function to strengthen the educational programs offered by UWC or to allow more students to attend UWC through various types of scholarship provision. In addition, individual UWC schools and colleges create partnerships with organizations in their local contexts. The UWC College in Norway for instance has a long-standing partnership with the Red Cross and has even been named UWC Red Cross Nordic to highlight this special relationship. Similar partnerships exist, for instance, in India with the Mahindra Group, in Germany with the Robert Bosch Foundation, and in the Netherlands with the Department of Education.

Particularly noteworthy is the long-standing co-operation between UWC and the International Baccalaureate Organization (IB). Over fifty years ago, UWC Atlantic College was instrumental in the creation of the International Baccalaureate Diploma Program, the two-year pre-university course offered by all seventeen UWC schools and colleges (Peterson, 1987). The IB was a partner when the UWC schools in Italy and Mostar were established, and the two organizations continue to collaborate on program development and curriculum design. This is a natural partnership as UWC and the IB are closely aligned in their missions to create a more peaceful world through education (van Oord, 2008b).

THE CONTEXTS IN WHICH THE MODEL WORKS BEST

UWC schools and colleges have been established in a wide variety of local contexts and geographical locations. Some colleges are based on very isolated campuses while others are located in highly populated cities or urban areas. Generally speaking, a UWC education can make a genuine contribution in post-conflict regions, where a young generation of students can embrace the UWC model of education to overcome the divisions of the past and model these values and attitudes as they find their place in society. UWC Mostar in Bosnia and Herzegovina is perhaps the most exemplary example of such a college. A recent study into the peacebuilding impact of UWC Mostar demonstrates that the college indeed plays its part in overcoming the ethnic tensions and divisions in Mostar (Malkamäki, 2017). In a different way, UWC Waterford Kamhlaba plays a vital role in Swaziland, as it is the only institution in the country that combines high-quality education with a generous scholarship program. For many able but disadvantaged youth in Southern Africa, obtaining a scholarship for UWC Waterford Kamhlaba is one of the few routes available to lift themselves and their families out of poverty (Smith, 2013).

CHALLENGES AND RISKS

Considering the ambition to offer a UWC education to students with promise and potential regardless of their economic means, it will be of no surprise that the main challenge faced by UWC is a financial one. This is apparent in the latest strategic plan, which focuses heavily on financial sustainability and the need to step up fundraising efforts across the movement (UWC, 2017). Another less apparent challenge stems from the dynamics of the selection process and the way UWC presents itself to prospective candidates. For the model to be successful it is important to select students from a wide variety of backgrounds, including different political contexts and worldviews. Yet there is a risk that the trumpeting of the UWC mission and values narrows the applicant pool and largely attracts students who already more or less agree with the UWC values. If this were indeed the case, an incredible opportunity would be missed. In a closely knit UWC community, there is also a risk that the student community develops a degree of conformist thinking rather than independence of thought among students. This, interestingly, is among the first criticisms UWC Atlantic College received when it was first studied by Robert Skidelsky in his survey of British progressive schools in 1969. He wrote that Kurt Hahn's students are not remarkable for their independence of thought. Though they may well hold minority views, it is because their school does, not because they have worked them out for themselves (Skidelsky, 1969).

For Skidelsky, this drive toward conformity was highly problematic. "A very good test for an educational institution is whether it affords any real opportunity for rebellion," he concluded. Forty years later there is still great truth in this statement. Like all values-driven organizations, the UWC movement runs the risk that its idealism grows increasingly dogmatic. To challenge this possible development, UWC would be wise to drill less on its successes of the past and instead investigate and embrace as many different practical applications to the UWC model of education as possible. This will ensure ongoing tinkering, progress, and transformation, allowing UWC to continue to be a movement in the most literal sense of the word.

A third risk to making the model a success results from developments in society. The notion of a post-trust society, and the risk-aversion that comes with it, poses a real challenge to the UWC model of education while, at the same time, making it more pertinent than ever before. By offering genuine trust, authentic responsibility, and real autonomy to relatively young adults, vital to the UWC model of education, UWC will have to seek an appropriate response to the societal forces that challenge this educational principle.

LESSONS LEARNED

For a well-established movement like UWC, the ongoing question is how to adapt and continue to be relevant amid changing times. There are three notable lessons learned, which can be captured under the headings seek, educate, and inspire (UWC, 2017).

- Seek refers to the audiences UWC wishes to bring to its schools and colleges and what it understands by a "deliberately diverse" community. The main lesson learned is that diversity itself should be defined as diversely as possible. While UWC traditionally defined diversity in national and later in ethnic terms, the movement is increasingly learning that the real divisions in society are created by socioeconomic tensions. Accordingly, UWC schools and colleges are challenged to seek ways to increase the make-up

of their diverse communities by bringing in more students from across the socioeconomic spectrum with an important focus on students from disadvantaged or disenfranchised communities.
- In terms of the UWC model of education, an important lesson learned (and decision made) is that UWC needs to actively seek ways to keep its educational offerings relevant and innovative. Consequently, UWC is developing new programs and initiatives that nurture the skills, attitudes, and dispositions needed for learning and living in today's world. Although UWC remains proud of its past educational achievements, there is a growing realization that in order to be relevant today, past achievements may no longer suffice. UWC is keen to step up its innovative capabilities and is undertaking a variety of initiatives to this end.
- In recent years, UWC has reached out to many other like-minded partners. The UWC movement has learned that it is not alone in its pursuit of a more peaceful and sustainable world and that it is more likely to succeed when working together with others. Although this is not an entirely new realization, UWC has made the explicit pledge in its 2017 strategy to "systematically form strategic alliances with organisations whose work aligns closely with UWC's mission of making education a force for good" (UWC, 2017).

FINAL RECOMMENDATIONS

Those interested in adopting (elements of) the UWC model of education are strongly advised to start with a thorough investigation of the context in which they wish to implement it. UWC has learned over the course of its history that context is the most important variable in determining success. The experiential nature of UWC's pedagogy determines that students should be offered real experiences in the real world, and the local community in the close vicinity of any UWC campus should be able to provide these experiences and engagements. Although the eighteen UWC schools and colleges have a lot in common, they are also, in many different ways, distinctly different. A school in the heart of Europe's most densely populated areas will inevitably offer different types of student experiences than a school on the slopes of Mount Kilimanjaro. As a consequence, UWC Maastricht allows students to participate in over one hundred different urban community projects, while UWC East Africa has a strong focus on opportunities for conservation work and intense outdoor pursuit. The result is that these contextual opportunities are a wealth of ways in which the movement has implemented its model of education in its schools, colleges, short courses, and summer programs. This demonstrates that the model is amorphous in nature and can be adapted and made to work in virtually every context in which tension reduction and peacebuilding are needed. Those interested in doing so should feel free to add new varieties to the myriad ways in which the UWC model of education is put to practice. This will make the model richer and allow more people to develop a changemaking mind-set.

REFERENCES

Allport, G. W., Clark, K., & Pettigrew, T. (1954). *The nature of prejudice*. Cambridge, MA: Addison-Wesley Pub.

Branson, J. (1997). *An evaluation of the United World colleges. Final report, June 1997*. London: University of London Institute of Education.

Brown, R. (1995). *Prejudice: Its social psychology*. Oxford: Blackwell.

Chung, C., Shanker, A., Lee, S., & Chinhao Qian, V. (2018). *Building bridges to the future: Global case studies of teaching and learning in the 21st century*. Cambridge: Connie K. Chung.

Dewey, J. (1897). My pedagogical creed. *The School Journal, 54*(3), 77–80.

Hahn, K. (1954). Gordonstoun and a European mission. *American-British Foundation for European Education* (privately printed).

Hahn, K. (1959, November 17). Address at the forty-eighth annual dinner of Old Centralians, Grocers' Hall, London. *The Central, 119*, 3–8.

Hall, R. (2016). *What does a global education look like?: What is the UWC (United World Colleges) movement?* Retrieved from https://medium.com/change-maker/what-does-a-global-education-look-like-863d7de321c2.

Mahlstedt, A. (2003). *Global citizenship education in practice: An exploration of teachers in the United World Colleges*. Stanford University, School of Education. Retrieved from https://stacks.stanford.edu/file/druid:th204gp6905/Mahlstedt_A_Monograph_2003.pdf.

Malkamäki, M. (2017). *The power of intergroup contact and experiential learning on individual perceptions in the United World College in Mostar, Bosnia and Herzegovina: A path towards bottom-up reconciliation?* (Master's thesis). University of Tampere, Faculty of Social Sciences.

Peterson, A. (1987). *Schools across frontiers: The story of the International Baccalaureate and the United World Colleges*. Chicago and La Salle: Open Court Publishing.

Project Zero. (2018). *Project zero classroom 2018*. Retrieved from https://pz.harvard.edu/professional-development/events-institutes/project-zero-classroom-2018.

Röhrs, H., & Tunstall-Behrens, H. (Eds). (1970). *Kurt Hahn: A life span in education and politics*. London: Routledge & Kegan Paul.

Skidelsky, R. (1969). *English progressive schools*. Harmondsworth: Penguin Group.

Smith, D. (2013). Southern Africa's first multiracial school celebrates fifty triumphant years. *The Guardian*. Retrieved from https://www.theguardian.com/world/2013/apr/29/southern-africa-first-multiracial-school-50.

United World Colleges. (2018). *UWC strategy 2018 and beyond.* Retrieved from https://www.uwcad.it/ProxyVFS.axd/null/r17361/UWC-Strategy-2018-and-Beyond-pdf?ext=.pdf&v=12057.

United World Colleges. (2019). *International annual review.* Retrieved from https://www.uwcad.it/ProxyVFS.axd/null/r17361/UWC-Strategy-2018-and-Beyond-pdf?ext=.pdf&v=12057.

United World Colleges Costa Rica. (2019). Retrieved from https://www.uwccostarica.org/.

Van Oord, L. (2008a). After culture: Intergroup encounters in education. *Journal of Research in International Education, 7*(2), 131–147.

Van Oord, L. (2008b). Peace education: An International Baccalaureate perspective. *Journal of Peace Education, 5*(1), 49–62.

Van Oord, L. (2010). Kurt Hahn's moral equivalent of war. *Oxford Review of Education, 36*(3), 253–265.

Van Oord, L. (2013). Moral education and the International Baccalaureate learner profile. *Educational Studies, 39*(2), 208–218.

Veevers, N., & Allison, P. (2011). *Kurt Hahn: Inspirational, visionary, outdoor and experiential educator.* Rotterdam: Sense Publishers.

Chapter 3

Community Connected Learning

Social Innovation in Education

Laura Hay

United Kingdom

A CASE STUDY OF THE NATIVE AMERICAN COMMUNITY ACADEMY IN ALBUQUERQUE, NEW MEXICO

Adversity affects learning, and how schools respond matters. This qualitative case study based on the Native American Community Academy (NACA) sought to understand how they are succeeding, well beyond the odds, in contexts where students experience compounding disadvantages of poverty, trauma, and structural inequality. The combined evidence revealed an intentionally spun web of "compounding advantages" for students and families that help to mitigate the effects of poverty, build resilient students, and cultivate caring and collaborative communities. NACA achieved this by reimagining the purpose of education, recoupling community values to concrete institutional practices, and reinforcing them through positive school culture and systems. This case provides a powerful conception of school communities as spaces that can offer nested layers of support. It also reveals some of the critical components of relational and structural empowerment. While highlighting several programmatic innovations, these findings ultimately point to the need for a school-wide approach to change. This provides a theoretical grounding for how schools can explicitly disrupt many of the damaging institutional logics of schooling that have negatively and disproportionately affected their communities and lay the foundations for new institutions based on principles of equity, agency, and well-being.

SOCIAL CONSTRUCTION OF PROBLEMS

The United States spends more per student than any other country and yet it has far from the best educational outcomes (OECD, 2018). National trends reveal multiple ongoing *achievement* or *opportunity* gaps across ethnicities, income levels, and geography that manifests in several ways. Native American students, in particular, are more likely to attend schools with fewer resources, teachers unconsciously hold lower expectations of them, the curriculum can often be subtractive of their cultural identities, they are more likely to get punished (Teasley, 2014), receive lower grades, drop out of high school, and are less likely to enter and finish college (Ansell, 2011). As a result, many Native Americans remain trapped in a cycle of poverty.

Poor academic and health outcomes are serious problems, but so too is how we define and frame these problems for particular students and communities. Relying on educational achievement statistics based on standardized test scores, for example, frames academic failure as individual social pathologies where young people are the problem. This discourse of school failure is often imbued with discriminatory biases and reproduces a deeply disempowering narrative that ignores the procedural and distributional injustices underpinning academic failure. The so-called patterned failure is usually a symptom of more complex, structural dynamics, including individual and social behaviors that marginalize certain communities, and proceed to normalize the ensuing inequality (Zhao & Wry, 2016). Critical race theory, for example, reveals how teacher prejudice (López, 2017) mainstream curricula (Yosso, 2002; Crowley, 2013), and fragmentation between cultural and academic frames (De Lissovoy, 2012) compounds to ostracize non-White students. Based on this understanding, it's vital that we shift the public discourse from *certain groups that are consistently failing school*, to *schools and policies that are systematically failing certain people and communities*.

How problems are understood and defined matters, because it often reflects specific norms, values, and beliefs that end up privileging some while penalizing others (Lawrence et al., 2014). How problems are framed also delimits the perceived legitimacy of certain solutions, including which actors and what actions constitute an appropriate response (Smith et al., 2017). It is vital to recognize how cultural values and assumptions shape the metrics we use to assess communities, especially when these stories come to define entire groups from a deficit perspective. Defining people only by their problems is the very meaning of stigmatizing them (Shorters, n.d.) and commonly yields policies designed to address statistics rather than engage complex, living people. If the *problem* is understood as *low achievement* and *bad behavior*, then the solution becomes episodic changes to curriculum, assessment, and discipline. Such *solutions*, founded on institutional logics of efficiency and standardization, command and control, and a harsh disciplinary environment can unintentionally compound existing inequalities by disproportionately affecting those already most at risk of social exclusion (Jojola & Lee, 2010). Data contradicts the key assumptions that these policies deter bad behavior and make schools safer for the other students. In fact, research shows that pathologizing individual students and communities instead of recognizing the structural roots to patterned failure can have a negative effect on overall school climate, mental health, academic achievement, and is associated with higher rates of school dropout (Skiba et al., 2006).

COMPOUNDING DISADVANTAGES

While it is important not to frame communities from a deficit perspective, it is critical to acknowledge the challenges they face. One of the essential features of social inequality is "overlapping and reinforcing advantages versus disadvantages" (Ragin & Fiss, 2017). Native communities particularly continue to face a web of challenges including racism, poverty, food and housing insecurity, substance abuse, and poor health (United Nations Permanent Forum on Indigenous Issues, 2010). These pose significant psychological, cultural, and socioeconomic barriers that continue to impede many young people from excelling academically. If the socioeconomic exclusion is further reinforced in schools through *logics* of command and control, *narratives* about the *achievement gap* rather than *opportunity gap*, *cultures* that reinforce quiet conformity and disempowerment, and *systems* that disregard students' background and experiences, rely on high-stakes standardized testing and inflict severe punishments for minor behavior infractions and the odds stack up against them, leading to patterned educational failure and feelings of hopelessness.

HOLISTIC DEVELOPMENT

Increasingly, school communities are focusing on enhancing the holistic development of young children and their families—based on an understanding of the nature of learning itself (Robinson & Aronica, 2015). Insights from child development science confirm that learning is social and emotional, and children actively construct knowledge based on their experiences, relationships, and social contexts. Adversity affects learning and the way schools respond to matters (Darling-Hammond & Cook-Harvey, 2018). The NACA has creatively taken up this challenge. The purpose of this study was to explore how NACA helps their students thrive, despite hailing from communities who have been chronically underserved by public education systems for generations. While it certainly poses a unique host of challenges, it also presents the opportunity to do things differently.

METHOD

A core ontological objective was to capture a more nuanced narrative of this school community from people's native ontology, lived experiences, and feelings, to their complex behaviors and cultural practices and offer insights into the social processes that often elude quantitative data (Yin, 2014). These relational elements of education are the most essential, but often also the most taken-for-granted. As such, this research is based on interdisciplinary literature and qualitative ethnographic case studies rooted in the grounded theory that prioritize the qualities, processes, and meanings that do not lend themselves to measurement (Denzin & Lincoln, 2005). The study used semi-structured interviews (n = 23) with school stakeholders (n = 30) (founders, principals, teachers, students, and parents), on-site observation, and document analysis.

While qualitative methods and case studies can appear to have only localized and partially valid findings (Moulaert, 2013), from the perspective of social innovation, *truth* and *transferability* become more about the relevance of knowledge for social transformation and empowerment of people and communities (Moulaert, 2013). I hope that the "thick descriptions" (Geertz, 1973) can inspire others with alternative visions for education and provide practical pathways for beginning the journey of transformation. Ultimately, studying the foundations of social innovation within innovative schools provides an unprecedented opportunity to explore the core cultural components of positive learning environments and offer examples of organization-wide practices that successfully respond to social exclusion and promote individual and community empowerment (Moulaert, 2013).

RESEARCH CONTEXT

Native American Community Academy

The NACA is a state-funded public charter school serving almost 400 students aged 5 to 18 in Albuquerque, New Mexico. More than just a school, NACA is part of a shared vision and purpose. Representing over sixty different tribes, they are the first community-led, urban charter school in the United States designed specifically to meet the academic, cultural, and wellness needs of native youth.

Context is critical. In the field of social innovation, great solutions often come from places where problems are most acutely felt, and solutions are best evolved out of *ecology* that can sustain them (Zakaras, 2016). The school's location is symbolic. It was once one of the American Indian boarding schools (AIS) where native children were sent to be Americanized in the late nineteenth and twentieth centuries. Historically, education was used as a tool to forcibly and often abusively assimilate minority students into mainstream American culture by separating them from their language, culture, and communities (Lomawaima & McCarty, 2002; Reyhner & Eder, 2004). At NACA, this history is still deeply felt. "Many families associate the school system with pain, trauma and loss" (executive director). Most community members spoke of the lack of cultural awareness of their own educational experiences. This was true across the board.

> Any one of the native staff that you talk to has a story that is very similar: going through public education, not seeing our faces in curriculum, not seeing Native American teachers in the classroom, and not having our voice seen or heard. (Principal)

They pointed to language loss and a "lack of role models and cultural-historical representation in the school curriculum" that made it difficult to "build a positive identity as students" (founder). While schools may no longer actively attempt to expunge the culture of Native American students, neither do they actively value and attempt to sustain students' cultural heritage (Westby & Roman, 1995). Overt discrimination, limited or no lessons on Native American history and culture, and a lack of native teachers to serve as role models have resulted in a public education system that, intentionally or not, perpetuates the erasure of Native Americans and contributes to a cycle of low expectations and achievement (Jojola & Lee, 2010).

Education is a complex social process, and contextual differentiation is critical for understanding organizational priorities, practices, structures, and activities (Konstantatos et al., 2013). Varying sociopolitical histories and systems define, in varying ways, why, when, where, and how socially creative strategies develop, and which is the pioneering element in each case (Moulaert, 2013). Thus, NACA's approaches and success are best understood in light of persistent disparities in educational opportunities and outcomes for Native American learners, as well as the opportunity to transform these patterns. The site has since been reclaimed and repurposed. Now, the school is a bright desert white, with a roof of terracotta tiles, and an entrance lined with stones and native plants. It is a place where the ancient meets the emergent. It is a site of community, healing, knowledge, and action.

Grassroots Innovation

In the context of social innovation, NACA can be considered a social purpose organization: aiming to satisfy the unmet and emerging needs of their students, families, and communities, while also consistently changing the odds and improving the outcomes for their community (Nussbaumer & Moulaert, 2004). True to grassroots innovation movements, NACA's change efforts stemmed from within their community. Inspired by shared negative experiences and commitment to improving educational opportunities and experiences of Native American children, over 100 community members gathered in 2004 to share their concerns and ideas. This cross-stakeholder community groups such as elders, teachers, parents, physicians, community advocates, and business owners convened to imagine a school that would serve the specific needs of their students. Knowing that many NACA teachers and parents suffered trauma in their own experience of schooling, NACA actively worked and continues to work to build their faith in education by including families in the educational journey of their children. Their vision of a desired alternative resonated so deeply with the everyday experiences of their members that it constituted a solid foundation for coordinated action (Benford & Snow, 2000). Drawing from the experience, ideas, and strengths of their community, NACA evolved their philosophy, mission, and pedagogy (See Figure 3.1). The design stemmed from discussion around a key question: *"how can public education embrace the future while sustaining our identities, culture and traditions?"*

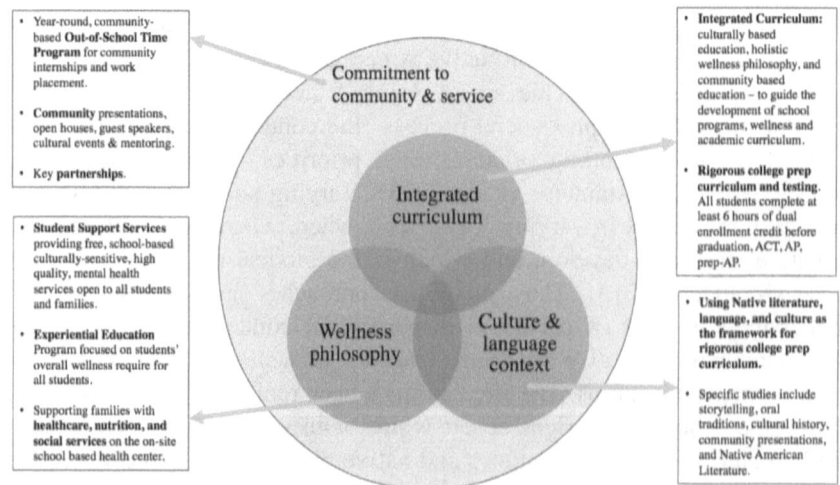

Figure 3.1 NACA Curriculum and Instruction Framework.

The community's answers provided the philosophical framework on which NACA is based: holistic personal wellness, cultural identity, academic preparation, and community leadership.

The whole community-led process of defining the problem, identifying solutions, and working together on a shared vision proved a great source of solidarity, validation, power, and pride. For many families, it continues to represent a key shift, a demonstration that *education can and should work as a lever in the hands of communities*, rather than as a *weapon wielded against them* (Founder). This process of mobilizing people around a shared vision and mission is core to the emergence of new institutions.

Institution-Building: Convening, Reframing, Cocreating, Reinforcing, and Institutionalizing

NACA's school community engaged in a process of institution-building by reconfiguring the three pillars of institutional order (and thus also change)—cognitive-discursive, social-relational, and material-structural connections (Lawrence et al., 2014)—in order to meet their community's needs (Smith et al., 2017). Together, school stakeholders reflected on, questioned, and challenged the systems of power that had traditionally caused their communities harm and worked together to transform them into sources of well-being and empowerment. It began with a different mind-set and narrative that provided the founding logic for a more empowering set of principles, policies, and practices that were then embedded and, over time, institutionalized in organizational culture and systems (figures 3.2 and 3.3).

- Reimagining the aims and scope of education based on a root paradigm of social-emotional health, well-being, and personal agency;
- Recoupling that vision with concrete practices and consistently reinforcing it through positive school culture;
- Transforming the physical environment to reflect these values and behaviors;
- Scaffolding several support systems, such as access to mental health services, family involvement, pedagogy and curriculum, and teacher professional learning and development.

REIMAGINE: PURPOSE AND SCOPE OF EDUCATION THROUGH SHARED SCHEMAS AND STORIES

Cognitive-Discursive

NACA, as an institution, is intentionally founded on an alternative set of beliefs and relationships, based on a new narrative around the purpose of

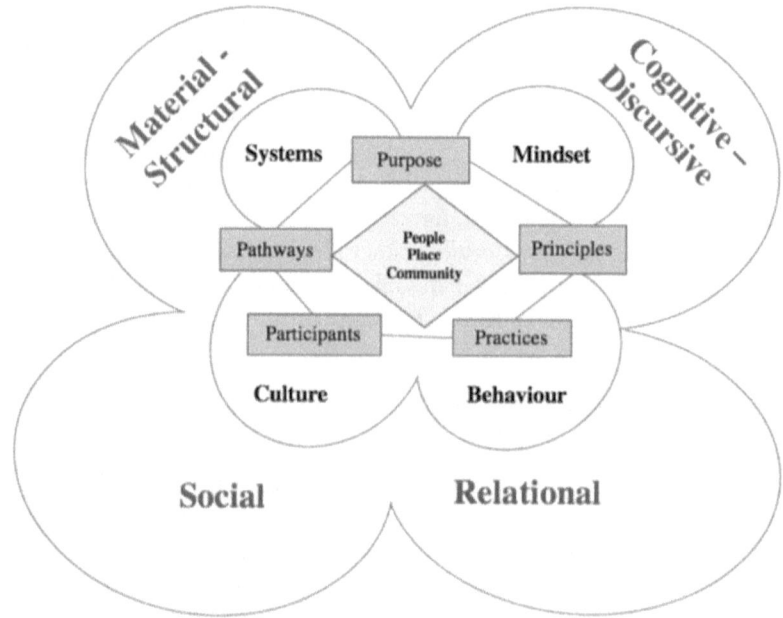

Figure 3.2 Institution-Building Theoretical Model.

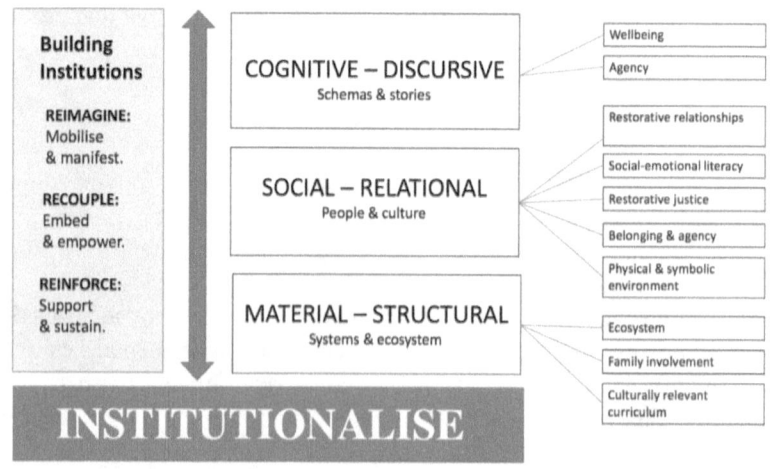

1. *Cognitive-discursive process of 'reimagining:' communities convene their constituents, surface shared schemas, mobilize around shared stories, and manifest collective values by founding a new organization.*

2. *Social-relational process of 'reinforcing:' people are empowered to foster more equitable social relations and enabling culture.*

3. *Material-structural process of 'recoupling:' stakeholders connect their values to concrete organizational practices and systems.*

Figure 3.3 Institution-Building Process and Practice Model.

education, and the role of students, teachers, schools, and the broader community. They have a clear understanding that educating a child is not just an academic process. Success is creating the conditions in which students are able and eager to learn. As such, they focus as much on children's emotional well-being as their academic engagement. Their expanded idea of well-being includes a strong sense of self (being self-aware and confident in your identity); a sense of belonging (feeling valued by family, school, community, and society); a sense of purpose, skills, and opportunities (agency to improve the situation for yourself and others and live a life of fulfillment) (RWJF and Ashoka Changemakers, 2016). To them, building social-emotional health *is* great pedagogy. It is not a separate add-on; it is critical to creating the conditions in which deeper learning can take place.

RECOUPLE

Values and Practices

NACA's whole child approach to education appreciates the fundamental interrelationships between all areas of human development and creates school policies and practices to support them. School leaders prioritize time and space for all stakeholders to participate in the intentional restructuring of their learning environments in order to make well-being and agency central to school culture and systems. The result is an intentionally spun web of "compounding advantages" for students' and families' physical and emotional safety; affirming relationships; trauma-informed pedagogy; rich, hands-on learning experiences; integrated academic, physical, cognitive, emotional, and social development; empowering norms and narratives; restorative approaches to discipline; culturally relevant curriculum; and supportive systems for students and their families that help to mitigate the effects of poverty/trauma, build resilient students, and cultivate a caring community.

Social-Relational: People and Culture

Culture

Positive school culture is central to reinforcing an alternative vision and practice of schooling. Studies show a positive school climate can reduce the negative effects of poverty on achievement and boost grades, student engagement, and well-being (Darling-Hammond & Cook-Harvey, 2018). Therefore, one of the key symbolic roles of school leaders is positively shaping these patterns and practices (Deal & Peterson, 2016).

NACA has a palpably positive school culture, underpinned by values and customs that bolster a strong educational mission, a sense of community, social trust among all stakeholders, and a shared commitment to continued learning and growth (Deal & Peterson, 2016). At the core of NACA's model are three essential ingredients: practices that make the students feel safe, valued, confident, and optimistic; practices that make students feel honored, empowered, and included; and instructional practices that give students opportunities to think deeply, take risks, and develop a sense of themselves as learners and leaders. This provides fertile ground for children to fully explore who they are in relation to the world.

Relationships

At its core, education is a social and relational process. While each child develops differently, every brain grows and changes in response to relationships and experiences throughout childhood and young adulthood (Schwartz, 2019). Given the sociocultural barriers to learning for native students—trust, stigma, labeling, and low expectations—part of the teachers' explicit role is to build secure-attachment relationships, foster physical, emotional, and identity safety, and nurture a sense of community (Darling-Hammond & Cook-Harvey, 2018). Teachers explicitly cultivate environments that support students' growth across all the developmental pathways: cognitive, psychological, social, emotional, and physical, while actively building their abilities to manage stress and anxiety. They grow their students' capacity for connection, learning, and growth by spending time and resources on creating a caring, culturally responsive learning community in which all students feel safe, known, valued, inspired, challenged, and supported. Several students mentioned they felt that their teachers and administrators cared about them and their growth and sought to build confidence and set high expectations.

The parents also marveled that the relationship between the teachers and students was much more positive and respectful and maintained that they could really see the difference in their children; they are much more confident in themselves. This approach is intentional. Teachers pointed to research that indicates that kids learn better from teachers they love and feel loved by. While robots learn in "abstract and formulaic" ways, human learning is founded on "embodied, emotive, subjective" experiences (Beard, 2018).

Nurturing, responsive, and stable caregiving in early childhood are linked to better physical and mental health, fewer behavioral problems, higher educational achievement, and more productive employment (Schweinhart et al., 2005; Heckman, 2007). In fact, some studies attribute the failure to break the cycle of disempowerment for minority communities to the fact that while the stakes and discipline mount, there is no change in the relationships between the adults and the students, and between the schools and their community (Cummins, 1986).

School communities like NACA, founded on restorative relationships that nurture the *whole child*, are more effective in mitigating the effects of trauma (Darling-Hammond & Cook-Harvey, 2018). Knowledge and skills are important, but, ultimately, it is motivation that determines what people actually *do* (Seelig, 2013). For students at NACA, having a strong sense of passion and purpose often helps build the courage, discipline, and resilience to transcend their circumstances (Wagner, 2014).

Rituals

Positive, school-wide culture can be seen as an active, coordinated, continuous process driven by teams of motivated people, connected through new relationships, supported in collaboration, who are critically, creatively, and compassionately engaging with and adapting their environment. Since culture serves as a reinforcement mechanism, it has enormous power as a pathway for negotiating agency at the level of interaction. Principals and teachers seed change by infusing new meanings into everyday experiences and reinforcing shared values through daily practice (Howard-Grenville et al., 2011). Teachers engage in "explicit, mindful tending" of the environment (Howard-Grenville et al., 2015), the people and place, values and norms, rules and rituals that define it matter.

Drawing on McLaren's concept of "root paradigms of the ritual system" (McLaren, 1999) and Mills' notions of "habitus" (Mills, 2008), as constituted by "reproductive and/or transformative traits," research at NACA revealed the possibilities of intentionally restructuring school environments for empowerment. Community rituals help set the tone.

It's Monday morning at NACA and teachers, students, and parents gather in a circle outside. Students begin with a greeting in their native language; they share an inspiring thought or something they are grateful for; they lead the school in meditation or prayer and then everyone joins together for a song, steadied by the sounds of drums.

These moments of shared attention and connection are meant to bring the school together to start the day in a mindful way. It provides time for pause, a moment to build a reserve of calm energy that will carry each person through the day. When school leaders make fostering community an explicit priority and lead by example, it changes the type of interactions teachers and students make time for and builds the foundation for culture change.

At NACA, rituals are a powerful force for producing patterned success. They build a sense of community and make compassion, connection, and collaboration the norm. Morning and closing circles create safe, open spaces for dialogue that build mutual trust; mindfulness and brain breaks offer a chance for feeling calm and connected; collaborative activities encourage communication and problem-solving; and empowering norms encourage students to take the lead. These positive cultural features foster success by creating the psychological and physiological conditions for meaningful learning (Deal & Peterson, 2016). Rather than aiming to improve academic achievement by increasing instruction time, discipline or adding more content to the curriculum, NACA is making school a more engaging, restorative, joyful place to be. This is just as well, because to fully engage in their learning experiences and share new ideas, children need to feel physically and emotionally safe to do so.

PEDAGOGY AND CURRICULUM

Social-Emotional Literacy (SEL)

Emotions and social relationships both deeply affect learning. Our brains are whole and work as an interconnected and interdependent system: emotional, cognitive, and social. While we know that learning is deeply emotional, the conventional curriculum focuses mostly on the outside world, with little attention paid to the inner world. In contrast, NACA makes the healthy growth and development of their students central to the design of classrooms, school culture, curriculum, and systems. They emphasize students' well-being as bedrock for academic excellence. Teachers take time to get to know their students, instill confidence in their cultural identities, encourage them to persevere academically, support their physical, emotional, social, and spiritual wellness, and prepare them for college. Everything can be looked at through the lens of "how am I growing my learners," both in what they need to know and be able to do, but also how am I honoring them as people?

While stress is a necessary part of growth, learning how to self-regulate, recognizing, and addressing overwhelming emotions are critical to academic and lifelong success (Tranter, 2018). Evidence from NACA confirms that SEL programming significantly improves children's school attendance and academic performance and decreases disruptive behavior and suspensions (Greenberg et al., 2003; Zins et al., 2007; Durlak et al., 2011; Taylor et al., 2017). These positive outcomes are attributed to the fact that SEL hones the interpersonal skills that improve children's social relationships, reduce antisocial behaviors, and increase their self-regulation and motivation to learn—all key predictors of achievement, especially for economically disadvantaged youth (Howse et al., 2003). Ultimately, SEL provides students with a toolbox for managing adverse experiences and the resilience to persevere through the challenges of school and life (Cappella et al., 2016). Students engage more deeply in learning and develop positive lifelong behavioral habits like working well with others, communicating clearly and respectfully, and resolving conflicts peacefully (Darling-Hammond & Cook-Harvey, 2018). Developing self-awareness also helps children understand their power to make choices and feel a sense of agency in shaping themselves and their community. With this foundation, they are more likely to graduate from high school, enter college, succeed in their careers, have positive family and work relationships, and have better physical and mental health (Zins et al., 2007; Moffitt et al., 2011; Greenberg et al., 2017).

Wellness

Wellness is one of the core components of NACA's holistic and integrated curriculum. The "wellness wheel" (see Figure 3.4) was often quoted by students, teachers, administrators, and parents alike. This tool centers Indigenous philosophies of holistic development and encourages students to be aware of how they are developing intellectually, physically, emotionally, socially, and communally. The whole school uses it as a self-reflection tool to identify their feelings, articulate their strengths, consider areas of possible growth, and set individual and collective wellness goals.

NACA has also created multiple layers of programs and support systems for their students and families. Each NACA student, family, and

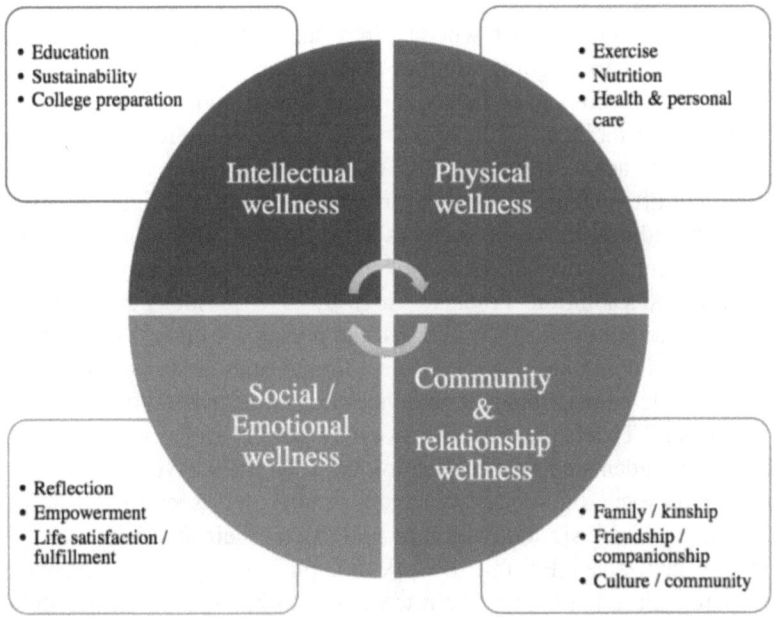

Figure 3.4 NACA Wellness Wheel.

staff have access to on-site free health care and dental services, emotional and behavioral health counseling, crisis intervention, and family and community nights (W.K. Kellogg Foundation, n.d.). In addition, they offer substance abuse and suicide prevention programs along with the Student Health Advisory Council that works in collaboration with students, parents, faculty, staff, administration, and community partners. NACA's Hiyupo Alliance is one of the programs that support boys and young men to heal, grow, and thrive so that they can become community leaders. They use trauma-informed, restorative strategies such as talking-circles, where students discuss highs and lows of the week, along with a weekly prompt. When students first arrive, they feel uncomfortable, because they are not accustomed to talking about themselves emotionally. The power of the program is that these conversations become normalized (counselor): "You see a person come to life as they get more and more comfortable talking about their inner and outer worlds. It's kind of like peeling back the layers of onions." Several students shared that when they started school, they "didn't have the confidence" to express who they were but that NACA helped them "explore their passions," "find themselves as leaders," and "contribute to the community."

Restorative Justice

Conflicts are inevitable, but whether they turn into opportunities to build empathy or lead to ongoing conflict depends on how the adults respond. Rather than classroom-wide behavior management approaches, teachers try to look at each incident as an opportunity to help children develop skills. Their approach acknowledges that negative behavior is a form of communication and often stems from unmet needs. They use a variety of problem-solving procedures to teach students how to calm their emotions, make respectful contact with the other, talk through each perspective, and work together to find a solution. Teachers use restorative questions to help students understand the reason for their actions, the reason for others' reactions, and how to prevent doing harm in the future. Ground rules are important. They do not use specific names; they use sentence stems like "when you did {blank}, I felt {blank}." This is the crux of restorative justice—repairing relationships and helping students see the connection between themselves and their community. This focus on social engagement rather than social exclusion taps into children's intrinsic motivation to understand their emotions and feel in control of themselves. For this to work though, it is important to have a culture where failure is ok and where teachers can be "real" with the students about their own mistakes.

Culturally Relevant Pedagogy and Curriculum

NACA's work also invests in the communities beyond their school walls by celebrating the histories of their students' families and the linguistic and cultural traditions that uphold them. One NACA student shared her experience of being bullied at previous schools, where the teachers were often part of the problem. In contrast, she feels that her experience at NACA has been "healing and empowering": *"It has been particularly empowering for me to be in an environment that supports my individual growth as a young native woman, but also fosters my connection to something bigger—my community, past and present"* (Student 1).

Talking to NACA teachers, parents, and students, it was common to hear stories of how learning their own native language mattered to them on a personal level and how it allowed them to connect with their history, culture, and community: *"It has not just allowed me to connect with my elders, but it means that I will be able to pass down so much knowledge to my own kids. That for me has been the greatest gift that NACA has given me"* (Student 3).

In the entrance of NACA, two large pieces of art face each other. One is a painting of a Native American woman, haloed by the sun, offering a basket of corn. The words "love, respect, responsibility, knowledge, culture, wellness, creativity, appreciation, community service, and perseverance" flow out from her. She is facing a collage of a bald eagle framed by a billowing American flag made from photographs of the faces of all NACA staff and students. A collection of unequivocal cultural symbols makes a powerful statement about the layered nature of identity. While NACA clearly emphasizes native cultural identities, they ultimately "engage identity as a multi-layered, fluid concept" in order to help students "embrace and be proud of who they are" (counselor). *"I have found a community that honors me for who I am and that has helped me become more myself. Each year I feel more empowered to explore and express who I am"* (Student 2).

Critical approaches in education can help educators acknowledge sociohistorical and contemporary contexts of school failure in their communities. NACA found that by integrating language and culture into the academic curriculum, they have been able to boost students' self-esteem, strengthen their sense of connection to their community, and instill a sense of purpose and belonging (Dessel et al., 2006; Spencer et al., 2008; Aldana et al., 2012; Frischen & Worsham, 2019). Teachers prioritize high expectations, cultural competence, and critical consciousness—three elements known to positively impact student engagement and critical to closing the opportunity gap (Ladson-Billings, 1995a, 1995b; Morrison et al., 2008; Christianakis, 2011; Sleeter, 2012; Rivas-Drake et al., 2014; Dickson et al., 2016). They also intentionally draw on students' knowledge, experiences, and cultural backgrounds as assets in the classroom (Gay, 2010), in order to affirm their identities (Byrd, 2016), help them unpack the role of race and culture in society at large (Hughes et al., 2006), and become resilient to their circumstances. This fundamentally changes the narrative from one of alienation and marginalization to one of connectedness, possibility, and agency (NACA founder). Core to this approach is encouraging students to identify problems in their classrooms and neighborhoods and work together to address them (Byrd, 2016).

Belonging and Agency

Young people need to feel that they are heard and respected. The adults either communicate to children that they are a valuable, contributing members of the community with the rights and responsibilities of shaping it for the better, or they signal that the rules have already been decided and students are just expected to follow orders. While NACA has a set of community-ratified core values that mobilize their constituents, guide leadership, seed school culture, and anchor systems, there are many ways in which students, teachers, and parents contribute to molding their school community.

Teachers frequently spoke of giving young people the power to realize that they can make a difference even in their smallest actions. They listen to them, foster their ideas, and provide official platforms where students can voice their opinions. Students are encouraged to think critically, creatively, and compassionately about the world around them and become leaders in the name of a cause they care deeply about. Small steps begin to add up to a bigger identity and students experience their own journey of being and becoming a changemaker. The walls inside and outside of the classrooms are lined with student work. Recurring symbols reinforce the power of community leaders throughout history, all changemakers with similar backgrounds to the students, in whom they can see themselves reflected. This helps students build a positive self-image and internalize that they can make a difference. Everything is pointing back to changemaking, from the inside out. Several parents mentioned that their children say that they want to be a changemaker: "*She explained to me that a changemaker is someone who makes positive changes in the world, for society, for their community.*" By challenging their students to be active participants of their community, teachers are ultimately fostering the most critical habits and processes necessary for social innovation: asking questions, framing and reframing problems, generating ideas, collaborating across differences, and persevering through challenges.

Enabling Environment

A school's physical and symbolic environment sets the tone for creativity, risk-taking, belonging, and learning. At NACA, the visible habitats signal that creativity and collaboration are welcome. Walking into each school, you are greeted with warm, earthy colors. It is a pleasant contrast with the fluorescent lights and clinical classrooms and corridors of traditional public schools. Their learning environments are diverse and adaptable, with flexible furniture so that students can self-organize. Students sit at round desks so that they can face each other and collaborate on assignments. They feel that the space is theirs because their work proudly decorates the walls.

Positive messages all around the school remind students of key mind-sets, values, and behaviors: curiosity, cooperation, empathy, persistence, tenacity, self-confidence, and community. The walls outside the kindergarten classrooms are splashed with photographs of students with an accompanying note celebrating how each of them had recently shown that they were living by the school's core values: being kind, helping others, and showing perseverance. In the corridor connecting the high-school classrooms, a graduation robe hangs vertically against a wall, with a mirror as a head that reflects the person standing in front. As students walk by, they catch a glimpse of themselves reflected in that future. Adjacent posters celebrate where past and present students have been accepted, and this helps current students see themselves as part of that same narrative. Longitudinal studies of NACA students show that they graduate at a rate 27 percent higher than local public schools, and four to five times the national average, and 100 percent of NACA graduates applying to postsecondary programs. Most of these students are and will be the first in their families to graduate from high school and attend college.

As curriculum shifts from memorization, following instructions, and completing individual tasks toward critical thinking, problem-solving, and collaboration, teachers have also begun to intentionally restructure the physical environment. At NACA, they conceive of *empowerment* as a construct that links personal competence to environments that offer opportunities for choice, autonomy, and creativity in demonstrating those abilities (Myrick Short et al., 1994). The key seems to be *flexibility* (Imms et al., 2017). Classrooms are comfortable, engaging spaces that offer students the freedom to "move, explore different materials, interact and collaborate with different people, and quietly work on individual tasks" (Robinson & Aronica, 2015). Their flexible furniture and tailored break-out spaces positively impact academic achievement by accommodating the variability in how children learn (Briggs, 2013; Barrett et al., 2015; Dornhecker et al., 2015; Gronneberg & Johnston, 2015). Thus the physical and symbolic environment of the transformative organization becomes a "living expression of the change that its members seek," giving it a significant ability to spark institutional renewal (Nilsson & Paddock, 2014).

MATERIAL-STRUCTURAL

Systems and Ecosystem

Education, more than most enterprises, is rooted in and underpinned by human development. Constantly learning, growing, and evolving with the times require multiple layers of support for students, families, and teachers. NACA leaders understand that the health and success of the students are also influenced by the health and support of their families, and the care and commitment of their teachers (Grigsby, 2019). They actively invest in people at all levels of the organization (the human side of organizational life) and build a web of integrated support structures for all school stakeholders: culturally sustaining pedagogy and curriculum, student advisory systems, teacher professional learning and development, and access to free, integrated, mental, and physical health. Principals dedicate significant time and resources to professional development for staff to grow themselves and their practice, and teachers leverage existing curricular pathways as chances to seed the knowledge, build necessary skills, and develop behaviors that underpin positive social change. Science, technology, engineering, arts, and mathematics (STEAM) are seen as opportunities to design, tinker, and create; history is used as a chance to choose which story to tell; and literature presents the opportunity to decide whose story matters.

Investing in families and neighborhoods is essential. Since children develop in an environment of relationships, strengthening the capacities of their caregivers and communities is critical to laying the foundations for future success (National Scientific Council on the Developing Child, 2010). NACA creates multiple layers of support for these key stakeholders: a web of partnerships between the school and home, teachers and parents, teachers and students, and teachers and teachers. When the classroom, family, and the community work together, children gain the mind-sets, skills, tools, and behaviors to manage life's challenges. Parents confirmed this sentiment, expressing gratitude for feeling welcome to participate in their children's education, connect with other families, and build positive relationships with the "relatives" at school.

Institutionalize: A Whole-School Approach

Congruent with social innovation theory and praxis, these findings reveal an intriguing perspective on school transformation: a story of people, purpose, and participation. The findings also highlight a collective process of reimagining education, aligning school practices to community values, and reinforcing them through positive school culture and systems. While highlighting

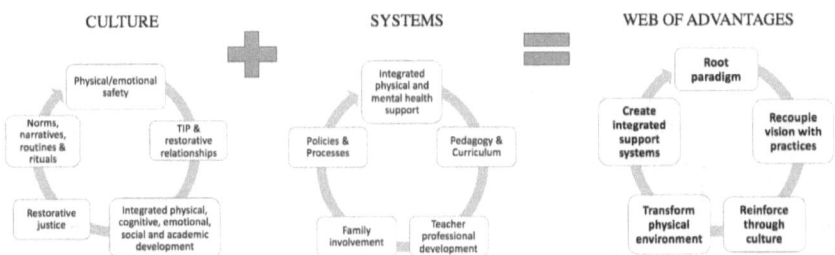

Figure 3.5 Compounding Advantages.

several programmatic innovations, these findings ultimately point to the need for a school-wide approach. In the case of NACA, both the structural pillars of change are institutionalized through a system of integrated support for students, families, and teachers, and the relational components of culture: positive relationships, integrated social-emotional learning, restorative justice, belonging and agency, and an enabling physical and symbolic environment, emerged as essential enabling conditions for a whole-school focus on wellness and agency. The result is an integrated web of compounding advantages (figure 3.5) that help students succeed despite their circumstances. The implication is a powerful conception of school contexts as consisting of "nested layers of influence on student learning" and community development (Bascia, 2014).

COMMUNITY TRANSFORMATION

A Dynamic and Participatory Angle

The story of NACA highlights the power of creating new pathways for sustainable development based on the premise that people at the grassroots level already have ideas, knowledge, tools, and capabilities required to create their own solutions (Smith et al., 2017). Their educators are culturally grounded in their communities and have come to understand the challenges intimately from within (Bornstein, 2007). This *insider's ontology* is a source of power and legitimacy. Where the traditional school system often frames Native American youth in terms of deficits, NACA frames young people in terms of their strengths, as assets to their community, and as the next generation of leaders. Teachers work together to create an environment where students' whole selves can unfold, including their connection to themselves, each other, their families, histories, languages, lands, and culture.

In schools, meaningful approaches stem from the recognition that the quality of education is inextricably tied to the overall quality of life for children and their families. To be successful, education should be conceived as a dynamic system tasked with preparing young people to be willing and able to learn for their entire lives. It is not about producing individual innovations, but a continuously evolving approach to solutions (Lawrence et al., 2014). Schools can turn spaces of disempowerment into places of agency through respectful relationships, empowering environments, participatory systems, community focus, and inspired learning and action. This process is underpinned by reimagining social relations in ways that remove the barriers to full participation and growth (Westley & Antadze, 2010), and trickling power downward such that every person can contribute.

By making "knowledge and cultural assets of communities central to the reconfiguration of social relations," NACA is enacting a new paradigm of deepening priorities and localized approach to education, rooted in the needs and realities of their stakeholders (MacCallum & Moulaert, 2009). They leverage the socio-psychological power of strong relationships, community traditions, and shared stories to affirm collective values and identity, nurture passion, seed commitment, and sustain rigor over time (Nettleingham, 2018). This socially innovative view of development integrates basic needs satisfaction, cultural emancipation, and social empowerment. As such, it becomes a particularly compelling framework for understanding the dynamics and processes of social change, thanks to root paradigms and design principles that put people at the center of solutions, prioritize stakeholder participation, foster enabling environments, and conceptualize transformation as a complex multifaceted process (Lawrence et al., 2014) aimed at community empowerment through relational and structural transformation (Smith et al., 2017). From this perspective, improving the quality of life in "area-based communities" (Moulaert et al., 2007) can best be driven by active citizens and strong local democratic institutions that own and embody sustainable development (Young, 1997). This kind of locally rooted action is more likely to generate socially embedded changes in behavior (Burgess et al., 2003) because it stems from the concrete circumstances and experiences of each community (hooks, 2003).

The story of NACA may seem small in scale, but it represents a larger movement of grassroots innovation efforts that are expanding the purpose and scope of education and changing the odds for their communities. Reimagining education demands that educators connect to their passion, reframe school priorities, and embrace the exceptional power that their profession has in shaping the world. It begins with understanding that notions of success are socially constructed and, as such, can be challenged and redefined. It also means being honest about what we value. As long as educators are promoted and schools are rated by students' performance on standardized tests, teachers will feel the pressure to drill content rather than spend time building the solid foundation of well-being and agency needed for most students to thrive academically

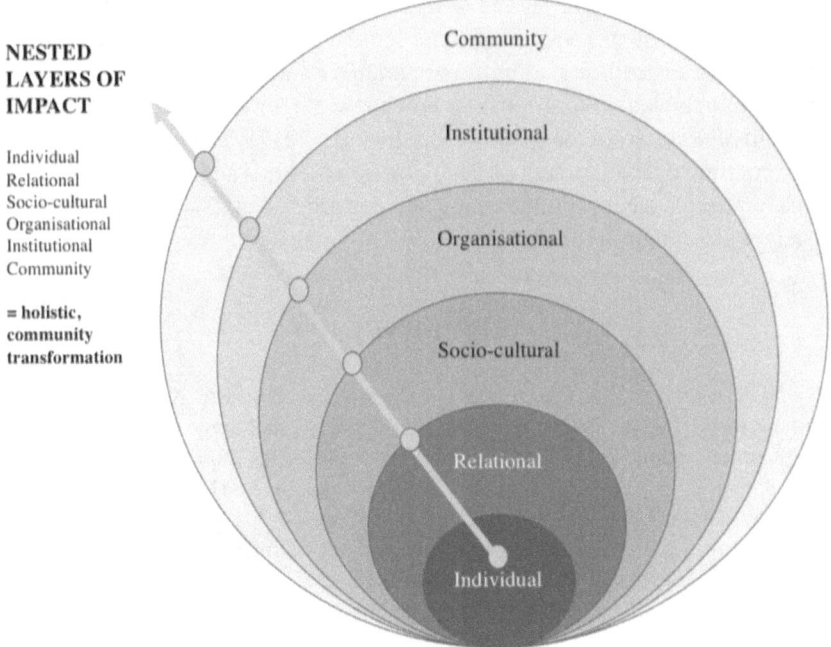

Figure 3.6 Layers of Impact.

in the first place. If we seek a society of "caring, creative, and committed people," and leaders who feel "called to service rather than to stature," then we need to make that clear (Cain, 2017) and create time, space, and opportunities for students to practice at school. Rather than another wave of reform, we need a conscious shift away from the efficiency, compliance, and standardized logic of management toward models that prioritize creative individual and social value and empowerment. This entails reconsidering the purpose, role, design, and objectives of education as envisioned and informed by the communities that they serve, while also focusing on a broader range of knowledge, skills, values, and behaviors, in service of motivating and enabling students to improve their lives and that of their community (see Figure 3.6). To do so, it is necessary for schools to expand their equation for academic success.

CONCLUSION

Implications for Research and Practice

This study aims to provide a functional and critical framework to help practitioners and policymakers rethink the purpose and possibilities of education, contextualize change efforts, and design and refine solutions that address the interconnectedness of social issues and lay the groundwork for deeper structural change. Instead of scaling up apparently innovative products and programs, policymakers might consider how to "scale down institutions" in ways that cultivate grassroots ingenuity (Smith et al., 2017). This could contribute to the continued development of emancipatory theories and practice of education and provide a base for imagining and enacting educational improvements based on a community impact model.

REFERENCES

Aldana, A., Rowley, S. J., Checkoway, B., & Richards-Schuster, K. (2012). Raising ethnic-racial consciousness: The relationship between intergroup dialogues and adolescents' ethnic-racial identity and racism awareness. *Equity & Excellence in Education, 45*(1), 120–137. doi: 10.1080/10665684.2012.641863.

Ansell, S. (2011). Achievement gap. *Education Week, 30*(30). Retrieved from https://www.edweek.org/ew/issues/achievement-gap/index.html?cmp=SOC-SHR-FB.

Barrett, P. S., Zhang, Y., Davies, F., & Barrett, L. C. (2015). *Clever classrooms: Summary report of the HEAD project.* University of Salford. Retrieved from http://ow.ly/Jz2vV.

Bascia, N. (2014). *School context model: How school environments shape students' opportunities to learn.* Measuring What Matters, People for Education. Retrieved from https://peopleforeducation.ca/report/qle-domain-paper.

Beard, A. (2018). How babies learn–And why robots can't compete. *The Guardian.* Retrieved from http://www.theguardian.com/news/2018/apr/03/how-babies-learn-and-why-robots-cant-compete.

Benford, R. D., & Snow, D. A. (2000). Framing processes and social movements: An overview and assessment. *Annual Review of Sociology, 26*(1), 611–639. doi: 10.1146/annurev.soc.26.1.611.

Biggs, S. (2013, November 26). Neuroeducation: 25 findings over 25 years. *Informed Ed Blog.*

Bornstein, D. (2007). *How to change the world: Social entrepreneurs and the power of new ideas.* New York: Oxford University Press.

Burgess, J. (2003). Sustainable consumption: Is it really achievable? *Consumer Policy Review, 13*(3), 78.

Byrd, C. M. (2016). Does culturally relevant teaching work? An examination from student perspectives. *Sage Open, 6*(3), 2158244016660744.

Cain, S. (2017). Not leadership material? Good. The world needs followers. *New York Times.* Retrieved from https://www.nytimes.com/2017/03/24/opinion/sunday/not-leadership-material-good-the-world-needs-followers.html.

Cappella, E., Aber, J. L., Kim, H. Y., Gitomer, D. H., & Bell, C. A. (2016). Teaching beyond achievement tests: Perspectives from developmental and education science. In *Handbook of research on teaching* (pp. 249–347). United States: American Educational Research Association.

Christianakis, M. (2011). Hybrid texts: Fifth graders, rap music, and writing. *Urban Education, 46*(5), 1131–1168.

Crowley, R. M. (2013). "The god damndest, toughest voting rights bill": Critical Race Theory and the Voting Rights Act of 1965. *Race Ethnicity and Education, 16*(5), 696–724.

Cummins, J. (1986). Empowering minority students: A framework for intervention. *Harvard Educational Review, 56*(1), 18–37.

Darling-Hammond, L., & Cook-Harvey, C. M. (2018). Educating the whole child: Improving school climate to support student success. *Learning Policy Institute*.

De Lissovoy, N. (2012). Education and violation: Conceptualizing power, domination, and agency in the hidden curriculum. *Race Ethnicity and Education, 15*(4), 463–484.

Deal, T. E., & Peterson, K. D. (2016). *Shaping school culture*. San Francisco, CA: John Wiley & Sons.

Denzin, N. K., & Lincoln, Y. S. (2005). Introduction: The discipline and practice of qualitative research. In *The Sage handbook of qualitative research* (3rd ed., pp. 1–33). Thousand Oaks, CA: Sage.

Dessel, A., Rogge, M. E., & Garlington, S. B. (2006). Using intergroup dialogue to promote social justice and change. *Social Work, 51*(4), 303–315.

Dickson, G. L., Chun, H., & Fernandez, I. T. (2016). The development and initial validation of the student measure of culturally responsive teaching. *Assessment for Effective Intervention, 41*(3), 141–154.

Dornhecker, M., Blake, J. J., Benden, M., Zhao, H., & Wendel, M. (2015). The effect of stand-biased desks on academic engagement: An exploratory study. *International Journal of Health Promotion and Education, 53*(5), 271–280.

Durlak, J. A., Weissberg, R. P., Dymnicki, A. B., Taylor, R. D., & Schellinger, K. B. (2011). The impact of enhancing students' social and emotional learning: A meta-analysis of school-based universal interventions. *Child Development, 82*(1), 405–432.

Frischen, K., & Worsham, E. (2019). The groundwater issue: Insights from social entrepreneurs about race. *Forbes*. Retrieved from https://www.forbes.com/sites/ashoka/2019/03/29/the-groundwater-issue-insights-from-social-entrepreneurs-about-race.

Gay, G. (2010). *Culturally responsive teaching: Theory, research, and practice*. New York: Teachers College Press.

Geertz, C. (1973). *The interpretation of cultures* (Vol. 5019). London: Basic Books.

Greenberg, M. T., Domitrovich, C. E., Weissberg, R. P., & Durlak, J. A. (2017). Social and emotional learning as a public health approach to education. *The Future of Children, 27*(1), 13–32.

Greenberg, M. T., Weissberg, R. P., O'Brien, M. U., Zins, J. E., Fredericks, L., Resnik, H., & Elias, M. J. (2003). Enhancing school-based prevention and youth development through coordinated social, emotional, and academic learning. *American Psychologist, 58*(6–7), 466.

Grigsby, S. (2019, February 20). Dallas is heading toward a reckoning: nonprofit boss wonders if we are doing it all wrong. *Dallas News*. Retrieved from https://www

.dallasnews.com/opinion/commentary/2019/02/20/dallas-heading-toward-reckoning-nonprofit-boss-wonders-wrong.

Gronneberg, J., & Johnston, S. (2015). *7 Things you should know about universal design for learning.* Retrieved from https://library.educause.edu/resources/2015/4/7-things-you-should-know-about-universal-design-for-learning.

Heckman, J. J. (2007). The economics, technology, and neuroscience of human capability formation. *Proceedings of the National Academy of Sciences, 104*(33), 13250–13255.

Hollweck, T. (2015). Robert K. Yin. (2014). Case study research design and methods. Thousand Oaks, CA: Sage. 282 pages. *Canadian Journal of Program Evaluation, 30*(1), 108–110.

Hooks, B. (2003). *Teaching community: A pedagogy of hope* (Vol. 36). New York: Psychology Press.

Howard-Grenville, J., Bertels, S., & Boren, B. (2015, June). What regulators need to know about organizational culture. *Best-In-Class Regulator Initiative.* Retrieved January, 19, 2017.

Howard-Grenville, J., Golden-Biddle, K., Irwin, J., & Mao, J. (2011). Liminality as cultural process for cultural change. *Organization Science, 22*(2), 522–539.

Howse, R. B., Lange, G., Farran, D. C., & Boyles, C. D. (2003). Motivation and self-regulation as predictors of achievement in economically disadvantaged young children. *The Journal of Experimental Education, 71*(2), 151–174.

Hughes, D., Rodriguez, J., Smith, E. P., Johnson, D. J., Stevenson, H. C., & Spicer, P. (2006). Parents' ethnic-racial socialization practices: A review of research and directions for future study. *Developmental Psychology, 42*(5), 747.

Imms, C., Granlund, M., Wilson, P. H., Steenbergen, B., Rosenbaum, P. L., & Gordon, A. M. (2017). Participation, both a means and an end: A conceptual analysis of processes and outcomes in childhood disability. *Developmental Medicine & Child Neurology, 59*(1), 16–25.

Johnson, N. (2014). Creating innovators: Can the library contribute? In *Issues in science and technology librarianship* (p. 76). West Lafayette, IN: Purdue University.

Jojola, T., Lee, T. S., Alacantara, A. M., Belgarde, M., Bird, C. P., Lopez, N., & Singer, B. (2011). *Indian education in New Mexico, 2025.* Santa Fe, NM: Public Education Department.

Konstantatos, H., Siatitsa, D., & Vaiou, D. (2013). 20. Qualitative approaches for the study of socially innovative initiatives.

Ladson-Billings, G. (1995). But that's just good teaching! The case for culturally relevant pedagogy. *Theory into Practice, 34*(3), 159–165.

Lawrence, T. B., Dover, G., & Gallagher, B. (2014). Managing social innovation. In *The Oxford handbook of innovation management* (pp. 316–334). Oxford: Oxford University Press.

Lomawaima, K. T., & McCarty, T. L. (2002). When tribal sovereignty challenges democracy: American Indian education and the democratic ideal. *American Educational Research Journal, 39*(2), 279–305.

Lopez, J., & Scott, J. (2000). *Social structure.* Buckingham, Philadelphia: Open University.

MacCallum, D., Moulaert, F., Hillier, J., & Haddock, S. V. (2009). *Social innovation and territorial development*. Farnham: Ashgate.

Madsen, J. A., & Mabokela, R. O. (2013). *Culturally relevant schools: Creating positive workplace relationships and preventing intergroup differences*. London: Routledge.

McLaren, P. (1999). *Schooling as a ritual performance: Toward a political economy of educational symbols and gestures*. London: Rowman & Littlefield.

Mills, C. (2008). Reproduction and transformation of inequalities in schooling: The transformative potential of the theoretical constructs of Bourdieu. *British Journal of Sociology of Education*, *29*(1), 79–89.

Moffitt, T. E., Arseneault, L., Belsky, D., Dickson, N., Hancox, R. J., Harrington, H., . . . & Caspi, A. (2011). A gradient of childhood self-control predicts health, wealth, and public safety. *Proceedings of the National Academy of Sciences*, *108*(7), 2693–2698.

Morrison, K. A., Robbins, H. H., & Rose, D. G. (2008). Operationalizing culturally relevant pedagogy: A synthesis of classroom-based research. *Equity & Excellence in Education*, *41*(4), 433–452.

Moulaert, F. (Ed.). (2013). *The international handbook on social innovation: Collective action, social learning and transdisciplinary research*. Cheltenham: Edward Elgar Publishing.

Moulaert, F., Martinelli, F., González, S., & Swyngedouw, E. (2007). Introduction: Social innovation and governance in European cities: Urban development between path dependency and radical innovation. Advance online publication. doi: 10.1177/0969776407077737.

Nettleingham, D. (2018). Heritage work: The preservations and performances of Thames sailing barges. *Cultural Sociology*, *12*(3), 384–399.

Nilsson, W., & Paddock, T. (2014). Social innovation from the inside out. *Stanford Social Innovation Review*, *12*(1), 46–52.

Nussbaumer, J., & Moulaert, F. (2004). Integrated area development and social innovation in European cities: A cultural focus. *City*, *8*(2), 249–257.

OECD, K. (2018). *OECD science, technology and innovation outlook 2018*. Paris: OECD Publishing.

Ragin, C. C., & Fiss, P. C. (2016). *Intersectional inequality*. Chicago, IL: University of Chicago Press.

Reyhner, J., & Eder, J. (2017). *American Indian education: A history*. Oklahoma: University of Oklahoma Press.

Rivas-Drake, D., Syed, M., Umaña-Taylor, A., Markstrom, C., French, S., Schwartz, S. J., . . . & Ethnic and Racial Identity in the 21st Century Study Group. (2014). Feeling good, happy, and proud: A meta-analysis of positive ethnic–racial affect and adjustment. *Child Development*, *85*(1), 77–102.

Robinson, K., & Aronica, L. (2015). *Creative schools: Revolutionizing education from the ground up*. Australia: Penguin UK.

RWJF & Ashoka Changemakers. (2016). *What is children's wellbeing?* Retrieved from https://www.changemakers.com/childrenswellbeing/framework.

Schwartz, K. (2019, March 20). *Why schools should be organized to prioritize relationships*. KQED.org. Retrieved from https://www.kqed.org/mindshift/53091/why-schools-should-be-organized-to-prioritize-relationships.

Schweinhart, L. J., Barnes, H. V., & Weikhart, D. P. (2005). Significant benefits: The High/Scope Perry preschool study through age 27. In *Child welfare: Major themes in health and social welfare* (pp. 9–29). Ypsilanti, MI: High/Scope Educational Research Foundation.

Seelig, T. (2012). *inGenius: A crash course on creativity*. London: Hay House, Inc.

Shonkoff, J. P., Duncan, G. J., Yoshikawa, H., Fisher, P. A., Guyer, B., & Magnuson, K. (2010). *The foundations of lifelong health are built in early childhood*. Massachusetts: National Scientific Council on the Developing Child, Harvard University.

Short, P. M., Greer, J. T., & Melvin, W. M. (1994). Creating empowered schools: Lessons in change. *Journal of Educational Administration*, *32*(4), 38–52.

Shorters, T. (n.d.). Asset framing: The other side of the story. *The Communications Network*. Retrieved from https://www.comnetwork.org/resources/asset-framing-the-other-side-of-the-story.

Skiba, R., Reynolds, C. R., Graham, S., Sheras, P., Conoley, J. C., Garcia-Vazquez, E., ... & Palomares, R. (2006). Are zero tolerance policies effective in the schools? An evidentiary review and recommendations an official report of the APA.

Sleeter, C. E. (2012). Confronting the marginalization of culturally responsive pedagogy. *Urban Education*, *47*(3), 562–584.

Smith, A., Fressoli, M., Abrol, D., Arond, E., & Ely, A. (2016). *Grassroots innovation movements*. London: Routledge.

Spencer, M. S., Brown, M., Griffin, S., & Abdullah, S. (2008). Outcome evaluation of the intergroup project. *Small Group Research*, *39*(1), 82–103.

Taylor, R. D., Oberle, E., Durlak, J. A., & Weissberg, R. P. (2017). Promoting positive youth development through school-based social and emotional learning interventions: A meta-analysis of follow-up effects. *Child Development*, *88*(4), 1156–1171.

Teasley, M. L. (2014). Shifting from zero tolerance to restorative justice in schools. *Children & Schools*, *36*(3), 131–133.

Tranter, D. (2018, January 29). The third path to student's psychological wellbeing and achievement. *Nelson Education|Blog*. Retrieved from http://www.nelson.com/blog/the-third-path.

United Nations Permanent Forum on Indigenous Issues. (2010). *The state of the world's Indigenous peoples*. United Nations.

Westby, C. E., & Roman, R. (1995). Finding the balance: Learning to live in two worlds. *Topics in language disorders*, *15*, 68–88.

Westley, F., & Antadze, N. (2010). Making a difference: Strategies for scaling social innovation for greater impact. *Innovation Journal*, *15*(2), article 2.

W. K. Kellogg Foundation. (n.d.). *Native American Community Academy: Developing strong identities*. Retrieved from https://www.wkkf.org:443/what-we-do/featured-work/native-american-community-academy.

Yosso, T. J. (2002). Toward a critical race curriculum. *Equity & Excellence in Education*, *35*(2), 93–107.

Young, S. (1997). 10 Community-based partnerships and sustainable development. In *The politics of sustainable development: Theory, policy and practice within the European Union*. (p. 217). United Kingdom: Routledge.

Zakaras, M. (2016). Let's redraw the map. *Stanford Social Innovation Review*, *14*, 59.

Zhao, E. Y., & Wry, T. (2016). Not all inequality is equal: Deconstructing the societal logic of patriarchy to understand microfinance lending to women. *Academy of Management Journal*, *59*(6), 1994–2020.

Zins, J. E., Payton, J. W., Weissberg, R. P., & O'Brien, M. U. (2007). *Social and emotional learning for successful school performance*. Oxford: Oxford University Press.

Chapter 4

Practice What You Teach
A Case for Emotionally Intelligent Educators
Amy McConnell Franklin and Kei Franklin

United States

> Our deepest calling is to grow into our own authentic self-hood, whether or not it conforms to some image of who we ought to be. As we do so, we will not only find the joy that every human being seeks—we will also find our path of authentic service in the world. —Parker J. Palmer

Educational institutions have a responsibility to develop the inner selves of their students in order to nurture the insight and aptitudes necessary to engage with social challenges and contribute to a better world. In this chapter, we assert the need to systematically develop social and emotional (SE) skills in young people in order to help them become effective and ethical changemakers. We argue that the most effective and efficient way to develop these skills in students is to surround them with teachers who embody these skills themselves—in other words, emotionally intelligent educators. We also present case studies that describe instances of emotional intelligence (EI) training of adults in several schools in Taos, New Mexico (USA), and the resultant impacts on the schools and the wider community.

A strong inner life provides a coherent foundation for dealing with the complexities of the outer world. In the midst of global uncertainty and ever more visible injustice, it is common to feel overwhelmed and powerless in a time that is calling for hope and innovative action. This burden falls especially heavily on young people as they—the anticipated "leaders of tomorrow"—confront a fractured world that is changing at an unprecedented rate.

Responding with nuance, equanimity, and insight to an increasingly polarized, reactive, and externally focused world is a humbling task. How, then, can young people develop not only an awareness of their own values but also the skills to know themselves and navigate their thoughts, emotions, identities, and aspirations in order to better align their actions with those values? How can education more intentionally nurture awareness of our interconnections and translate motivation into movement, insight into action, and personal transformation into social justice?

Now more than ever, young people need role models who embody the characteristics they strive to manifest in themselves. Students need teachers who have confronted their own reflections with such intimacy, humility, and radical acceptance, that when they invite students to look in the mirror, the students trust them and have the courage to look and really see themselves for who they are and who they can become.

> *We can make our minds so like still water that beings gather about us that they may see, it may be, their own images, and so live for a moment with a clearer, perhaps even with a fiercer life because of our quiet.* (William Butler Yeats)

In this chapter, we assert the need to systematically develop the SE skills required to live an authentic life of integrity, connection, and contribution. Authenticity requires self-awareness and courage, and integrity calls for clarity of values and conviction. The ability to connect deeply depends on respect, empathy, and honed communication skills.

But how do we foster these core SE skills in order to nurture balanced, healthy inner lives as a foundation for creating ethical change in the world?

We assert that a framework for developing effective changemakers rests on two crucial concepts: social and emotional learning (SEL) and emotional intelligence (EI). Educational institutions have a responsibility to focus on the development of their students' inner selves in order to nurture young people with the insight and aptitudes to solve social problems and contribute to a better world. In this chapter the following definitions will be used:

- EI: the capacity to (a) effectively blend thoughts and feelings, (b) use emotional information to enhance reasoning, motivations, and decision making, and (c) create and sustain more mutually respectful relationships.
- SEL: the process through which students acquire and effectively apply the knowledge, attitudes, and skills necessary to understand and manage emotions, set and achieve positive goals, feel and show empathy for others, establish and maintain positive relationships, and make responsible decisions. EI is both the foundation for and an outcome of effective SEL. SE skills are the inter and intra-personal skills that are the subject of the model highlighted in this chapter. Please see the end of the chapter for more comprehensive definitions.

We ground these assertions in case studies of adult EI training in schools in the small town of Taos, New Mexico (USA). We present details about what these EI trainings comprised, lessons learned through their implementation, and the resultant impacts on the schools in question as well as the wider community.

Notable impacts include: (a) shifts in school culture to nurture more mutually tolerant relationships across the community, (b) regularly articulated shared values and intentions, (c) increased self-awareness, accountability, and compassion, (d) increased sense of personal responsibility, agency, and understanding of motivations in both adults and students, and (e) improved skills and willingness to constructively engage in difficult conversations, (f) evidence of practice in creating lasting change for the greater good.

While these outcomes were regrettably not measured in a quantifiable way, they are based on observations by teachers, students, parents, and school administrators, conveyed via verbal correspondence to the author. Beyond self-reported observations, evidence of these stated outcomes can be seen in the schools, programs, and initiatives that spun off from the initial adult EI trainings, spearheaded by training participants.

Educational institutions have a responsibility to develop the inner selves of their students in order to nurture the insight and aptitudes necessary to engage with social challenges and contribute to a better world. In this chapter, we assert the need to systematically develop SE skills in young people in order to help them become effective and ethical changemakers. We argue that the most effective and efficient way to develop these skills in students is to surround them with teachers who embody these skills themselves—in other words, emotionally intelligent educators.

We present case studies that describe instances of EI training of adults in several schools in Taos, New Mexico (USA) and the resultant impacts on the schools and the wider community. Notable impacts include: (a) shifts in school culture to nurture mutually tolerant relationships across the community, (b) regularly articulated shared values and intentions, (c) increased self-awareness, accountability, and compassion, (d) increased sense of personal responsibility, agency, and understanding of motivations in both adults and students, (e) improved skills and willingness to constructively engage in difficult conversations, and (f) evidence of practice in creating lasting change for the greater good.

CASE STUDIES

Taos is a small community in northern New Mexico marked by a unique mix of cultural exchange and ethnic discord. Taos' population is composed of four culturally and historically distinct groups: the Taos Pueblo Native Americans, Hispanic peoples, Anglo-Americans, and Mexican Nationals.

The many communities that now fall under the common name of Taos share a range of overlapping histories that actively shape current race and class relations. Social inequality and cyclical poverty are prominent issues facing the town today. Communities suffering under the pressures of drug abuse and teen pregnancies exist side-by-side with those enjoying immoderate wealth. More than three of every four children in the Taos school district live at or below the US poverty line, while at the same time Taos is known for affluent artist communities and wealthy retirees.

Two existing schools—Anansi Charter School (ACS) and Taos High School (THS)—are the primary focus of these case studies, with one former school, Yaxche Learning Center (YLC), playing an important role in the history as well. These three schools implemented EI training for the adults and simultaneously integrated SEL into their classrooms. While ACS and THS continue to integrate EI and SEL as core components of their schools' pedagogies, educators and parents who learned, taught, nurtured, and lived EI and SE skills at YLC (which eventually closed due to lack of funds) went on to incubate several new schools and service agencies in the community which are grounded in and explicitly incorporate and teach EI skills and concepts. These individuals continue to play very significant roles in embedding the concepts and skills in schools and families throughout the community and region. These case studies demonstrate that intensive EI training for adults created opportunities for the effective development of SE skills in youth and left a lasting impact on the culture of the schools, families, and surrounding communities.

While the details of the schools varied—ACS is a K-8 grade public charter school that admits students via a lottery system, Yaxche was a K-8 grade private school, THS is a ninth-grade to twelfth-grade public school—the training model and impacts were similar.

Anansi Charter School (ACS)

Originally a private school focused on early childhood development, in 2001 ACS became a publicly funded charter school, serving students in grades K-2. Prior to becoming a charter school, the Anansi preschool program integrated SE skills development into the early childhood program. With the advent of students in kindergarten via a lottery system, many of whom had had no prior schooling experience, classroom management became more challenging. ACS recognized the need to address SEL more systematically and began integrating EI training for the adults and SEL for students early in its transition to a charter school and continued intensive training in EI over the next three years and beyond.

ACS is now a K-8 grade school and was recently recognized for having the highest academic achievement among charter primary schools in the state. EI development of adults remains a sustained top priority of ACS, and SE skills development in students is a core focus. This section will explain how this transformation occurred.

Implementation

In January 2003, staff, teachers, administrators, interested board members, and parent representatives participated in three days of EI training with trainers from 6 Seconds, an international not-for-profit organization and EI network. This was the first of three intensive trainings held over the next three semesters. Concurrently, as a parent at the school and a trained instructor in the 6 Seconds model, coauthor Amy McConnell Franklin (hereafter Amy) was hired as a consultant to the school to model-teach SEL lessons, write lessons, coach and mentor teachers, and facilitate parent education classes throughout the first year and a half of implementation.

The first goal of this initiative was to develop EI concepts, skills, and shared language within the adults, individually and as a collective, so that they could model and instruct these skills in the classroom. Through professional development coaching and consultation by the 6 Seconds consultants, and with local mentorship by Amy, the teachers were supported to eventually confidently impart the SEL lessons to students.

While in Taos, the 6 Seconds trainers also provided parent training and public lectures to introduce EI to the greater Taos community. This meant that as EI concepts and tools became more deeply embedded into the culture of ACS, the school became a valuable flagship for EI and SEL development in the wider community.

The 6 Seconds approach provides a framework of skills and concepts rather than a set curriculum. The philosophy is that once educators have experienced and begun to incorporate core EI insights and competencies into their own personal lives and professional interactions, they can be supported to seek out and create age-appropriate lessons to build the same skills in students. This approach initially proved to be challenging as teachers felt they neither have the time nor sufficient understanding to translate emerging concepts into customized lessons. Two solutions emerged:

- In advance of the periodic training by 6 Seconds, teachers provided the 6 Seconds consulting trainers with particular themes that had emerged in their classrooms, and the trainers prepared customized, prototypical lessons which they taught to students during their scheduled visits
- Amy was hired to develop and model-teach lessons and to meet with teachers individually and collectively to continue the integration of EI skills, identifying student needs and coaching teachers as they began to build and teach age-appropriate lessons to develop core EI competencies.

Below is an example of a customized lesson addressing the theme of "It's not fair!"—a cry frequently heard in the kindergarten class of ACS. Marsha Rideout, one of the original 6 Second trainers, developed and taught this lesson.

Start the lesson by reading aloud "The Little Red Hen Makes A Pizza"—the classic children's story retold with an empathetic and generous twist by Philemon Sturges and illustrated by Amy Walrod. Have everyone sit in a circle. Each child writes his/her name on a piece of paper which is put into a basket in the middle of the circle. Each child receives a red and a green "flag," made of construction paper (fancier flags can be made by attaching the construction paper to tongue depressors). Two names are selected from the basket and each child of this pair receives a brown paper bag filled with small items that are similar but distinct, for example, one bag contains two small cars of distinct colors and the second bag contains two small bouncy balls, also of distinct colors. Everyone in the circle gets to vote on the relative 'fairness' or 'unfairness' of the contents of the two the brown paper bags, but only the members of the selected pair have the ultimate "vote." The pair can ask for suggestions from the circle as to the fairness of the contents and/or ways to make the contents more fair. Once the first pair decides on the "fairness" of the contents of their bags, the question is asked, shall we put these names back in the basket? Would that be fair? Children can vote and voice their reasoning as to whether or not putting the names back in the basket to be potentially chosen again, is fair or not. The items are part of the lesson, so not kept by the children.

Next a second pair of names is selected and that pair receives another set of bags, this time with items that are a bit more distinct, but still similar, for example, a paint brush and palette of paints in one bag and a box of various colored chalk in the second bag. Again, all the children vote on the fairness of the contents of the bags and the pair whose names were selected have the ultimate say about the relative fairness of the contents and how to make the set more fair. Again, ultimately the decision about the fairness of the contents of the bags rests with the selected pair of children. They can ask for suggestions, negotiate or simply accept the contents as presented.

The lesson continues in this way until all of the children have had the opportunity to receive and consider the contents of a pair of bags. With each set, the contents become a bit more unequal. The third set of bags might contain copies of the same book, one in paperback and one in hardcover. A fourth set holds hats; one sun hat and one ski hat. One set might contain candy, four small bars, and one large bar, of the same candy.

The subjective nature of "fairness" becomes evident as the lesson progresses. Children have multiple opportunities to consider, share their thoughts and hear others perspectives on the relative fairness of items, to think about equality, and whether or not it is "fair" or possible to try to create greater "fairness." Perhaps most importantly the children have the opportunity to hear and see the feelings of their classmates when the perception of unfairness, inequality, injustice emerges. Fairness is a complex concept yet the feelings associated with perceived injustice are apparent even in the young and unsophisticated children. Having some agency in allocations is often key to re-calibrating a sense of justice.

The "Fairness Bags" lesson became

- a foundational SEL lesson for generations of ACS students and
- a prototype of a successful SEL lesson.

It provided:

- the structure of a good SEL lesson,
- shared experience, language, and a reference point for students and staff in many discussions, and
- a springboard for additional lessons created over subsequent semesters and years initially by Amy and eventually by ACS staff.

The themes of equity, empathy, inclusion, justice, and respect for diverse perspectives and needs, collaborative problem solving, self-awareness, and choice were embedded in this lesson and are aligned with values held by the ACS staff for both their classrooms and the world.

This lesson provided a prototype that included all of the foundational components of an EI experiment. EI lessons are designed to be experiential, interactive, and reflective. Lessons start with a shared experience or "hook" to evoke feelings and thoughts about the theme—in this case, the Little Red Hen story. Participation considering the contents of the bag and "voting" provides an "experience" that evokes emotions. Students practice constructive social interactions sharing diverse reactions which build healthy communication skills. As students share and consider alternate perspectives, they nurture empathy, humility, agility in problem solving. Comfort considering diverse perspectives evolve. EI lessons usually take place in a circle to reflect the values of inclusion, democracy, respect, and interdependence. Lessons are age-appropriate, relevant, and transdisciplinary, and typically explore real, current, and complex issues that require nuanced and contextualized consideration. The lessons help create collaborative, empathetic, cohesive groups that practice constructive engagement with one another, even in difficult conversations. SE lessons are customized to the age group, responsive to a stated need, inclusive of skills from across disciplines, and invite action.

As the ACS teachers' own capacity in EI continued to develop, Amy modeled for them how to teach SEL lessons. In the first semester of EI integration, she taught weekly lessons to each of the three classes with the classroom teacher and assistants actively participating in the classroom experiments and discussions. The interactive *Rainbow Kids* curriculum by Barbara Porro was selected to be taught to all grade levels as this curriculum was aligned with the goals, values, and intentions of the EI model and could provide a good baseline and shared story for all of the children in the school. She also met with teachers during weekly staff meetings to talk about lessons and continue the development of EI skills and practices within the team. Watching Amy model-teach and noting student responses to the lessons and the impact of the lessons on student behavior, reinforced and encouraged teachers' confidence and commitment to integrating SEL.

In the second semester, Amy observed classes as the teachers taught weekly lessons she had developed. Amy continued to meet twice monthly with the teachers to discuss the lessons and responsively prepare upcoming lessons and themes. Teachers began to experiment with building lessons to address social and emotion-related needs in their classrooms.

In the third semester, Amy continued to write lessons and source literature to highlight SE topics, and she met monthly with the staff to discuss implementation and consult on the next steps.

Through this coaching and consultation, Amy supported the staff so that they could confidently impart SEL lessons to the students, integrate the SE themes across the curriculum and disciplines, nurture healthy social and emotion-related skills on the playground, and revise disciplinary processes, policies, and procedures to reinforce EI skills and tools. All the while the group of adults further embodied EI skills themselves and integrated aligned concepts, pedagogy, modalities, and procedures in staff meetings, interactions, and parent trainings. Teaching lessons and watching the development of EI skills in the students, in turn, reinforced the adults' understanding of these skills, creating a positive feedback loop.

As teachers became increasingly interested in and comfortable eliciting and addressing SE needs of the students, several shifts began to happen. First, teachers began to more often attend to, elicit, and trust students' feelings and needs and began to interpret these as indicators of change needed. Students were encouraged to verbalize their feelings, needs, and requests for change which fostered in them confidence and agency to request and initiate change. As the students' empathic curiosity was respected and increasingly trusted, they in turn began to trust themselves more. As the students became more skillful at recognizing and constructively articulating their own emotions, needs, and wants, and noticing those of others, emotions became data to motivate change. This newfound skillset was foundational to students initiating changes that benefited themselves and others which in turn demonstrated to students their own capacity and agency as changemakers.

The following story demonstrates a concrete example of how the mutual respect and trust purposefully engendered at ACS led to changes needed by students and responsively created by teachers, increasing agency and commitment to changemaking.

Early cohorts of students graduating from ACS (when it was initially a K-2 grade school) reported considerable "culture shock" when entering conventional schools as third graders. One male Hispanic student reported feeling like "just a number"—anonymous and unseen when he transitioned from ACS to a local public third grade classroom. In one of the early student cohorts instances of classroom, misbehavior increased as the spring semester progressed and graduation approached. Eventually, some students shared with their teachers the worries that they had. Amy designed an EI exercise to give voice to these worries. The second graders were given the time and materials to create collages to describe their feelings about moving to new schools for third grade. One boy who had repeatedly struggled with focusing his attention in the class created a collage of a man inside a cage with claw marks down his back, the tiger on the outside of the cage. Sharing the collages with one another gave the students the chance to make more conscious and articulate their feelings in order to constructively engage with the questions and uncertainty they felt. Following this lesson and in response to the students' sharings, the ACS school administrator arranged for the students to go on field trips to the new schools in order to help mitigate their fears and begin to talk about impending transitions and skills that might mitigate anticipated challenges. The school visits were an effective intervention to help students grapple with their natural fears and questions about the unknown. By committing to identifying and paying deliberate attention to the students' feelings as legitimate sources of information that indicated a need for action, the adults nurtured in the students a sense of agency—their emotions warranted action. The adults in this situation helped the children identify and utilize their emotions to bring about needed change. As the adults noted the impact of EI skills in their personal lives, they became more invested in the approach. They reported being better able to articulate the benefits of self and social awareness, self-regulation, and responsible decision making, and noted improvements in their own relationship skills. Emotions became data that motivated intentional change.

Summary

The transition from an independent, fee-paying early childhood center to a publicly funded elementary school had created some discord and discontent among the ACS community. The first need was therefore to identify the challenges at hand, repair relationships, and build bridges.

EI skills were called on, implemented, and practiced as the 6 Seconds consultants guided the administrator and staff

- to become more self-aware and literate about their emotions, thoughts, and choices, and to impart these skills to others,
- to clearly and inclusively articulate shared values, intentions, and goals for the school community, and
- to build shared agency and responsibility in individuals and the collective so that the schools' structures, pedagogy, and discipline policies were more aligned with the articulated goals.

EI skills and concepts were both taught explicitly and simultaneously experienced in lived, meaningful ways as tools and lessons were used to build a more agile, resilient, cohesive, and self-aware team of educators.

As the team of adults became better able to communicate and engage constructively—as they became more self-aware, empathetic, intentional, and responsive as individuals and as a collective—they became more cohesive, trusting, and comfortable creating classrooms that integrated and reinforced EI skills. When teachers responded to student emotions and needs with respect and appropriate action, students in turn recognized their own agency. The ACS school administrator gave the teachers trust and agency in order for the teachers to communicate this same trust and ownership to their students.

When actions are aligned with intentions/values, the feelings that follow inspire further bold and aligned action. This positive feedback loop reinforces parallel processes and compels similar action. Teachers were educated in EI and developed a shared language and body of concepts and skills as a team. Reinforcing practices were built into the daily/weekly processes at the level of both the adults and the students. Structures and procedures aligned with intentions enabled sustainability, depth, and growth of EI competencies that continue to today, eighteen years later.

Critical Components

The following components seem essential to the sustained integration of EI at ACS:

- Felt Needs: There were felt needs within the community, which EI skills could address namely (a) incoming students lacked the emotional and social skills to effectively learn, and (b) there were relational fractures within the team of teachers and administrators in need of mending.

- Vision: There was a strong vision of where school wanted to go, enabled by exposure to the field of EI as (a) a foundation for SEL and (b) a skill set for improved communication and team cohesion.
- Resources: There were resources available for EI professional development and local EI expertise to support curriculum development, modeling, mentoring, and coaching to build capacity.
- Integration: The commitment to developing and embodying EI skills on every level—from ongoing professional development for school administrators and EI classes for parents—meant that SEL practices, modalities, processes, and policies were integrated at all levels, from board meetings to classrooms to home life. This integrated model created mutually reinforcing processes.
- Community: Dissemination of the EI concepts, language, and skillsets, and consequent interest and support throughout the community gave rise to increased energy and commitment to the development of EI for all children.

Additionally, ACS relied heavily on literature from the field of SEL, using this literature as a basis to create lessons that enhance foundational skills and weave SEL across the curriculum. Besides needs-specific lessons, like the "Fairness Bags" one described above, the ACS teachers also integrated classroom practices including *check-ins, circle or council time, communication charters*, and other rituals that developed SE skills and highlighted the importance of feelings, relationships, and choices. Please refer to the end of the chapter for more details about such practices.

Initially, the same SEL curriculum was taught to all students, from K-2 grade to introduce concepts and shared language. In subsequent semesters, Amy worked alongside teachers to create a variety of age-appropriate lessons as teachers gained confidence in creating lessons to develop foundational EI skills. For a more granular Timeline of Implementation, please refer to the end of the chapter.

Key Lessons Learned

- Adults need to be trained in EI before and simultaneously with students. For accountability, whole team training is essential and can be followed by individual or small-group mentoring, but it is important that the whole team of teachers is familiar with the same material and is on board with the universal commitment to shared praxis.
- Both individuals and structures need to embrace the concepts so that EI is understood and modeled by the community at every level.
- It takes three to five years to intentionally change the culture of a school. The level of external time and resources required for integration decreases

over time as internal skills and self-sufficiency increase. Intensive training with modeling leads to coaching and eventually observation and mentoring.
- As EI grows in a community, more opportunities arise to discuss SE dilemmas; to embrace diversity, nurture empathy, and consider multiple ways to address challenges; to emphasize long-term thinking, intrinsic motivation, and ethical decision making.
- A curriculum is a tool, not the essence of the teaching. At the offset, teachers may depend on an SEL curriculum, but as the foundational EI skills are understood, teachers create their own lessons, seek out literature, design writing assignments, and most importantly embody pedagogy that nurtures SE skills. Multiple curricula enrich and diversify learning.
- Beyond custom-made lessons, simple classroom routines including *check-in*s, *circle time*, and other rituals that highlight feelings, relationships, motivations, and responsible decision making, all contribute to the growth of SE capacities.
- Discipline policies and procedures need to be aligned with SE skills. When this alignment is present, the goal of discipline is more clearly identified (e.g., to rebuild relationships, restore community, and repair harm rather than to punish offending behavior). With systemic changes that better align with SE values, disciplinary referrals decrease as pro-social behaviors increase. *Rules broken* become opportunities to reflect on, learn, and grow SE skills individually and collectively.

The positive impact of EI skills on the culture and learning at ACS was so outstanding that the school's leadership decided that EI training was an innovation worth spreading. In 2006, ACS was awarded a Federal Dissemination Grant to provide two years of EI training to schools in the region. Although ACS was an early childhood center, the EI training was disseminated to two charter middle-high schools (sixth to twelfth grade) in Santa Fe, New Mexico. Assisted by Amy, the ACS teachers conducted EI skills training, which further strengthened their own fluency and understanding of EI. In 2014, ACS was recognized as an Ashoka *Start Empathy* School.

Ongoing, systematic professional development in EI, mindfulness, and kindred approaches to SEL continues to expand and deepen the understanding, skillsets, and repertoire of the adults at ACS so that in turn the SEL integration has maximum integrity and impact on students, families, and the school culture as a whole.

Teachers, I believe, are the most responsible and important members of society because their professional efforts affect the fate of the earth. (Helen Caldicott)

Taos High School (THS)

The majority of high-school students in Taos County attend THS. Approximately 70 percent of students identify as part of an ethnic minority community and approximately two-thirds of the students come from homes that are economically disadvantaged ("How Does Taos High Rank Among America's Best High Schools?" US News & World Report, (n.d.)).

In the case of THS, the most visible consequence of the adult EI training showed up in a surprising form. Unanticipated by the adults, the most enduring impact has been a student-designed response to the endemic problem of entrenched racism at the school. The teachers created conditions for students to constructively engage with the reality and the students, in turn, devised an innovative solution in collaboration with the adults—a solution that became and continues to be a core communal event supported by the entire community.

Implementation

Between 2003 and 2011, disparate members of the THS community encountered SEL skills from multiple entry points:

- Individual teachers recognized the need for SEL-related skills development in students and consulted with Amy who coached them in integrating SEL into specific classes.
- Amy was contracted to teach teen-parent students SEL as a part of their in-school parenting classes.
- Some twelfth-grade students took Amy's course on EI at the local university.
- THS English department had the opportunity to participate in the beta development phase of an assessment to measure EI in youth.
- Some teachers attended training in restorative practices and processes—essential approaches to discipline problems in a school culture committed to EI and SEL.
- Students and families from the primary schools embedding SEL joined the high-school community.

This diffuse approach over time prepared the soil and helped identify and connect the dots between (a) entrenched challenges to learning, counterproductive patterns in decision making leading to destructive habits and conditions and the lack of social cohesion widespread in the school and (b) the promise and potential of teachable individual and collective emotion-related and social skills to create alternate decision-making skills, increased personal responsibility and agency, and greater social cohesion in the richly diverse community.

In June 2011, utilizing a small pot of funds needing to be spent at the end of the district's fiscal year, a small cohort of seven teachers from the English, science, and math departments, as well as the librarian, joined Amy in a four-day intensive EI training. The question was: *could teaching SEL increase student engagement and address various relational, emotional, and behavioral challenges experienced by the students?* These self-selected teachers were paid a small stipend for attending the training as a part of their professional development.

In addition to core EI skills and concepts, a pivotal component of the training was a presentation by the local chapter of PFLAG (Parents and Friends of Lesbians and Gays). Topics such as sexuality, mental health, abusive relationships, drug and alcohol use were not readily addressed in the classroom due to a lack of time, vocabulary, and appropriate forum, as well as discomfort on the part of teachers. Teachers said that they recognized that some students felt emotionally and physically unsafe on campus and that they were not holding space for difficult but critical conversations to take place constructively. Connecting with PFLAG provided a model of a socially and emotionally informed, educational approach to skillfully engage the community in sensitive, controversial topics that needed to be addressed. This brief experiential EI training provided the small cohort of early adopting teachers with a glimpse of how social and emotional skills could be mobilized to engage complex topics with skillful respect, compassion, courage, and transparency. The cohort of teachers identified the following areas as essential needs to be addressed during the full-staff training which would take place two months later, at the start of the school year:

- Building group cohesion through deliberate, diverse, and frequent regroupings of students into different tables in class
- Cocreating and displaying a signed adult *communication charter*, highlighting the need for adult cooperation with a concrete commitment to specific values and practices
- Developing emotional literacy in teachers and students
- Articulating shared values for the community
- Combating "emotional hijacking" through effective emotional navigation skills
- Creative and pluralistic thinking for problem solving
- Increase empathy for underrepresented perspectives and marginalized groups through exposure to the PFLAG presentation

Although the value of integrating EI into the full-staff training in August was not appreciated by every member of the THS community (some teachers did not feel SEL fell within the scope of their responsibility), a committed group of staff and teachers prevailed and rallied the group to continue to engage and learn together. In addition to the full-staff August training, Amy was contracted to be engaged for sixteen days on campus. Every six weeks she spent two consecutive days on campus helping the four departments; math, science, English, and social studies use their designated "professional learning community" meeting times constructively to build SE skills that would both positively impact departmental interactions and efficacy and prepare the teachers to integrate SEL into their classrooms. As a result of these periodic meetings, the teachers' interest and understanding about the potential impact of EI training on student engagement and learning grew. During her days on campus, Amy was also called into a variety of classes to help teachers address ongoing social, behavioral, and learning challenges.

The Birth of the "EQ Retreat"

In January 2012, Carla Chavez—a THS science teacher—approached Amy, lamenting the fact that the students in her class clustered into social groups determined by ethnicity. Having noticed the impact on her department and their capacity to communicate constructively and make decisions, she wondered if the EI skills being developed in the adults might be able to support her students in having constructive experiences and conversations that might help them overcome the entrenched racialized discriminatory dynamics. Ms. Chavez and Amy worked together to devise six, ninety-minute lessons to explore ethnic identity and promote constructive conversations about race and culture in the science teacher's classroom. The lessons explored questions such as:

- *What is race, ethnicity, and culture?*
- *What benefits and challenges had students experienced based on their ethnic identity?*
- *How, where, and why have ethnic categories emerged?*
- *Is ethnicity a choice? Why or why not?*
- *Can one challenge history, exercise agency, forge a new path, or choose their identity? How so?*

Students engaged eagerly with the questions, keen to critically explore their own histories, ethnicities, cultures, races, and identities. Word spread to other departments. Toward the end of the weeks of engagement, a group of grade 12 students said, "We should have done this earlier." We understood this to mean earlier in the year, as it was already late February and graduation was fast upon us. "No," they said, "when we first came to high school!" While we knew that the skills were useful in helping individuals become calmer, more self-regulated, and happier, we had not anticipated that these skills would provide the venue, language, and skills to empower students to imagine a different social reality and more comfortable school culture. It was important that the students' initiative was embedded in a developing culture among the adults who had a shared body of experiences, language, and emerging skills to understand and creatively support the nascent student initiative.

The politics and tensions of ethnic discrimination underlie many interactions and decisions in the small Taos community, and perhaps even more apparently at THS. After completing the six lessons on ethnic identity in Ms. Chavez's class, the students conceived of a way to help future generations of students avoid falling into similar patterns of narrowed intercultural relations and discrimination. Supported by a cadre of adults, the students went on to organize a retreat that would welcome new students, where they could relay "words of wisdom" that they wished their seniors had told them and ultimately contribute to building more inclusive and kind school culture. A month later, the students led the inaugural "EQ Retreat," a gift from the graduating class to the school. The retreat required considerable commitment and collaboration from students, teachers, administrators, and the wider Taos community.

Implementation

Teachers used their knowledge of student friendship groups to arrange groupings for the retreat to intentionally disrupt established cliques and created space for new bonds to form. They volunteered to lead sessions with the twelfth-grade students, providing direct instruction and guided practice of core SEL skills. The English department assigned writing projects in advance of the retreat that highlighted personal experiences requiring core EI skills, stories that could be shared during the retreat. Students in the woodworking class designed a puzzle of which each piece would be decorated by one of the eleven retreat groups. Local businesses donated supplies and snacks. The local university awarded one academic credit (a mandatory prerequisite for graduation) to students who attended all three days of the retreat, eliminating a barrier to high-school completion.

The THS administration allocated three school days to the EQ Retreat, aligning the timing with standardized testing so that many teachers were available to lead workshops and provide mentorship to the twelfth-grade students who were organizing the retreat to train the ninth graders. The PFLAG panel shared their stories of marginalization on the basis of gender and sexual identity. This skillfully led session modeled for students the possibility of respectful and constructive discussions about sensitive, complex topics. For three days, the students rotated through workshops, learning core SEL skills from seniors, teachers, and community mentors.

The first session of each day involved a group gathering in which the participating twelfth-grade students stood before the entire assembly—their classmates, teachers, ninth graders, and community members—and shared stories of challenges that they had faced during high school and what helped them survive and even grow through them. These were difficult stories to hear and took great courage and strong EI to share. There were stories of betrayal, forgiveness, loss of a parent, abuse, and neglect, as well as stories of the skills and support systems that helped the students carry on. THS, like many long-established institutions, was known for being reluctant to change and slow to innovate. Yet in just six short weeks, a committed group of students—with the support of peers, teachers, administrators, and the wider community—designed the highly successful inaugural EQ Retreat, a powerful example of SEL in action that has now become an annual tradition at THS.

On the final day of the retreat, the students fit together eleven uniquely decorated puzzle pieces to form a single piece of art—a united world—to hang in the THS lobby. A second EQ Retreat was scheduled for October of the following school year. This year the community will hang its tenth EQ Retreat art piece in the THS lobby. While by no means a fix-all solution, the EQ Retreat has become a treasured innovation that is recognized for helping the community come together and engage constructively around complex and long-standing circumstances. It has also become a respected and institutionalized forum for student engagement and contribution that was imagined, created, and is sustained by students.

Critical Components

The following components seem to have been essential to the sustained integration of EI at THS:

- Emotions began to be seen as data rather than a distraction for a majority of the community.
- A signed communication charter (Emotions Matter. Yale Center for Emotional Intelligence, n.d.) for the adults was created and displayed publicly.
- The promise and potential of EI skills that could be taught, learned, and could become more permanent and available through practice were developed through training a majority of the teachers and administrators. The students learned through both direct instruction at the EQ Retreat and through integration and modeling by a cadre of adults on campus.
- Adults and students had a shared body of language, experiences, and skills that permitted constructive communication and support/trust in students needs.

- Students took the lead as changemakers and the success of the innovation reinforced trust in the students.

For a more granular Timeline of Implementation, please refer to the end of the chapter.

Lessons Learned

- As the THS staff began to embody EI skills, they recognized the potential of these skills to respond to endemic challenges to learning and relating. They began to "connect the dots" between SEL skills and entrenched emotional, relational, and behavioral challenges.
- Training the whole staff was essential for the evolution of the EQ Retreat. Shared language, tools, goals, and intentions allowed the administration and teachers to allocate the time and resources necessary to carry forward this innovation.
- Building trust within the staff and between the staff and Amy at the beginning of the year and throughout the year led to effective communication and conviction regarding the importance of SEL. Without this trust building, Carla Chavez would not have approached Amy, and the EQ Retreat would likely not have materialized.
- The EQ Retreat originated from the concern of a single teacher within the context of a particular class. Students engaged and devised an innovative solution that was authentic, respectful, and tailored specifically to what they perceived as the needs of their community. This innovation and its success resulted from students who felt they were being seen as the whole human beings they are, by staff and teachers who shared some common understanding and values.
- Since 2012, the EI training sessions and the EQ Retreat have been fundamentally changing the culture of THS. Teachers and school administrators verbally report fewer fights in the halls and say that disciplinary referrals have decreased and enrollment is up. The school is now reputed to be a kinder, more inclusive place to learn for the diverse students that comprise its community.

In 2015, a team of THS students and teachers attended the Emotion Revolution Conference at Yale University sponsored by Yale Center for EI (YCEI) and the Born this Way Foundation. The same year, the "Taos Pod"—composed of THS students and peers from the neighboring Taos Academy—was recognized by the YCEI as *Ambassadors for Change* and a Pioneer EI School. In 2016, the Taos Pod was awarded an InspirED Changemaker Award, sponsored by Facebook and the YCEI. THS students and faculty from the pod attended the 2016 InspirED Changemaker Summit. THS staff and students intend to disseminate the innovation to communities within and beyond the state of New Mexico.

CONCLUSION

As social beings, it is through social interactions that we begin to understand who we are, what we care about, what we stand for, and what we won't stand. Teachers have a choice. They can deliberately create classroom structures that invite and, in fact, depend on participation by all and encourage diverse voices, experiences, and perspectives or they can create pedagogies and structures that privilege a single story and reinforce a dominant narrative.

Classroom structures and pedagogy can invite authentic engagement and model democracy while nurturing critical thinking, empathy, and responsibility. Teachers must both embody and value these outcomes if they are to model and foster these qualities. Teachers who understand and have explored these questions themselves are necessary if the students in their care are to learn who they are and what aligns with their own values, experiences, and truths versus simply following rules, directives, and established norms.

In order to constructively participate in an uncertain future, youth need SE skills, and creativity; they need hope and confidence in their own agency; they need awareness of themselves and others in order to recognize their strengths, limitations, and interdependencies, and to practice putting into action changes that are aligned with their values, needs, and dreams, individually and collectively. Teachers and classrooms that model the characteristics needed—empathy, engagement, curiosity, and agency—have a chance to nurture these qualities in students.

Different age groups require different processes. Young children will model the SE skills in the adults around them. For better or worse, they mostly trust the adults in their lives to be honest and wise and will act as they see others acting. Older students who have often already realized that not all adults have integrity need a cadre of adults who believe in them and understand SE the concepts and skills well enough to support students in their efforts to create a more socially and emotionally skillful, equitable, respectful, and inclusive world.

Schools that envision and articulate the intention to create ethical, self-aware changemakers, and align pedagogy and structures with this outcome model these characteristics and create mutually respectful interactions, policies, and procedures with these intentions and empowered students with the skills to be ethical and effective changemakers.

Impact on a Community

The EI trainings at ACS, Yaxche, and THS had widespread effects on the community, far beyond the walls of the schools. The intentional and systematic training of EI in adults and the commitment to SEL in schools have permanently changed the lives of many individuals and families. Just as they can empower students to innovate compassionate, respectful solutions, EI skills empowered an array of adults in Taos to innovate. Leaders of the programs described below were all parents or educators involved in EI trainings in one of the three schools highlighted.

- *First Steps Home-Visiting Program*: Weekly home visits for all first-time parent are organized and funded by the local hospital (Enson & Imberger, 2017). The focus is on developing responsive, informed, compassionate parent-child interactions starting from infancy. Staff are trained and coached in EI skills, which form the foundation of the organization's culture, and these skills are taught, modeled, and practiced with the new parents over the first four years of the child's life through ongoing contact with each family. First Steps is disseminating their model of Infant Mental Health home visiting across the state and nationally.
- Community-wide parenting classes: Incorporating EI skills and concepts with a broad swatch of parents, across diverse groups, these classes are sponsored by the local Community Foundation and held in public spaces like the local public library. The same foundational EI skills are taught through experiential learning, reflection, and interaction. Parents from across the community participate and include parents who were court-ordered to attend parenting classes, grandparents, and parents of students from every school in the community.
- Taos Academy: A seventh to twelfth-grade charter school based on an online academic learning model embeds EI skills through staff training, weekly direct instruction with students, and integration across the curriculum as a core component of leadership skills for the twenty-first century.
- Sixth-grade EQ "boot camp": Taos Middle School, a full-inclusion program for a sixth-grade classroom in which fundamental EI skills were taught and integrated intensively for the first six weeks of each school year. Results of the program included increased collaboration and inclusion, improved relationship and conflict resolution skills, and decreased disciplinary interruptions and referrals throughout the year.
- The Taos branch of the University of New Mexico sponsors the following programs that integrate EI and SEL practices:
  - Kid's Korner—an early childhood lab school where EI forms the foundation for staff development and student learning and informs teachers' interaction with students and families.

- Taos Education and Career Center—an SEL-focused adult education program wherein participants learn social and emotional life skills while simultaneously developing basic academic knowledge. The program combines SE and technical competence for lifelong learning.
- Semester-long courses on EI—an introductory and an advanced course on EI were taught by Amy for four years under the Psychology department.
* Professional training in masters in social work: Integration of EI training into social work programs across the state consequent to ACS Dissemination Grant.

GLOSSARY OF TERMS

Emotional intelligence (EI) is the ability to process complex information about one's own and others' emotions and to use that information as a guide to thinking and behavior. High-EI individuals pay attention to, use, understand, and manage emotions in ways that help them interact effectively with their environment, benefiting themselves and others.[1]

Social and emotional learning (SEL) is the process of acquiring and effectively applying the knowledge, attitudes, and skills that help students and teachers to understand and manage emotions, set and achieve positive goals, feel and show empathy for others, establish and maintain positive relationships, and to make responsible decisions

EI is a building block of SE competence, as it allows a person to use emotion to enhance reasoning and decision making.

Collaborative for Academic, Social, and Emotional Learning (CASEL) is an internationally recognized research-based organization that advocates SEL programming in schools. CASEL's model of SEL[2] includes the social and emotional competencies of self-awareness, social awareness, relationship skills, decision-making skills, and self-management.

SEL promotes cognitive, affective, and behavioral education; as people learn to connect respectfully with one another and their environment, they choose to more often think, feel and act in caring and compassionate ways. This increases their ability to consider alternative perspectives and motivates them to navigate complexity while accounting for the internal experiences of self and others.[3]

Mindfulness—"Being aware, on purpose, of things as they are at the present moment, with curiosity and kindness." An outcome of the practice of meditation, mindfulness permits[4] focused awareness of the bodily experience of the present moment and aids the development of perspective taking, genuine curiosity, and empathy.

Kindred educational approaches that aspire to promote children's social-emotional cognitive competencies[5] and enhance the environmental conditions and contexts that influence their learning and development go by various names including character education, global citizenship, ethics, peace, civics education, positive behavior supports, twenty-first-century skills, mind-sets, and whole-child education.

Robust research indicates that these are teachable, learnable skills that become more permanent with practice and convey myriad academic as well as nonacademic benefits.[6]

An Integrated Model

The skills to create and sustain mutually respectful relationships and to make circumspect decisions that benefit the whole rest on (1) awareness of the thoughts, feelings, and context of self and others, (2) clarity of intention grounded in values, empathy, and respect, and (3) a robust sense of choice and agency (See Figure 4.1).

When these three domains interact effectively EI emerges, resulting in more mutually respectful relationships, choices that are aligned with values, and decisions that contribute to the greater (common) good.

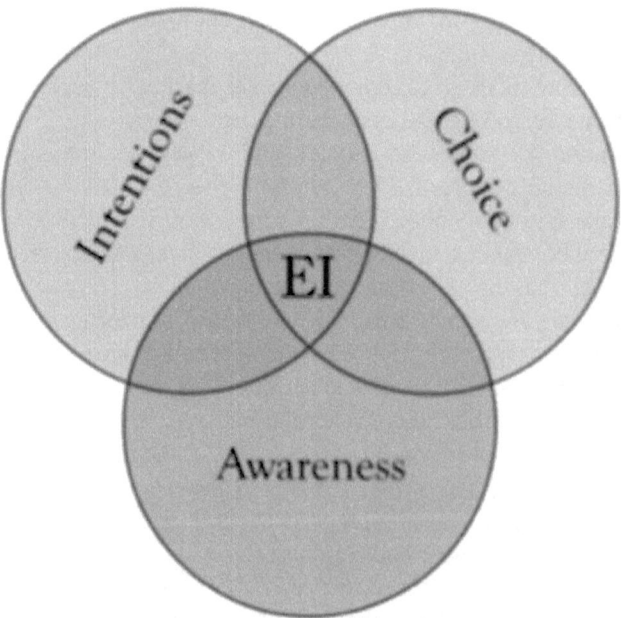

Figure 4.1 An Integrated Model of Emotional Intelligence.

The model integrates various theories of EI to capture three fundamental domains: (1) Awareness: being conscious of thoughts, feelings, actions in self and others, mindful of context, the connectivity of identity, history, personality, tendencies, focus of attention, and patterns in thoughts, feelings, and action, in self and others. (2) Intention: clarity of purpose, reason and desired outcomes of an interaction, action, decision, in order to more frequently align actions with intentions. Values guide choices and motivation compels movement. (3) Choice: a strong sense of agency, the belief that one has options and alternatives about possible courses of action and agency in one's own life. Skills that contribute to accountable, compassionate decision making include consequential thinking, deepened intrinsic motivation, choosing an optimistic outlook, and recognizing that with choice comes responsibility.

Restorative Processes When things "go wrong" as they inevitably will when a community grows, experiments, culture shifts, risks are taken; discipline processes must be aligned with and reflect the values and purposes of the new culture. The field of restorative justice and restorative processes provides many examples, guides, tools, and processes that share the fundamental values and principles of the model described in this chapter. The authors believe any school truly committed to the integration of SEL and EI must adopt a restorative discipline policy for students.

The guiding principles of a restorative community are that everyone wants and needs to belong and that positive interpersonal relationships are a major influence on behavior. When we look at a restorative community more broadly, the restorative practices that are implemented in these communities devote time and energy to creating a sense of interconnected relationships, fostering trust and openness. At the same time, space is made for each person to show up as an individual in the interconnected whole. Each person's voice is given an opportunity to be heard and each person's strengths are given an opportunity to make a positive contribution. In a restorative community, Individualist and Collectivist views do not need to be at odds. The things that make us unique and different from others can be honored within a deeply felt understanding of interconnected social relationships (Pointer, 2016)

Additional resources are listed below.

FOUNDATIONAL LESSONS

Check in

A *check in* is a structured routine that provides practice in self-awareness and respectful listening. As a whole group, in pairs or small groups, a check in is an invitation to look inward and report on the present state of their inner landscape.

Physical objects such as a collection of cards, rocks, cars, or flowers can be used to metaphorically represent and help describe the inner landscape. For example, a miniature ram to one student might represent strength, fleet-footed maneuvers, and readiness to fight. Similarly, identifying a particular imagined image such as a weather pattern, landscape, or movie could provide insight and be a useful aid for communicating. For example, the question "What landscape would best describe how you are doing right now?" might invite responses ranging from an open plain with mountains in the distance to a jungle with many vines and roots.

The first response might indicate an open mind and long-range perspective, while the second might represent a feeling of being too busy and penned in. Crucially, however, the insights could vary from person to person: for another individual, a jungle might represent abundance and multiple options. It is thus important to state that there are no right or wrong answers and that everyone has the right to pass. No one should challenge anyone else's check in.

Check-ins are based on individual perceptions and require trust and vulnerability. Sharing such information creates a culture of empathy and inclusion and highlights the importance of feelings and relationships. Metaphorical thinking is a valuable skill in many arenas, and teachers report being grateful for the opportunity to learn more about the inner lives and minds of their students as their students weave stronger bonds with one another and their teacher.

Communication Charter

A communication charter is a document collaboratively created by members of a community that outlines how they aspire to treat one another. Its purpose is to establish a supportive and[7] productive environment for learning. Cocreating and displaying a signed communication charter signals the commitment to mutual cooperation and dedication to specific values and practices.

Circle and Council[8]

It is a practice that involves bringing people into a circle to authentically share their personal experiences while listening without judgment to others doing the same. These processes[9] draw on indigenous practices from around the planet and have been advocated by many organizations including the Center for Justice and Peacebuilding and The Ojai Foundation.[10]

Deliberate, Diverse, and Frequent Regroupings at Tables

Random mixing of members of a group offers them opportunities to engage meaningfully with myriad peers and builds group cohesion. Groups can be creatively designated in a variety of ways. For example, participants could organize themselves in a line from youngest to oldest, then split them into groups based on age. A teacher could hand out playing cards to participants and have them organized according to the suits on their cards. Another approach could be to get participants to line up based on how far they are currently located from their birthplace and then group according to that criteria.

Emotional Literacy

Developing a rich and nuanced, accurate vocabulary for feelings is a foundational building block for all models of EI and SEL. Several curricula focus specifically on this skill set. The authors are most familiar with the curriculum RULER and anchor tool—Mood Meter—both from the Yale Center for Emotional Intelligence. Below is a preliminary lesson to build curiosity about emotional literacy:

1) Give students three minutes to individually jot down in whatever language they choose, as many words as possible to describe feelings, that is, mad, sad, happy, ashamed, confused, and so on.
2) At the end of the three minutes, ask students to indicate with a raised hand if they have at least five words, ten, fifteen, twenty, over twenty.
3) Have each person categorize the words they listed by (a) feelings they have when their needs are being met and (b) feelings they have when their needs are not being met.[11]
4) Count which category has more words for individuals and the group. Explore why this might be from an evolutionary perspective, from cultural, individual viewpoints, and the meaning and purpose of communication around feelings.
5) Categorize feelings by intensity—do some words have more energy and some less? Does this depend on individuals, cultures, histories, modeling?
6) Explore the following. Some models identify seven core emotions. Some identify eight. What are they? Do you agree? Are emotions hardwired or taught? What are the implications if they are biological responses? What would be some evolutionary advantages of them being hard wired? How are emotions communicated? What percentage of communication is verbal, body language, tone? Create lessons and research assignments to explore these questions.

Value Sort Experiment

Value sort experiment is an exercise to help participants identify and prioritize values and motivations, providing the opportunity to more closely align actions with values.[12]

1) To begin, provide students with a set of eight cards, each with one of the following words: friendship, beauty, riches, wisdom, peace, family, popularity, or long life. These are aspects of life that are commonly "valued."
2) Invite participants to organize the cards according to the order of importance to them—there are no right or wrong answers.
3) Once ordered, ask them to eliminate three that they could do without.
4) Then eliminate two more so that they have three values remaining.
5) Discuss in pairs or small groups personal interpretations of the values—words on the cards and the process of elimination.
6) Finally ask people to describe concrete examples of behaviors or choices that indicate that in fact what they say they value is in fact what they value.

Once established as a tool for values clarification, a modified version of the tool serves in myriad circumstances and can be an anchor for school culture. For example:

- Eight intentions for a school trip: new sights, group bonding, stay in budget, sport, explore a new area, learn new content, reinforce learning, and social skills in public.
- Eight variables in choosing universities: cost, location, pedagogy, departments, quality of professors, prestige, location, and quality of students.

Six-Second Pause[13]

> *Between stimulus and response there is a space. In that space lies our freedom and power to choose our response. In our response lies our growth and freedom.*
> (Victor Frankl)

This lesson develops a tool for creating a pause or space essential for responding rather than reacting.

Ask students to privately think of a time when they reacted to a trigger in a way they later regretted. Choose a small incident. Have them write on a paper some of the ripples or impacts of this reaction.

1) Ask them to imagine an alternative response they might have chosen and list the anticipated consequences of that choice.

2) Explain that being able to create a space or pause between a stimulus and a response is a capacity we can all develop, and it is often a crucial tool for choosing an optimal response. What is needed is to engage our neocortex in order to be able to most effectively access the thinking part of our brain and respond from a position informed by both thought and feelings in order to respond in a way we will feel good about in the long run. This lesson introduces a technique for creating that space by engaging the neocortex.
3) Ask students to list six colors or six bands, six countries that border Germany or six seas, six words that start with the letter "m," or six flavors of ice cream—customized for the age group and their interests. Keep asking for items in different categories until students have to really think to come up with at least six items.
4) Explain that by thinking of these items, they've just engaged their neocortices.
5) Ask them to write down three categories of items, activities, adjectives that have some interest to them; for example, breeds of dogs, ways to cook an apple, sports, pairs of shoes they have, names of cousins, and countries they'd like to visit. The categories should have personal relevance and interest.
6) For practice, ask students to write down six items in one of the categories and then to pair share these six items and the organizing category as well as the other categories they chose.
7) Group share categories if students are interested.

An Illustrative Anecdote: A university student shared a dramatic example of implementing the six-seconds pause. On the weekend following our class practicing the "six-second pause," she had a party at her house and walked into the bathroom to find a friend using drugs. Rather than "rearrange the bones of her friend's face," she stepped back out of the bathroom and listed the names of six of her cousins—a category she had identified in class. This pause permitted her to remember that (1) her friend was probably in big trouble, addicted to drugs, (2) that she would not tolerate this behavior at her house, (3) that her friend probably needed help, (4) that she needed to stop the behavior and get her friend home as quickly as possible, (5) to think who she could ask for help, and (6) consider long-term help for her friend that she could call on.

She stepped back into the bathroom, spoke to her friend firmly, respectfully, and compassionately. They dealt with the matter and got the friend home.

In reflecting on the situation, the student was able to identify several beneficial outcomes of the decision including de-escalating the situation, helping her friend, not injuring her friend, not embarrassing the friend, not disrupting the party, not endangering herself or anyone else. It was a notable example of a six-second pause put to practical use.

Six Ways to Peel a Banana[14]

This lesson provides a fun, memorable introduction to divergent thinking skills and creative problem solving. Once experienced, it becomes a quick reference point for a community and a reminder that there are always multiple ways to respond to a problem, question, or choice. Ideally, this exercise should become a standard tool for decision making.

There is an unfortunately graphic expression used in parts of the United States: "there are lots of ways to skin a cat." A teacher at the Yaxche School proposed an alternative metaphor that later evolved into this lesson:

1) Break students into small groups of three to four people.
2) Give each group one banana and one knife. Ask them to find at least six ways to get to the fruit of the banana and record the different methods.
3) Have each small group share with the class their various approaches, until all of the techniques have been listed. Don't repeat the same techniques.
4) Discuss as a class the process of decision making. Possible prompting questions include:
    Is there a "right" way to peel a banana? How would your technique change if you have one banana and six hungry children? Are there advantages to starting at the bottom vs the top of the banana? What if you want to share the banana with a friend but you have a sore throat?
5) Deductions: There are always multiple ways to address a problem and context and values inform solutions. For example, the context may be six hungry children and one banana. The core values of the people involved may be: inclusion, fairness, empathy, and responsibility. Combining these two will help determine which approach is most aligned with the core values and most appropriate for the context.
6) Provide two or three age-appropriate role-play prompts for the students to practice the lessons. For example, one child is using the orange pencil and when she goes to the bathroom, her pencil rolls onto the floor. Another child picks it up and starts using it. What are the first child's options of how to respond when she returns to her table?
7) It is important to insist on listing at least six ways to address the challenge. The first four possible responses are easy to generate; they often evolve spontaneously from patterned thinking. However, the discipline to insist on at least six responses pushes thinking beyond established patterns and generally results in more creative and compassionate solutions.

8) After having completed the exercise, the prompt "there are always six ways . . ." is frequently enough to remind a trained community to pause, consider multiple solutions, discuss values, and make choices that are aligned with values.
9) The lesson provides an opportunity to revisit and remember core values, think creatively, and make circumspect decisions.

GRANULAR IMPLEMENTATION TIMELINES

Detailed Timeline of Implementation of EI at ACS

Preservice professional development at the beginning of the year: two-day training with six-second consultants; experiential training and capacity building in core EI skills: self-awareness, self-navigation, and self-direction. These three domains are broken into eight core competencies: emotional literacy, pattern recognition, consequential thinking, emotional navigation, intrinsic motivation, choosing optimism, empathy, and noble goal. Foundational exercises to develop skills in these competencies include: communication charter, check-ins, lists of feeling words, six-second pause, ripple effect, six ways to peel a banana, optimism, values clarification, and aligning actions with values. The consultants returned approximately every semester to continue experiential training and capacity building with the ACS administrator and staff. Amy participated in all trainings as well.

- **Semester 1**: Amy led weekly SEL lessons in the classrooms with the active participation of teachers, initially using the "The Rainbow Kids" curriculum in all classrooms k-2. Monthly staff meetings dedicated to EI provided the opportunity for teachers to debrief lessons, share insights, prepare for upcoming lessons, and continue staff development.
- **Semester 2**: ACS teachers led weekly SEL lessons with Amy's input and consultation. Monthly EI staff meetings continued wherein Amy provided coaching and mentoring.
- **Semester 3**: ACS teachers taught weekly SEL lessons alone. Monthly EI staff meetings continued and Amy remained available for individual consultations. A final intensive whole community training with six seconds continued to build EI capacity in the ACS adults.

DETAILED TIMELINE OF IMPLEMENTATION OF EI AT THS

- **2003–2011**: Sporadic exposure to EI concepts and skills created interest and familiarity among THS staff and students

- **June 2011**: Intensive four-day EI training of a small group of self-selected pioneer teachers
- **August 2011**: Four half-days of EI training with all staff prior to the arrival of students
- **2011–2012 academic year**: Sixteen days interspersed throughout the year of modeling SEL lessons, coaching, and mentoring
- **January 2012**: Six, ninety-minute lessons with Ms. Chavez' class exploring ethnicity/identity; these students then designed and created the EQ Retreat with teachers, peers, and the community at large

March 2012: First-ever EQ Retreat

RESOURCES OR FURTHER READING

Gratefully there are numerous resources available for further reading. These works originate from the fields of neuroscience, psychology, public health, education, and peacemaking. Below are some of the authors most frequently referenced.

Emotional Intelligence and Social and Emotional Learning

- Collaborative for Academic, Social, and Emotional Learning (CASEL) (casel.org/)[15]
- Yale Center for Emotional Intelligence (ei.yale.edu/)
- Six Seconds International Network for Emotional Intelligence (www.6seconds.org)
- The Greater Good Science (greatergood.berkeley.edu)
- The Organization for Economic and Community Development (www.oecd.org/education)
- Nonviolent communication—Marshall Rosenberg (www.cnvc.org/)
- Paul Ekman—human micro-expressions (www.paulekman.com/)
- Ashoka Start Empathy Initiative (startempathy.org)
- Plutchik Model of eight basic emotions by Robert Plutchik (www.6seconds.org/2017/04/27/plutchiks-model-of-emotions)
- Edutopia Celebrating and Promoting Innovations in Education (www.edutopia.org/)
- Mindfulness training in schools (mindfulnessinschools.org)
- "Handbook of Social and Emotional Learning" (full reference in Works Cited)
- "The Impact of Enhancing Students' Social and Emotional Learning: A Meta Analysis of School Based Universal Interventions" (full reference in Works Cited)

- "Choose to Change: A step by step teaching guide for fostering emotional intelligence in the classroom" (full reference in Works Cited)

Restorative Circles and Processes

- Books by Kay Pranis and others (www.livingjusticepress.org/)
- The Center for Justice and Peacebuilding (emu.edu/cjp/programs/)
- The Ojai Foundation (ojaifoundation.org/)
- The Center for Council (www.centerforcouncil.org/)
- Constructive Engagement of Conflict (www.uwc-usa.org/page.cfm?p=543)

On Teaching

- "The Courage to Teach, exploring the inner landscape of a teacher's life"—Parker Palmer
- The Center for Courage and Renewal (www.couragerenewal.org/)
- "Earth Ed: Rethinking Education on a Changing Planet"—The WorldWatch Institute

NOTES

1. Brackett, Marc A., Susan E. Rivers, and Peter Salovey. "Emotional Intelligence: Implications for Personal, Social, Academic, and Workplace Success." *Social and Personality Psychology Compass* 5, no. 1 (2011): 88–103. doi: 10.1111/j.1751-9004.2010.00334.x.

2. "History of CASEL. "Collaborative for Academic, Social, and Emotional Learning (CASEL)." Accessed September 2, 2018. https://casel.org/history/.

3. Franklin, Amy M., and Pamela Barker. "Social and Emotional Learning for a Challenging Century." In *EarthEd: Rethinking Education on a Changing Planet*, 96. Washington, DC: Worldwatch Institute, 2017.

4. Mindfulness in Schools Project. "Mindfulness in Schools Project (Misp)." 2018. https://mindfulnessinschools.org/.

5. Durlak, Joseph A, Celene E Domitrovich, Roger P Weissberg, and Thomas P Gullotta. 2015. *Handbook of Social and Emotional Learning: Research and Practice*. New York: The Guilford Press.

6. Durlak, J. A., Weissberg, R. P., Dymnicki, A. B., Taylor, R. D., & Schellinger, K. B. (2011). The impact of enhancing students' social and emotional learning: A meta-analysis of school-based universal interventions. *Child Development*, 82(1): 405–432.

7. Yale Center for Emotional Intelligence. "The Anchor Tools." Accessed September 2, 2018. http://ei.yale.edu/ruler/the-anchor-tools/.

8. Learn more at: https://ojaifoundation.org/about-us/our-mission/

9. Center for Council. "What is Council?" Accessed September 2, 2018. https://www.centerforcouncil.org/what-is-council.html.

10. Read more on the Center for Justice and Peacebuilding at: https://emu.edu/cjp/spi/instructors/kay

11. For further reading on this ways to categorize emotions, see the work of The Center for Nonviolent Communication: https://www.cnvc.org/

12. A personal anecdote: The first time I participated in this lesson I confidently put "family" as my highest priority. However, when made to provide examples of this priority, I had to admit that my actions indicated I had another priority—wrapping up my day. When picking up my children from primary school, rather than listening to the stories they were eager to share, I chose to check phone and email messages and finalize my own day's work. Once I was ready to listen, they had often already moved onto another focus. I resolved to align my actions to my values and reordered my afternoon schedule to be fully present with my children when I first re-engaged with them after school. This experience continues to serve as a reminder to be to monitor and honestly evaluate the alignment of my daily choices with my values.

13. This exercise is adopted from the six-seconds pause formulated by 6seconds.org. Learn more at: https://www.6seconds.org/2004/02/05/why-six-seconds-about-our-intriguing-name/

14. Franklin, Amy M. 2009. Choose To Change. Taos, New Mexico: Missing Peace Press.

15. CASEL screens SEL programs through two criteria: Is the curriculum informed by developmental psychology? and Is the goal of the social and emotional development ethical and for the benefit or the greater good?

REFERENCES

Barker, P., & Franklin, A. M. (2017). Social and emotional learning for a challenging century. In *EarthEd* (pp. 95–106). Washington, DC: Island Press.

Brackett, M. A., Rivers, S. E., & Salovey, P. (2011). Emotional intelligence: Implications for personal, social, academic, and workplace success. *Social and Personality Psychology Compass*, 5(1), 88–103.

Center for Council. *What is council?* Retrieved from https://www.centerforcouncil.org/what-is-council.html.

Durlak, J. A., Dymnicki, A. B., Taylor, R. D., Weissberg, R. P., Schellinger, K. B., Dubois, D., . . . & O'brien, M. U. (2007). Collaborative for academic, social, and emotional learning (CASEL).

Durlak, J. A., Weissberg, R. P., Dymnicki, A. B., Taylor, R. D., & Schellinger, K. B. (2011). The impact of enhancing students' social and emotional learning: A meta-analysis of school-based universal interventions. *Child Development*, 82(1), 405–432.

Enson, B., & Imberger, J. (2017).Weaving emotional intelligence into a home visiting model. *Zero to Three*, 38(1), 26–35.

Franklin, A. M. (2009). *Choose to change*. Taos, NM: Missing Peace Press.

Mindfulness in Schools Project. (n.d.). *Mindfulness in schools project (Misp)*. Retrieved from https://mindfulnessinschools.org/.

Pointer, L. (2016, April 25). *The restorative community: Between individualist and collectivist cultural orientations*. Lindsey Pointer, Ph.D. Retrieved April 13, 2022, from https://lindseypointer.com/2016/04/25/the-restorative-community-between-individualist-and-collectivist-cultural-orientations/.

U.S. News & World Report. (n.d.). *How does Taos high rank among America's best high schools?* Retrieved from https://www.usnews.com/education/best-high-schools/new-mexico/districts/taos-municipal-schools/Taos-high-13014.

Weissberg, R. P., Durlak, J. A., Domitrovich, C. E., & Gullotta, T. P. (2015). *Social and emotional learning: Past, present, and future*. New York: Guilford.

Yale Center for Emotional Intelligence. (2021). *Emotions matter*. Retrieved from http://ei.yale.edu/ruler/the-anchor-tools/.

Chapter 5

Preparing Student-Teachers as Changemakers

The Case of the School of Education Universidad del Desarollo—Chile

Josefina Santa Cruz, Kiomi Matsumoto,
Josefina Valdivia, Trinidad Ríos,
and Paulina Guzmán

Chile

OUR VISION TO FORM CHANGEMAKER TEACHERS

Founded in 1990, Universidad del Desarrollo (UDD) is among the highest-ranked private universities in Chile, with over 13,000 students enrolled across its 22 undergraduate and 70 graduate programs. We are the only Chilean university certified by Ashoka as a Changemaker Campus since 2017. In 2014, the Ashoka team showed interest in our university's unique effort to form changemaker agents. A consequence of a rigorous three-year process, their certification honors our role as leaders in social innovation and changemaker formation. Since 2008, more than forty universities worldwide have received this prestigious designation. We feel proud to be part of Ashoka's changemaking network, contributing from our corner of the world to this global and dynamic community of students, staff members, professors, and partners that share a commitment to social innovation.

AT UDD'S SCHOOL OF EDUCATION, WE COMMIT TO?

We offer our future teachers four specialization tracks, two of which align with our changemaking commitment: public responsibility and entrepreneurship.

Students who choose these tracks enroll in courses such as "personal leadership and teamwork," "digital tools for entrepreneurship," and "forming citizens for the twenty-first century." They also engage in social projects like building basic houses in rural areas in Chile or supporting teachers who work at underserved schools in Nicaragua.

Besides our focus on their academic formation, we also educate our future teachers in the ethical practice of "exerting the leadership and authority that the teaching role implies" while "respecting the unique character of each student and, therefore, the diversity that exists among them." We take seriously our concern for the development of these ethical practices by explicitly teaching, practicing, evaluating, and prescribing them in our practice-based curriculum.

Inspired by Deborah Ball and the work conducted at the University of Michigan School of Education, our curriculum closely links pedagogical theories to daily teaching practices within and beyond the classroom. We have worked with Dr. Ball for more than three years in an effort to train teachers who change the lives of the children and young people they encounter. Like Dr. Ball (2018), we believe that "teaching [pedagogy] is the most important profession in our society" given that teachers "train the next generation [. . .] to imagine and make a fair world possible."

THE FIFTH INTERNSHIP AS A MEANS TO FORM CHANGEMAKERS

Commissioned with such a crucial endeavor, teachers must be made aware of the "ethical obligations inherent in pedagogical work" and of "their responsibilities to young people, their families and communities" (Ball, 2018). To develop this community awareness, as well as their teaching skills, students in the School of Education work as interns beginning from their first semester. The intensity of these internships increases from a single morning per week during their first year to four mornings per week by the end of their studies. Working mostly in underserved neighborhoods, our students are mentored to develop innovative capstone projects to benefit these communities.

In this article, we describe one of the seven internships our students complete. During this internship, teacher candidates work at institutions that serve infants and children whose rights have been violated and whose care has been commissioned to the National Service for Minors (NSM). The NSM is a government agency under the Ministry of Justice responsible for the adoption, prevention, protection, and rehabilitation of children and adolescents between the ages of zero and eighteen. Most children under the NSM's charge live in centers, hoping to go back to their families or be adopted by a new family.

The NSM supervises all these centers, but about 93 percent of them are run by ONGs and privately administered organizations.

In 2015, reports revealed cases of abuse—and even death—of children who were living at NSM care centers. We transformed our concern into action by creating an internship for our students at these facilities. The challenging conditions of these centers provided a unique training setting for our teacher candidates. We wanted them to experience that they can—and must!—improve the well-being and learning conditions of all boys and girls, especially those who are most vulnerable to the detrimental effects of poverty and violence.

Framed within our practice-based curriculum, the internship is part of a required third-year course ("Fifth Internship: Learning Experiences in Different Contexts") for students who are pursuing an early childhood education major. It is the students' fifth semester-long internship in an educational institution, but it is the only one (out of seven) that does not occur in schools. Organized in teams of three or four, teacher candidates are challenged to identify a problematic issue at the care center they attend and to provide a solution that benefits the children. Example implementations include projects that promote emotion recognition and expression, renovating the playground, and creating a mobile library that goes where the children are.

Teacher candidates are taught to apply the Design Thinking for Educators (Ideo, 2012) methodology, which relies on the iteration of ideas following users' input. The Design Thinking model divides the challenge of implementing innovative solutions into five stages: discovery, interpretation, ideation, experimentation, and evolution. It proposes the consideration of users' emotional state in the face of a problematic issue, the redefinition of the initial problem and the understanding that it might evolve, the integration of all relevant actors' skills, the early detection of errors in the proposed solution, and the promotion of an open mind-set that welcomes new ideas.

The course that frames the internship has two components: an on-campus workshop (once a week, eighty-minutes long) and field experience at the centers (twice a week, five hours per day). In total, it accounts for approximately 180 classroom hours per semester plus 48 hours of students' independent work. The workshop is taught at the university by a designer and an early childhood educator, whose combined expertise reflects the interdisciplinary nature of the course. In the workshops, students learn about the stages of Design Thinking, develop their ideas, and reflect on the process. Onsite, they engage in the daily activities of the center and gain valuable insight to improve their designs.

At the end of the internship, student-teachers display the processes and results of their experiences in public spaces within our campus, benefiting the entire educational community. Centers' staff members—who often lack formal studies for the tasks they perform—also benefit from the students' work, since their solutions optimize existing resources while maximizing the children's well-being. Lastly, this hand-in-hand work between the communities our students serve and our School of Education provides an opportunity for professional development for our staff.

THE DATA AND HOW WE ANALYZED IT

At the end of the internship, we ask students to write their takeaways in a final paper. For this article, we analyzed the papers of the thirty-five teacher candidates who interned at care centers in 2017. The purpose of our analysis was to determine whether their testimonies indicated declarative and discursive appropriation of changemaking principles and abilities.

We examined the data using content-analysis methods (Roller & Lavrakas, 2015; Weber, 2004) and NVivo, a qualitative analysis software. In some cases, we also explored data that needed further clarification using elements of discourse analysis (Wortham & Reyes, 2015). First, we imported the data into NVivo and carefully read it. After this initial reading, we annotated each testimony, identifying possible themes and inductive codes. To find other inductive codes, we analyzed text frequency using word cloud queries. We recorded the frequency of words and phrases for later analyses. Then, we coded the data using deductive codes obtained from Ashoka's changemaking characteristics and inductive codes obtained from the data. We studied each code and, in some cases, identified additional denotational indexes—for example, person deictic such as "us," "them," and so on (Wortham & Reyes, 2015)—to aid our analysis. Afterward, we wrote a memo for each code identifying themes, meanings, and connections. We wrote and outline the findings we report here using those memos.

Ashoka defines changemakers as people who have developed the abilities to effectively identify and solve problems. Using empathy, creativity, and collaborative skills, changemakers work with the community to imagine and put into practice innovative solutions. They know and feel that they have a role in the problem, but they also recognize their ability to solve it. To sustain these changemaking efforts, they build rapport within their communities and include others in the process (Ashoka, 2018).

OUR RESULTS: KEY SUCCESSES AND AREAS TO GROW

Students who participated in this study demonstrated high levels of conceptual appropriation of changemaking terms. In their own words, their writing referred to concepts like empathy, collaboration, problem, and creativity. Further, all students used the expression "educational needs" several times, which suggested the centrality of empathetic thinking during their work at the sites. Indeed, student-teachers explained how getting to know the communities, their opinions, and their cultural contexts were necessary to identify a relevant educational need: "[. . .] we can conclude that it was important to know the children's cultural context to develop our internship and to select an educational need to solve" (Group 3). "It was essential to stop to observe and listen to all staff members, *tías*, mothers, and also children at the center. Thanks to their testimonies, we could detect the educational need around which we created our program" (Group 4).

Besides empathy, student-teachers constantly referred to collaboration skills using the term "teamwork." For them, teamwork meant effectively distributing tasks among team members and acknowledging that each person had skills suited for particular jobs (e.g., Group 4). Students sometimes identified differences between team members as problems that needed to be "left behind" (Group 3) to effectively achieve the team's goals. Nevertheless, most students valued differences between team members as sources for potential benefits (e.g., Groups 4, 7, and 9).

The data also suggested that student-teachers saw themselves as changemakers, crucial in the design and implementation of solutions amid the educational community. More than half of the student-teachers' testimonies used the concept "changemakers" to refer to themselves, while many others used similar words to explain their position as promoters of change.

All groups but one presented themselves as essential in the solution of the identified problems. They mentioned that the implementation of creative solutions required the employment of specific skills: "As student-teachers, we needed certain skills to achieve significant change in the context where we were developing our work, we presented ourselves as perseverant, patient, neat, optimist, observant, and professionally committed to the work we had to do" (Group 4).

We identified an area for growth in the way students' testimonies defined who was and who was not a changemaker. Teacher candidates showed that they believed in their ability to effect change, yet they did not perceive others in the educational communities as changemakers. The student-teachers discursively constructed an "us-them" symbolic boundary between themselves and the adult members of the centers who were never positioned as changemakers. They also constructed themselves as knowledgeable in contraposition to their description of staff as ignorant or incapable (e.g., Groups 1, 7, 8, and 9, with one clear exception of Group 2).

Further, although most students' testimonies stated that knowing the local contexts was important to identify educational needs, they did not seem to appreciate the staff and children's input. One group even presented such input as an obstacle to be sorted out (Group 7). Thus, even though the testimonies acknowledged the importance of empathetic processes to gather relevant information, the actions students described relegated members of the community to mere recipients. The student-teachers presented themselves as competent enough to create and implement solutions but they did not include other members of the educational community in the implementation of their ideas.

These thirty-five students showed high levels of conceptual incorporation of changemaking values and abilities. The student-teachers described and expressed the importance of collaborative and empathetic skills—for example, celebrating the different skills of team members and valuing onsite research to be able to "walk in others' shoes." They declared to have worked with the community to identify educational needs and presented themselves as capable and creative problem solvers. The texts also conveyed some shortcomings, such as excluding the educational communities from the changemaking process. The testimonies suggested a relationship between empowered students and passive community members, yet students did not question this verticality.

CHALLENGES

The future challenges of this project are the following:

- broadening the communication of the experience,
- assessing and scaling its impact,
- sustaining students' implementations in the long term,
- developing a changemaking ecosystem where everyone contributes as a relevant agent.

Broadening the Communication of the Experience

Students shared their experiences within the university. However, to inspire other institutions to train their future teachers as changemakers, we need to reach an audience beyond our campus. (We move toward that aim with this chapter.)

Assessing and Scaling the Project's Impact

We need to systematize our desired outcomes into measurable impact tools. To do this, we need to collect more qualitative and quantitative evidence from different stakeholders during and after the internship. The use of systematic assessment will help us improve and scale up our project, which will allow us to compete for grants.

Sustaining the Implementations in the Long Term
We need to incorporate sustainability in the design of the projects and also encourage our students to keep in touch with the people at the centers.

Developing a Changemaking Ecosystem
We must identify the methodological and theoretical devices needed to make our students feel that both they and the people in the local communities are changemakers. We could think of this ecosystem as developing across two stages: once students see themselves as agents of change, we must strive to get them to recognize others as changemakers, as well.

LESSONS LEARNED

Following are some of the lessons we have learned in these three years:

- The value of having teachers see themselves as changemakers. We learned that it is critical to include changemaking preparation in the teacher training curriculum across several required courses and never solely as an extracurricular activity. In particular, we realized that internships present a unique opportunity to develop changemaking skills, especially when the hosting institutions are committed to the training of teachers candidates and open to join them in the implementation of solutions.
- The importance of including local community members in the changemaking ecosystem. We learned that it is not enough for students to feel empowered. To develop sustainable change, students need to share their changemaking skills with people in local communities.
- The value of interdisciplinary work in education. The project owed its success to the collaborative efforts of a designer and an educator. The use of professional design tools greatly contributed to the process. In particular, we discovered the benefits of prototyping—rarely done in education—which allowed for trial-and-error before having the final product, saving valuable resources.
- The value of Design Thinking as a tool to develop changemaking skills. Instead of being based on pure intuition, our improvement project gained professionalism and quality by following this methodology's systematic process.
- The value of working in non-school settings as part of teacher training and the importance of nurturing our partnerships with these institutions to continue to develop joint projects. Internships like this pull future teachers out

of the classroom and away from the traditional learning experience format, thus enhancing their training in collaborative and problem-solving skills.
- The value of communicating the outcomes to the educational community. Student-teachers' experience of talking in front of their peers was a preview of what the academic exchange between professionals will look like in the future.
- The value of having internships every semester as a critical tool that supports the theory-practice link. We know that teachers are the most impactful factor in the quality of schools (Mckinsey, 2008; OECD, 2018; European Commission, 2017; Darling-Hammond & Richardson, 2009) and we have learned that the most effective way to prepare expert teachers is to provide them with frequent opportunities to practice their future role.
- The importance for future teachers to have contact with children who live in extreme conditions. In 2017, we conducted a similar project with elementary education majors who were working as interns in private schools. When comparing the results of both interventions, we saw that the level of commitment and the quality of the projects were lower for students who worked in more affluent settings. Students might be better able to empathize with children who display profound needs and become more motivated to work as they see that their work can truly make a difference.
- The importance of having mentors from our university that share our vision of "everyone a changemaker." We learned that it is important to have expert tutors who can teach, guide, and accompany students throughout the process and who use a rigorous and systematic methodology to seriously and creatively address the search for solutions to the identified needs.

To conduct a project like this, we needed conviction, inspiration, and collaboration. It was very important for us to feel that university authorities believed and supported our project. We are grateful for the contributions of each member of our team. We value our systematic work and the humbling mistakes that helped us improve. We are glad to be part of the great Ashoka network and to contribute to it by training teachers as changemakers. So many children and young people are waiting for a better world. The more we believe it is possible, the sooner it will come.

REFERENCES

Ashoka. (2018, March 6). *My changemaker toolkit*. Retrieved August 28, 2018, from https://www.ashoka.org/en/story/my-changemaker-toolkit.

Darling-Hammond, L., and Richardson, N. (2009). Research review/teacher learning: What matters? How teachers learn, Volume 66|Number 5, Pages 46–53.

Design thinking: A method for creative problem solving. (n.d.). Retrieved August 28, 2018, from https://www.ideou.com/pages/design-thinking.

European Commission. (2017). Quality assurance for school development: Guiding principles for policy development on quality assurance in school education. Produced by the ET 2020 Working Group Schools 2016–18. Retrieved from https://ec.europa.eu/education/sites/education/files/2017-school-development-quality-assurance_en.pdf.

Facultad de Educación Universidad del Desarrollo. (2016a). *Modelo de Formación Práctica*. Santiago, Chile.

Facultad de Educación Universidad del Desarrollo. (2016b). *Plan de Desarrollo 2016–2020*. Santiago, Chile.

Facultad de Educación Universidad del Desarrollo. (2017). *Malla curricular carrera-Pedagogía en Educación de Párvulos*. Santiago, Chile. Retrieved from http://www.udd.cl/mallas/parvulos.pdf.

Facultad de Educación Universidad del Desarrollo. (2012). *Programacurso Práctica V Experiencias de aprendizajes en contextosdiferentes*. Santiago, Chile: Pedagogía en Educación de Párvulos.

McKinsey & Company. (2008). How the world's best-performing school systems come out on top.

OECD. (2018). World class: How to build a 21st-century school system. In *Strong performers and successful reformers in education*. Paris: OECD Publishing.

Roller, M. R., & Lavrakas, P. J. (2015). Qualitative content analysis. In *Applied qualitative research design: A total quality framework approach* (pp. 230–283). New York: Guilford Publications.

Weber, R. P. (2004). Content analysis. In C. Seale (Ed.), *Social research methods: A reader* (pp. 117–124). London: Psychology Press.

Wortham, S., & Reyes, A. (2015). *Discourse analysis beyond the speech event*. New York: Routledge.

Chapter 6

Born to Live

The Transformative Journey of Colombian Youth as Changemakers through Peace Education

Catalina Cock Duque and Ariel Safdie

Colombia

WHEN A YOUNG PERSON HAS NEVER KNOWN PEACE

Colombia's civil conflict has raged for over half a century. As a result, the country's youth have never known what it is to live in peace.

Multidimensional violence has permeated Colombian society as the country's complex conflict has evolved with each new generation—from Liberals against Conservatives to guerillas against paramilitaries, and criminal conflicts between organized crime mafias and drug lords.

Throughout this devastating violence, which continues in many forms today despite the 2016 peace agreement between Colombia's oldest guerrilla group, the FARC, and the national government, youth have been disproportionately impacted: they account for 28 percent of Colombia's population and make up 32 percent of the country's registered victims of the armed conflict (GOV.CO, 2020). They have also been negatively impacted by the country's structural violence, living in situations of extreme poverty and inequality. These complex challenges are intensified when, in the eyes of Colombian society, youth go back and forth between being stigmatized as only aggressors or, to the other extreme, only as victims.

The author Alonso Salazar captured the desperation many youth feel when trapped in these cycles of violence with the famous quote of a young gang member in Medellín who articulated, *"We are born to die"* (*No nacimos p´a semilla*).

For twelve years, Fundación Mi Sangre (FMS), a Colombian NGO with national reach founded in 2006 by Juanes, the Grammy Award-winning Colombian musician and social activist and led by Ashoka fellow, Catalina Cock Duque has sought to support youth to change this narrative. The organization envisions a world in which young people are leaders in building a culture of peace. Since its founding, Mi Sangre has placed youth at the center of peacebuilding processes, holding them up not as part of the problem but as a key part of the solution.

Instead of being born to die, Mi Sangre has worked for hand-in-hand with young people using a peace education model to create a present and future in which youth discover deep within themselves that they were *born to live, and live for the greater good.*

WHY A PEACE EDUCATION APPROACH— MEDELLÍN, COLOMBIA

Medellín is now known as the world's "most innovative city." But as on the national level, Medellín's children and youth have been some of the most impacted by the violence that has plagued the city, driven in part by the organized crime rings that emerged with the rise of Pablo Escobar. In 2014, it was estimated that the city had 247 street gangs which in 2016 were estimated to have around 13,500 members. The Ombudsman identified that 10 percent of the city's youth are at-risk of forced recruitment into armed groups or criminal networks.

During its first three years, Mi Sangre focused on providing psychosocial support to victims of violence. In 2009, after a process of deep observation, we learned that young victims were eager to transcend their situation as victims to become active agents of change in their communities. As an organization seeking to build a culture of peace, we questioned what steps could be taken to support the most vulnerable youth escape cycles of violence and discover their best selves, and their role as changemakers and peacebuilders.

With this question in our hearts, in 2010 FMS began a pilot in partnership with three public schools in Medellín neighborhoods severely impacted by urban violence. We began to work with children and youth, and their teachers, using art and play as tools to develop socio-emotional skills that could contribute to building a culture of peace in the school environment and in this way mitigate violence.

As is the case with all experiments, Mi Sangre began the pilot with a question: *Can risks be mitigated if children and youth strengthen their socio-emotional skills? Under these conditions can participants transform into peacebuilders?*

In the eight years since, FMS has continued testing and strengthening this theory and the pilot marked the launch of Mi Sangre's peace education model, called in Spanish, *PAZalobien* which seeks to form curious citizens capable of building a world in peace through strengthening life skills using tools such as art, play, and social entrepreneurship. *PAZalobien* has reached 122,980 participants directly, in 114 municipalities and 17 departments in the country in both urban and rural settings.

THE MODEL'S AIM—DEVELOPING THE TWENTY-FIRST-CENTURY SKILLS NURTURES HOPE

Globally, peace education has been conceived as a way to promote coexistence and a culture of peace from within and outside the school system. UNICEF has defined peace education as

> The process of promoting the knowledge, skills, attitudes and values needed to bring about behaviour change that will enable children, youth and adults to prevent conflict and violence, both overt and structural; to resolve conflict peacefully; and to create the conditions conducive to peace.

At the heart of Mi Sangre's peace education model, *PAZalobien*, is the aim of forming changemakers or peacebuilders, free and responsible human beings, capable of living at peace with themselves and their environment, conscientious of their rights.

Through *PAZalobien*, Mi Sangre began to identify that transforming vulnerable youth into changemakers is closely tied to the possibility of young people being able to imagine a better life for themselves. While it may sound intangible, imagining and dreaming individually and collectively is key to peacebuilding and to the possibility of ending cycles of violence. That is because the ability to dream is tied to hope, and we have seen time and time again that hope is essential to achieving change. As the United States activist, founder, and director of the Equal Justice Initiative, Bryan Stevenson articulated "in your hope you believe the things that others have not seen and you begin to change the world."

In the context of the realities of many Colombian youth, hope is scarce. And without it, a culture of illegality is nurtured because this seems like the only alternative available. Youth feel fear, and along with it a sense of isolation and anger, which is too often channeled into violence.

PAZalobien has given Mi Sangre tools that facilitate the development of two factors essential to cultivating hope. One is the strengthening and weaving together of protective ecosystems made up of parents, decision makers, and community leaders. The other is the development of the twenty-first-century skills in youth such as self-awareness, positive relationships, the capacity to make healthy decisions, and to transform their ideas into concrete actions.

HOW IT WORKS—PEACE EDUCATION USING A SYSTEMIC APPROACH

As the *PAZalobien* model (See Figure 6.1) developed over the years, Mi Sangre recognized that deep change could only be reached by seeking to impact society through a multidimensional approach. We have come to see the strategy of addressing the problem at the individual, community, and societal levels as a key part of the model's success. This approach helps lay the foundations for more systemic change in Colombia in which young people are the center of building a culture of peace. As *PAZalobien* developed, three programs emerged within the model, each one seeking to impact a different level of society.

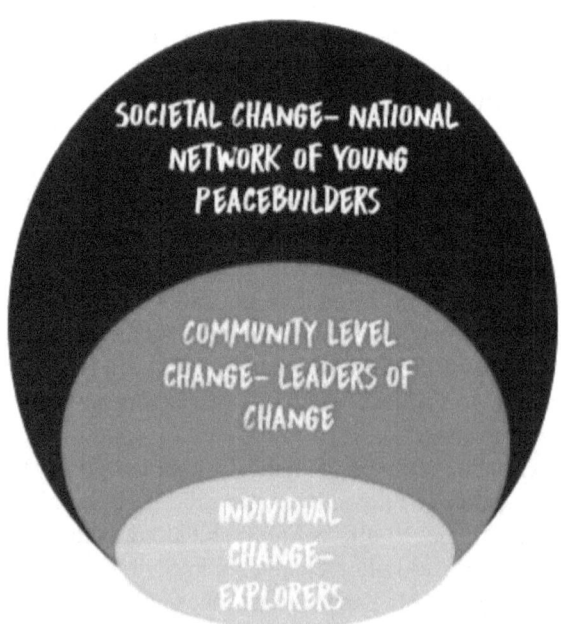

Figure 6.1　PAZalobien's Systemic Change through Peace Education Model.

LEVEL 1: PAZALOBIEN EXPLORERS—PEACE BEGINS WITH EVERY INDIVIDUAL

PAZalobien Explorers, the original *PAZalobien* model launched in 2010, seeks to foster an individual transformation in students, aged five to fourteen, within the school system in which they have a better understanding of themselves and of others and so can become peacebuilders. It does this by using pedagogical tools such as art and play to develop ten socio-emotional skills: self-awareness, effective communication, empathy, managing emotions, stress management, conflict management, critical thinking, creative thinking, interpersonal relationships, and decision making.

Art and Play as Pedagogical Tools

While favoring art and play as tools in working with young people, the key to the model's success has been the message that Explorers does not seek to train artists, but rather, peacebuilders. With that approach in mind, any educator can feel confident in implementing the model with their students without having artistic training. In its curriculum, Explorers identifies nine artistic tools including dance, photography, and theater, among others. We have found that the most successful replicas of Explorers incorporated urban and alternative art forms favored by Colombian youth, like hip hop, rap, and graffiti. The flexibility of being able to choose which artistic tools to use with students also means that Explorers can be implemented with minimum supplies, depending on the resources available.

Train-the-Trainer

While FMS began implementing Explorers directly in classrooms, soon after the launch the model shifted to a train-the-trainer approach with public school educators, which furthers the program's sustainability and leaves capacities instilled in the school system. We work in alliance with the Mayor's Secretaries of Education to identify which schools would most benefit from the program and form close partnerships with principals. Explorers complies with national education requirements that teachers must meet regarding citizenship development and peace education in students which further incentivizes its use in the classroom. As a result, over 3,000 teachers have been trained in Explorers in 150 rural and urban Colombian schools.

With individual coaching from the Mi Sangre team, public schools teachers implement thirty-two Explorers workshops within their classrooms, ideally during an academic calendar year, taking their students down a three-stage pedagogical route: *Travel* in which young people strengthen ten life skills,

Create in which students work together to use artistic tools to develop a class project that puts their life skills into practice, and *Share* in which students share their class project with the broader educational community.

Transforming the Trainer

In implementing this model, FMS found that educators faced many challenges both individually and professionally that prevented them from creating the conditions necessary for their students to transform into changemakers and peacebuilders. Teachers in Colombia, just like their students, have been victimized by Colombia's armed conflict. Often, they work in classrooms with forty or more students. In the rural setting, teachers can be very isolated with little support. Teachers are low paid and studies have documented widespread mental health issues and burnout. Many Colombian educators, just like their students, teach without a sense of hope and purpose.

With this analysis, Mi Sangre began to understand that *unless an individual transformation was achieved within teachers, they would not be able to transform their students into changemakers*. Mi Sangre is not alone in coming to this conclusion. More and more studies demonstrate that the inner journey of an educator or community leader is key to societal change. For a teacher to arrive at their maximum potential as an educator, they must have a positive sense of well-being, understand their purpose, and how it connects to their profession. For this reason, FMS now incorporates Conscious Leadership training into the Explorers program rendering results that affirm the importance of this approach.

> *When I look inside myself, I can get to know myself as a person and what I am capable of. This helps me understand what tools I have, what I can share and give it to others. If I see and recognize my gifts, and potential as a human being, I can give.* (*PAZalobien* Explorers teacher)
>
> *If I am not happy, how can I be happy to all these people that surround me?* (*PAZalobien* Explorers teacher)

LEVEL 2: PAZALOBIEN LEADERS OF CHANGE—LOCAL CHANGE, BIG RESULTS

When we met Candelo, he was seventeen years old, living in one of Medellín's most vulnerable neighborhoods. Candelo's father was involved in criminal networks. When his father was killed in the conflict, Candelo vowed to avenge his death. Like many young men, he was approached by a local gang. But when Candelo was given an order to commit an assassination, he realized that killing another person would be like killing himself. That was the moment he joined Mi Sangre's Leaders of Change program. Through the program, which leads youth who are fourteen to twenty-eight years old through a pedagogical route based around social entrepreneurship, Candelo began to strengthen his own social change initiative called the Hip Hop Nursery, where he trains children and youth from his neighborhood in socio-emotional skills using rap and hip hop. Today, years later, he is a Global Shaper Fellow with the World Economic Forum and has presented his work in Mexico and Argentina. Candelo is one of 13,000 youth who has completed the Leaders of Change program in Colombia, discovering not only their inner strength as leaders but also their power to positively impact the broader community as a changemaker.

Leaders of Change was launched as part of *PAZalobien* in 2013. Targeting at-risk youth outside the school system who have not yet had the first experience of leadership, the program seeks to create opportunities for young people to create inclusive, peaceful, and innovative solutions to community problems. It uses a three-step program involving twenty-five experiential workshops, implemented ideally over a period of six months to a year. First, leadership skills are developed in participants, giving them the confidence to understand their powers as changemakers. Young participants then identify the challenges and opportunities in their communities, and through this analysis begin to collectively identify possible solutions. Finally, they work as a team to develop proposals for change initiatives—small social entrepreneurial activities led by youth, which last between one day and a month.

The purpose of this activity is not to generate income, as is the focus of traditional entrepreneurial initiatives, but rather to explore their entrepreneurial capacity and the positive social impact that such an action can create in the community. As part of the program, youth are given a small seed fund of up to $150 USD to invest in their initiative. However, this resource can also be provided through in-kind donations from community allies and is not essential to the model's implementation. After presenting the initiative to the community, receiving feedback, and building alliances, the youth teams implement their change initiative.

So far, we have supported youth in implementing 548 change initiatives in over a dozen municipalities throughout the country, estimated to have reached 30,000 community members. Mi Sangre does not dictate the agenda of these change initiatives but rather leaves it to the youth participants to identify what they consider their community's priorities, asking only that youth reflect on what would help them build a culture of peace. As a result, the initiatives have ranged from planting trees to advocating in public policy, and to actions of memory with victims of the armed conflict.

Mi Sangre experimented with social entrepreneurship as the lens to Leaders of Change because worldwide entrepreneur organizations such as Ashoka have shown that if young people live an experience of social entrepreneurship, they are likely to continue making social changes the rest of their lives regardless of the professional field they enter. Every change initiative, however small, represents a conscious choice by youth to intervene creatively in their environments to solve problems and build a culture of peace.

LEVEL 3: NATIONAL NETWORK OF YOUNG PEACEBUILDERS—ECOSYSTEMS FOR CHANGE

With every new Leaders of Change program, we found ourselves in awe of the resilience, inner strength, and dignity demonstrated by countless young women and men participants who despite the challenges they faced were driven by something deep within them to work for the greater good of their communities. FMS began asking ourselves what would happen if these incredible young leaders from around Colombia joined forces to imagine and build a country in peace together.

What emerged from these reflections was the National Network of Young Peacebuilders. In 2015, we launched a small network of 150 graduates of the *PAZalobien* Leaders of Change program from the Colombian department of Antioquia. Since then, it has expanded to include a community of 900 youth from 30 municipalities in 10 Colombian departments.

Through this network activity, FMS has begun to discover what happens when so many inspiring young leaders are connected. They learn from each other by sharing experiences around what has worked and what has not in their community interventions. As a result, young network members have received and replicated the strategies successfully used by their peers across the country, no small feat considering the great challenges in connectivity resulting from Colombia's weak communications and transport infrastructure.

> *It helped me recognize all the tools and people I have at my side that can make my job easier as a leader. Also I realized that many of my friends in the network want to do the same thing I do in different ways.* (Network Leader Antioquia)

The second opportunity we found through the network is the possibility it holds for youth to empower and inspire each other through shared life experiences. Friendships have been formed over the years—a community, a tribe of young leaders working for the greater good. The importance of this human connection cannot be underestimated; many studies in Colombia have demonstrated that one of the reasons so many youth join gangs is to break a sense of isolation and seek companionship, loyalty, and affection through an alternative family unit.

> *It is inspiring because we listen and exchange experiences with youth from all over Colombia, with other realities and circumstances. This lets us value our territories and environments and gives us new visions to confront situations that are going on in our processes.* (Network Leader Pasto)

Finally, we have seen how facilitating physical and virtual spaces in which youth from different regions and departments of the country connect increases their voices in decision-making processes, both locally and nationally. By identifying common needs that unite them across the country, youth are now using the network to organize and mobilize. They are linking their local change initiatives, and, in doing so, a much bigger force is emerging: a youth-led peacebuilding movement. We saw this when youth joined together through the network in a national campaign to increase the youth vote in the Colombian 2018 Legislative and Presidential elections or when they coconstructed a national agenda to present to political candidates around the issues important to young people. Strategic actions such as these break the stigmas of youth as victims or aggressors and give them a place on the national stage as decision makers. Attempting societal changes such as these is only possible by working as a network.

> *Meeting other young people who are just as empowered as me, and even more so, who swim against the current, changing the ways we see our contexts, exposing alternatives and engineering them to make their dreams a reality is something surprising and rewarding. When I met the other network leaders, with their ideas and experiences, I got so excited. I realized that I was not just someone alone in my city but I was part of a group of people who were fighting for our country.* (Network Leader, Antioquia)

WHAT PRINCIPLES GUIDE OUR WORK

The three levels of this model share certain principles or what we call pedagogical pillars.

Breaking rigid vertical education structures has been key to the model's success, especially in the school system, where educators are often trained using traditional education methods. Creating horizontal learning processes in formal and informal education settings has allowed Mi Sangre to ensure that youth are at the center of *PAZalobien*. The model uses simple tools to shift the balance of power between educators and participants. Sitting with participants in a circle, for example, has introduced new ways of learning. When these barriers are broken, the entire pedagogical process is transformed, including the relationship and connection between educators and students. One public school teacher expressed this transformation as, "Before I was lemon, now I am honey."

Flexibility has proven to be another key pillar in adapting the methodology to diverse and complex settings. We discovered that when working with unique groups, ages, personalities, life experiences, and needs, it was essential for educators to read the context of each group and adapt to the model's activities accordingly, often spontaneously, in order to dig deeper into the needs of a specific group. While the *PAZalobien* model proposes activities, giving step-by-step instructions, they are meant to be used by educators as a guidebook and not a rule book.

The *PAZalobien* model permits children and youth to learn by doing. Activities are designed at every stage for youth to be active and directly engaged. Using games is key to this approach because learning is facilitated when a participant is having fun and is physically active.

Another pillar of the model is socio-emotional support. For many youth in situations of vulnerability, the need to be recognized and appreciated is essential, and something they may not receive from society or in the home. Meeting this need by incorporating socio-emotional affection into the learning process can be as simple as ensuring that as educators we learn the names of our students or participants, look them in the eye when they speak, and really listen and take the time to learn their likes and dislikes.

Finally, educators are often taught that they should have the answers. However, our model believes that children and youth are capable of discovering their own solutions and that we as educators can mostly contribute through instead of planting questions. This approach encourages youth to approach the world with curiosity and critical analysis.

THE IMPACT—*PAZALOBIEN* AS A SUSTAINABLE PEACE EDUCATION MODEL

The three levels of Mi Sangre's peace education model, *PAZalobien*, have yielded many successful outcomes. A quantitative impact study carried out with *PAZalobien* participants and a control group in the formal education system demonstrated that *PAZalobien* has a significant impact on young people's life skills, especially in the areas of creative thought, self-awareness, critical thought, and assertive and effective communication. In addition, the model has been evaluated using focus groups and the tool "Most Significant Change," as part of a qualitative evaluation of youth's perceptions of themselves before and after the program, as well as educators' perceptions of youth before and after the program. These studies also revealed a positive impact on the ten life skills that are the focus of the model.

> *My group is much more united. We learned to accept each other, to take our differences as a positive thing, to help each other mutually, to not be apathetic to the problems of our peers, to become friends.* (*PAZalobien* youth participant)

In the classroom setting, this has resulted in teachers reporting more focused students, better academic results, less aggression in the classroom, and more coexistence between students and between teachers.

> *The students were apathetic. They were in a very aggressive environment, and the process allowed them to connect. The aggression decreased.* (Teacher *PAZalobien*)
>
> *It was a cleansing experience with the students, because in each workshop they shared very deep experiences that they had lived to the point that we would all cry and we would all reflect on the life of the other.* (Teacher *PAZalobien*)

The extent of the direct impact of replicating the model with educators was an unexpected but important outcome. After receiving the model through methodological transfers and individual coaching sessions, as well as by living the experience and its pedagogical pillars, educators have questioned and altered their teaching methods, developed closer relationships with their students, and a greater understanding of their inner selves and their purpose as educators.

The impact of the 548 change initiatives led by youth leaders as part of the Leaders of Change program has permitted youth not just to experience an inner transformation but put that transformation to work for the greater good of their community.

> *After my change initiative, I realized that just because it is not happening directly to me, does not mean it is not happening around me. I learned that we can change and help others. I realized I could help others, and if not, at least think about the future we want.* (*PAZalobien* participant)

Finally, the outcomes of young leaders working as part of a broader network and ecosystem have been significant, especially the impact the network has had on their capacity to advocate at the local and regional levels. Through sharing advocacy models and strategies and forming alliances, network members have successfully begun to influence change in public policy.

WHERE CAN THE MODEL BE IMPLEMENTED?

After over a decade of working with young people for systemic change, we are convinced that just as in Colombia, youth from around the globe have the capacity to discover solutions to problems that previous generations have been unable to address. While the model has great potential to be replicated in countries or areas in situations of conflict or violent settings with vulnerable youth, we believe it would have an impact even in more stable environments. Mi Sangre has published a step-by-step guide allowing *PAZalobien* to be more easily replicated and adapted to different settings.

COLLABORATIONS

Mi Sangre has learned over years of implementation that the success of *PAZalobien* is determined by alliances. Whether working with the government's Secretaries of Education or directly with educators, parents, the private sector, or civil society organizations, we have found that putting youth at the center of decision-making processes and creating more safe and stable environments in which they can grow and reach their full potential cannot be done alone, *but it needs the minds and creativity of all members of the community.* Involving champions and influencers in this has been key whether they be politicians, YouTubers, faith-based leaders, or influential bloggers.

CHALLENGES

There are, of course, many challenges to implementing a peace education model like *PAZalobien*. One such challenge is amplifying its reach. Having piloted, evaluated, and systematized a successful model over the long term in Colombia, Mi Sangre believes that a huge value of the model lies in being able to share it as a resource with other educators to replicate in Colombia, the Americas, and around the world. Mi Sangre continues to experiment and explore innovative ways to scale and replicate *PAZalobien*, through methodological transfers or using technology and online tools.

Another challenge of which educators working in conflict or violent settings are well aware is the violent threat that many community leaders in Colombia and other parts of the world face. This danger sadly implicates that many young people must question their security as they begin to exercise their positive power as changemakers. Because of this potential risk when implementing peace education models like *PAZalobien* in these contexts, the safety of participants and educators must always come first, and a thorough risk analysis is essential before embarking on this transformative learning journey.

RECOMMENDATIONS AND LESSONS LEARNED

Our experiences in implementing *PAZalobien* as a peace education model that helps youth become leaders in building a culture of peace have shown us the importance of putting educators at the center of the program. Too often, educators suffer from exhaustion and feel distanced from their sense of purpose. However, for peace education to be sustainable and for at-risk youth to be reached, educators must be part of the change. We have found that, when possible, working both inside and outside the school system has allowed us to broaden our reach and achieve a deeper impact. In the case of working within the formal school system, it goes without saying that the buy-in of principals and teachers is essential and that entering through official government bodies when possible can at times give the program an additional sense of legitimacy.

Mi Sangre has favored pedagogical tools based around art and play; however, any didactic instruments that engage youth creatively and physically can be effective in working with this population and Mi Sangre has incorporated sports, recreation, social communications, and new technology. More important than the tools themselves is the understanding that these tools are a means to an end: transforming young people into peacebuilders and changemakers.

Finally, FMS has learned the importance of working with the focus that all of us, not just youth, are born to live for the greater good. Our strategy is based around systemic change, of which both participants and the FMS team must be a part. FMS has sought to incorporate this internally, within every team member, and through the way the organization operates, as well as externally in our work with the community—in other words on all levels Mi Sangre tries to put into practice living on the inside what we share with the outside. Through this approach, by recognizing ourselves in others, we have seen we can change the realities of many.

CONCLUSION

We are not going to get stuck in the problem. We are moving forward to find solutions. We will show people that if adults were not capable, we will do everything possible to resolve it ourselves. Because what is to come, is for us.
(Participant, *PAZalobien* Leaders of Change, Urabá Colombia)

After twelve years of developing, implementing, and strengthening the *PAZalobien* model, we hope that other educators around the world look to Colombian's youth as Mi Sangre does, not as aggressors, victims, or passive actors, but as inspiring examples of changemakers that against the odds are working for the greater good of their communities.

Our peace education model has shown us that while peace begins with every individual, as has been the case through *PAZalobien* Explorers, peace spreads through networks, communities, and alliances, as has been the case through *PAZalobien* Leaders of Change and the National Network of Young Peacebuilders.

By planting questions instead of answers, not only in Colombia, but around the world, peace education models like *PAZalobien* have the potential to be an important tool in working with youth, opening the spaces necessary for their creative, innovative, and critical solutions to come to the forefront. By putting tools in place that ignite young people's imaginations, walls are made more surmountable by a sense of hope. Youth are already leading the way, it is our job as educators to support them in their journey.

REFERENCES

El Inspector. (2014, June 27). El listado de los combos que azotan Medellín. (Web blog post). *EL Colombiano*. Retrieved from https://bit.ly/2qVEse6.

Loiza Bran, Jose F. (2016, February 25). Menores son mano de obra más barata para las bandas. (Web blog post). *EL Colombiano*. Retrieved from https://bit.ly/1UmEa6F.

Milligan, K., & Schwab, N. (2017). *The inner path to become a systems entrepreneur.* Skoll.org. Retrieved from https://skoll.org/2017/03/27/the-inner-path-to-become-a-systems-entrepreneur/.

Personaria de Medellín. (2017). *Rompiendo la lotería y el azar: situación de los grupos de especial protección de Medellín.*

Registro Unico de Victimas (RUV). (2020). *Unidad Para Las Victimas*. Retrieved from https://www.unidadvictimas.gov.co/es/registro-unico-de-victimas-ruv/37394.

Salazar, J. A. (1991). *No nacimos pa' semilla: La cultura de las bandas juveniles en Medellín.* Bogota: Aguilar.

Semana. (2016, August 8). *Las enfermedades mentales de los maestros*. Semana.com. Retrieved from https://www.semana.com/educacion/articulo/enfermedades-mentales-por-carrera/484690/.

Stevenson, B. (2015, May 22). *Commencement Address.* [Keynote Address]. Worcester, MA: College of the Holy Cross. Retrieved from https://www.holycross.edu/commencement-2015/2015-commencement-address-bryan-stevenson.

The Wall Street Journal. (2012, March). City of the year (Advertisement). *The Wall Street Journal Magazine*, sponsored by Citi. Retrieved from https://www.wsj.com/ad/cityoftheyear.

United Nations Children's Fund. *Peace education 2011*. Retrieved from https://uni.cf/2NQh4pQ.

Chapter 7

Passion Projects

A Case Study of Changemaker Education in Action

Kate Dickinson-Villaseñor

United States

There are numerous practices, projects, and ways in which changemaking is happening in classrooms across the country and around the world. A central reason why there is no handbook, playbook, or specific curriculum that educators can follow to lead changemaking in their classrooms is that a curriculum guide in itself would in some ways minimize one of the core principles of changemaking: namely the critical importance of student agency in shaping the inquiry and projects. This agency is a part of the very essence of changemaking which we view as a dynamic, interactive, vision that is driven by student passion and energy. With this in mind, the following is a discussion of passion projects as a case study exemplar of changemaking in action. I will explore the practice of engaging students in creating passion projects and discuss the organizational, philosophical, and contextual influences that frame the pedagogy for this model.

PASSION PROJECTS

The central idea of passion projects is for students to engage in an extended inquiry experience of their own choosing and then use their passion to teach and inspire others through celebration and sharing. Embedded in this process are academic skills, research, literacy, numeracy, scientific and social inquiry, writing, speaking, and the visual and performing arts. Beyond these academic skills, the essential questions at the heart of passion projects are about growing changemakers within our schools:

- In what ways can we support students in developing agency and self-awareness as changemakers?
- How can we align curriculum and pedagogy across content areas in the classroom so that it reflects core values and long-term goals of growing changemakers?
- How do we design experiences that develop the core essentials of change-making: empathy, teamwork, leadership, and creative and critical problem solving?

HISTORY AND CONTEXT

Education has changed throughout history as a function of societal context; changes in contemporary education are being driven in part by advancing technology, globalization, and the future of work. These changes have shifted what are considered the most important skills for the jobs of the future. In their "Future of Jobs" report, the World Economic Forum (2020) identified analytical thinking and innovation, active learning and learning strategies, and complex problem solving as the three most important skills for employment in the future. These contextually flexible skills work across settings and disciplines and provide access to new discipline-specific skill acquisition in emerging and yet unknown fields.

The transmission model of education remains, unfortunately, the dominant approach around the world, though it is neither relevant nor effective in providing opportunities for students to practice applying the knowledge to new contexts, communicating it in complex ways, using it to solve problems, or using it as a platform to develop creativity. Changemaker education on the other hand is marked by a few key critical shifts that move away from:

- privileging having answers over posing great questions,
- fostering competition to developing the skills of collaboration,
- focusing on content to a focusing on making connections across knowledge domains.

Passion projects seek to reflect these shifts. Outlined below are the practical goals and some of the challenges that can occur when implementing passion projects in the classroom. I also provide a discussion of the philosophical and cultural underpinnings for why schools and classrooms provide such fertile ground for these projects. I count myself fortunate to have had the opportunity to experience passion projects through multiple lenses—as a classroom teacher, instructional mentor and coach, as a school administrator, educational consultant, as a provider of in-service and professional development, and as a parent.

The narrative that follows reflects this diverse experience in leading and supporting the implementation of passion projects in five different school environments over the last seventeen years. This model of passion projects originally grew out of my own individual teaching experience in K-8 public charter school classrooms in Southern California. Public charter school law in California was intended to provide opportunities for small publicly funded schools to actively engage in innovation and hopefully the dissemination of effective practices that truly meet the needs of students and which would stand up to the scrutiny of authorizing public agencies at the district and state levels. In this way, the local control, academic freedom, and autonomy of public charters were designed to allow teachers and schools to experiment with instructional design, curriculum, and pedagogy, which is exactly what happened with passion projects.

The description of passion projects I present below has evolved considerably over time and taken on a variety of forms in order to adapt to specific student needs and various organizational contexts, including K-8 public charter schools, and individual classrooms in traditional public schools in Southern California and Oregon. As a student-centered model, passion projects provide differentiated instruction by design and seek to capitalize on the individual strengths, motivations, and interests of students. Because of the open-ended nature of passion projects, the model has been successfully adapted in practice in kindergarten through eighth-grade classrooms, with student populations who are ethnically, racially, socioeconomically, and linguistically diverse.

THE FIRST STEP: DEFINING PASSION PROJECTS

In action, passion projects have three key phases. We invite children to:

- Think and identify something you are passionate about.
- Reflect on what you know, ask new questions, and dedicate time and energy to knowing more.
- Create a way to share your knowledge, curiosity, and passion with others.

Defining what it means to be passionate for children in a way that is practical and accessible is an important step in the process. To begin with, it is important for students to feel free in order to bring questions to the process. Sometimes identifying a passion can feel like a burden; so, it's important to let things emerge organically through conversation and modeling. While the conversation about defining passion projects might feel unnecessary, time after time our experience was that it helped engage people in the process, whether in classroom meetings, one-on-one discussions, or formal teacher-student conferences. A few of the definitions that students and teachers have developed collaboratively over the years include:

- A passion is being so interested or in love with a topic, that you lose your sense of time when thinking about it or doing it . . . something that if you dreamed about it, you wouldn't feel like waking up from that dream.
- A passion is something that maybe you would want to do as your job one day.
- A passion is a strong feeling about something . . . so that you can't stop feeling it and need to share it with the world.

THE LAST STEP: MAKING PASSIONS VISIBLE

All the way on the other end of the passion project is the final presentation, which is best conceived of as a project night/project museum event to which families and community members are invited. This culminating event began as a celebration evening for one classroom at one school, has grown to be a school-wide K-8 event for at least one school, and is taking root in individual classrooms. The duration of this project has varied over the years from two to six weeks, from beginning discussions about passion project selection to the final culminating celebration. Often this is done at the end of the school year after children have had an opportunity to develop the capacity and skills to engage in independent research, writing, speaking, and sharing. As an end-of-the-year tradition, passion projects serve to celebrate learning and keep children intrinsically motivated and engaged through the final weeks of school that can be so challenging. There is something beautiful in finishing the school year by celebrating passionate inquiry, rather than celebrating the impending break from learning.

EXPOSURE AND TOPIC SELECTION

In an ideal world, parents, teachers, and peers encourage each other each day to identify and pursue their passions, learn more about the world, discover and share their findings, and take action to make a difference. Practically, the reality of encouraging both new and veteran teachers in engaging in this process in urban public settings is challenging. Passion projects are the final culminating projects of the school year. The topics are chosen by students, the ideas and nature of the project are conceptualized by student, teacher, community, and peer collaboration. Especially for the younger grades, it is necessary for the benefit of both students and teachers to engage an inquiry around integrated thematic instruction, creating a variety of different products and projects throughout the year. But, less is more when it comes to passion projects.

There are countless anecdotal stories about those who were passionate about their hamster, in part because they didn't know the asteroid belt or the pacific garbage patch existed. Six-year-olds rarely arrive on the first day of school effusively and eloquently passionate about symbiotic relationships; however, after a year of exposure to inquiry-driven integrated thematic instruction, students shift in their perceptions of what's possible with a passion project. For example,

In order to figure out your passion you have to ask a lot of questions and think about your thinking and you also have to try a lot of different things, because you never know what you might find out you're passionate about. (Student, age 8)

Table 7.1 lists sample topics, products, and student groupings for passion projects for the last several years. Topics vary widely in K-8, and this list is in no way exhaustive. Notable is the fact that some of the youngest learners were those who were open and willing to tackle some of the biggest topics.

Of course, school and classroom culture matter a lot. Based on the local situation, the projects can be sequenced throughout the year whether for the whole group, across grade levels, as partner projects across grade levels, or structured to be fully independent for each classroom and student.

What we do, and how we do it, will always be undergirded by who we are. Thus, passion projects are both a process of learning and doing, as well as a product. These projects work best when supported by strong project-based learning pedagogies (PBL) and student-centered instruction and universal design.

Passion projects help lay the groundwork for young people to embrace their identity as changemakers and to start their "changemaker journey." The spark for these projects can come from their lived experience, especially of hard times, suffering, stress, and trauma, or from inspirational examples, leaders, and role models, whether historical or peer, family, or community-based. While passion projects provide plenty of opportunities to apply, deepen, and connect with academic learning and curriculum-based content areas, what helps them rise beyond academic knowledge and skills to changemaking are the outcomes of empathy, sophisticated teamwork, leading, and creative and complex problem solving, which are the core attributes of changemakers.

Table 7.1 Topics, Products, and Groupings for Passion Projects

Sample Topics	Sample Groupings	Sample Products
Being biracial	Truffles	Clay models
Cake decorating	Temote	Comic books
Decay and decomposition	Controlled cars	Field guides
Diamond cheetahs (a mythical creature that a kindergartner invented)	Sea slugs	Fundraising
Fairies	Service animals	Campaigns
Homelessness	Tacos	Instructional videos
Magic	Things we use from animals: when do we have to kill them and when can they stay alive?	Interactive museum
Picnics	Transgender rights	Displays
Pillows	World War II	Magazines
Board games	Weaponry	Magic shows
Brochures	Small group	Maps
Campsite	Whole class	Movies
Character acting	Mixed class (e.g., four classes collaborate to identify four to eight topics)	Mural
Chocolate		Music videos
Simulations		Piles of soil
Independent		Plays
Same-age partner		Posters
Cross-age partner		Redistributed to work with teachers who lead passion project topic Groups 1–2 hours a day

EMPATHY

In recent years in schools known for changemaking (like those in this volume), and in schools across the country and the world, there has been a strong turn toward understanding the importance of social-emotional learning as critical and foundational to academic learning. Empathy is a highly developed area of research and theory but can be practically defined as the ability to recognize emotion in others, suspend judgment, communicate understanding, and take the perspective of others. This kind of empathy is important for both teachers and students and forms the foundation of trust and safety that is required for students to be vulnerable enough to share their passions with peers and teachers. Empathy is more than just an instructional goal, though it is that, and it is more than an element of the curriculum, though it is that too; empathy is both the method and the outcome of passion projects, for while coming to understand the world around them with empathy, young people, and indeed all of us, can also find out personally and deeply how we too fit into the world. Empathy is not just about walking in other's shoes, it's about valuing the lived experience of others and discovering that experience through active listening. When thinking through the implementation of passion projects, instructors and coaches must look carefully for the opportunities to help deepen empathy for it is the true foundation of all changemaking and changemakers.

In the context of the passion project, empathy allows space for children's products to vary widely in content and skill. A classroom culture that begins talking openly about differences, differentiating instruction, and honoring the process of thinking and wondering is one that is able to support growth and risk-taking throughout the year in ways that validate all students. The discourse of empathy must be embedded in the fabric of the larger community so that visitors to passion project presentations are able to stay out of judgment, communicate understanding, and connect with children whether they are passionate about mythical creatures, Hinduism, or blueberry pie.

You get to try things that you feel safe trying, but also things you might feel safe trying in the future. The teacher has to let you learn and ask questions. Everything connects into your future. —(Student, Age 9)

LEADERSHIP

Oftentimes when we talk about leadership with regard to changemaking in education, the focus is on the role of the leadership team at the school or district. While it is necessary for school leaders to be committed to a culture of supported risk-taking, innovation, and activism, understanding leadership as the responsibility of *leaders* is insufficient. Leadership in a changemaker school includes teacher leadership, student leadership, and community-based leadership. In further defining the leadership role of a changemaker teacher, it is useful to consider the academic literature from the business community that makes a critical distinction between what it means to function as a leader versus a manager. Leadership requires self and group awareness, is rooted in relationships, and is mission and vision-oriented. Management is rooted in transactional power, control, and is task-oriented. Effective leadership inspires, motivates, and provides a long-term, future-focused, and idea-driven direction. Good management provides short-term, bottom-line focused, expectation-driven details to reach a predetermined destination. Good management is effectively and efficiently following a map, which is sufficient insofar as there is a prescribed destination, but it takes effective leadership to understand, support, and integrate the experiences and perspectives of a team to forge a new path in uncharted territory. The call to changemaking in education is one of innovation, creativity, and inspired action, the ability to seek solutions to complex problems, and the power of possibility and imagination.

In the twenty-first century, everyone can be a changemaker and everyone can be a leader. While there have been recent fundamental shifts in how scholars envision the purpose and future of school, the concept of classroom management remains a central focus of teacher education coursework, professional learning, and common discourse in the teaching profession. Teachers are explicitly trained and conditioned to focus on management that is characterized by control and methods to facilitate compliance rather than foster community and agency. In reframing the role of teachers as *leaders* in their classrooms rather than managers, teachers must be provided time, space, and tools to grow, learn, and change.

Teachers must come to recognize themselves as the professionals they are with voice, agency, and a vast community of educational leaders, like them, who are sharing in a commitment to supporting the next generation of changemakers. In leading passion projects, the role of the teacher is one of a servant-leader, serving and supporting students through empathy, listening, awareness, and commitment to the growth of each individual for the betterment of the community. In order to effectively support students through the process of pursuing their passions, teachers must embrace uncertainty, accept the possibility of unknown destinations, and (very practically) be willing to guide children through unknown content. Passion projects honor children as the owners of knowledge, experience, and wonder. In a changemaker school, leadership is also in the opportunities we provide for children to lead. The opportunity for children to lead, try, fail, reframe, and recommit to their passion develops student agency and nurtures the changemaker spirit.

TEAMWORK

The expression of teamwork throughout the passion project process takes many forms. Active collaboration in a network of classroom/school, families, and the larger community is essential in leveraging connections and matching resources to needs. Leading deep and authentic learning that honors the uniqueness of each child is impossible to do alone. Here are a few examples of teamwork that makes passion projects powerful:

Teacher/School-Student

Students must understand their relationship with their teacher and their school as one of care, trust, engagement, and investment.

Teacher/School-Families

An asset-minded approach to family engagement that is consistent throughout the school, and throughout the year, lays the groundwork for being able to support children. An open door for families to take supported risks paves the way for families to share and provide resources in class. Knowing the jobs, histories, and talents of families at the school allows for primary source experience for students.

School Community

Community engagement, university partnerships, connections with community organizations, museums, businesses, and nonprofits are helpful tools in supporting children in pursuing their passions. Phone interviews, video conferences, backstage tours, personal field trips, guest speakers are often possible with a simple ask. Students have collaborated with college volleyball players, longshoremen, former Olympians, construction workers, business owners, geology professors, zookeepers, city council members, and community activists. These add to the richness and authenticity of student passion through community connection.

Student-Student

Student teamwork, driven by empathy, creates a social environment for collective efficacy and independence, supportive learning, and active collaboration. Students feed off one another, learn from one another, share resources, mentor one another (within grade-level clusters or in cross-grade-level teams).

Teacher-Teacher-All School Community

Passion projects are an all-hands-on-deck endeavor. Adults come together to create innovative ways to share students and resources. Front office staff members, custodial staff, instructional assistants, parents, older siblings all can play minor and major roles—making phone calls, setting kids up for video calls, phone interviews, sewing, cooking, dancing, singing, and imagining. All adults in the school community shift into serving kids and supporting them in fulfilling their dreams.

PROBLEM SOLVING

Embedded in the concept of problem solving are creativity and innovation. Creativity can be supported by frequent opportunities to make associations, play, investigate, explore, and tinker. *But how do we get kids to think creatively? How do we guide them toward selecting a big topic to dive into? How do we free kids so they can think out of the box on what their project product possibilities may be?*

The short answer is that we must practice all the time. Teachers who are new to student-led inquiry often have a desire to have students create with a wide-open and innovative heart when they are conceptualizing projects. The pathway toward this kind of creativity is in the mundane decisions of everyday classroom practice. The focus of creativity cannot only be on a project but on ensuring our actions and words are congruent and consistent with students trying, risking, failing, and growing. What this means in practice can feel challenging, because it means that teachers must seek to understand student intention and honor student agency in measured acceptances of noncompliance, and active questioning of systems in the status quo. The reality is that we can't move children from a place of compliance to creativity. We can't create a classroom based on the culture of control, and then control kids into being innovative. Students need opportunities to solve many small problems in an iterative way.

NUTS AND BOLTS: PRACTICAL TIPS FOR IMPLEMENTATION

Organization

- Whole class meetings to frame the conversation
- Individual student-teacher planning meetings.
- Small group planning or teaching meetings

Passion Project Plan example: Planning sheets including

- Goals, materials, plans, essential questions, subheading questions
- Folders for books, materials, planning forms
- Calendar/timeline
- Writing forms/templates available (brochures, maps, magazines, etc.)
- Dictation—students of all ages benefit from an adult-led interview where the adult takes dictation with or without prompts, providing students to talk about their process. This is a helpful archive for student portfolios and can be a powerful piece to display alongside the student's work.

Project Topic

- People will read:
- How do I want to organize my writing?
- What are the sections?

Reminders/Notes

- What will people do?
- What will my project look like?

What supplies might I need? Family Communication

- Prepare families for the continuum of student work.
- Provide prompts for visitors: scaffolds for visitors such as sentence frames and guided questions help focus visitors on the children and will lead to them developing their own questions.

Scavenger hunts for child and adult visitors—Resources

- Passion projects *can* be done with few resources other than time, energy, and passion; however, in order to truly support children in realizing their vision (life-size anacondas, electrical circuits, carved wooden masks, etc.) a budget for supplies such as paint, poster board, clay, tools and other materials is incredibly helpful.
- Tech resources for video conferencing, movie-making, song-recording, and so on.
- Having a variety of supplies available at school provides equitable access for all children.
- Teachers, assistants, and school personnel work hard to find resources for children to cook, build, and make things that they may not have access to at home.

Project Night

Students look forward to having an authentic audience and purpose for their work. Teachers invite:

- Families and extended families
- Student-teachers
- Community partners
- Arts organizations
- University volunteers

- City council members
- Experts in the community called upon for interviews or resources.

Environment

- Create a museum space. Many teachers and students have done this by moving furniture, hanging curtains, covering day-to-day supplies, and *transforming* the classroom space.
- Hold student work at the center. It is tempting for families to want to tag a bake sale or other activity on to this event. Though having food available has a positive impact on participation and attendance, it is important to help guide the energy toward the children and their learning. This is supported by clear expectations for visitors.

REFLECTIONS AND FIELD-TESTED FORMATIVE FAILURES

Expanding Spheres of Influence

Throughout the school year, opportunities for students to reflect on their learning, thinking, and action in the context of different spheres of influence can frame later passion project conversations. Conversations over time can encourage students to extend their sphere of influence, regardless of the topic of their passion. For example, a kindergarten student who was passionate about magic tricks began her exploration as a purely personal endeavor but later was able to reflect on her passion and reframe her influence as a way of bringing joy and amazement to her community. Simple graphic organizers can help facilitate this process and can serve as a developmental archive of student growth.

Schoolwork at School Example

- The world
- My school or neighborhood
- My friends/my class/my family
- Me

The practice that has helped the school community focus on the children and their individual and collective passionate learning is that ALL work is done at school, by kids. Adults are invited to come into the classroom and are welcome to support their child in attending community events or activities related to their project. In my practical experience, this is an equity issue and an issue of maintaining fidelity to the process, without the intervention and presence of parents' products. I joked once that if parents felt compelled to make a passion project, they were welcome to do so; but they were not allowed to make their child's. I was surprised when more than one adult took up on my offer—evidence of the innate human desire to wonder, learn, and create.

The Storm before the Calm

The reality is that this, like much great work, is figuratively and literally messy. The time commitment in class means suspending classroom routines and reconciling some elements of classroom organization and cleanliness as students take over the space as theirs. Strong classroom structures and routines for independence (including access to supplies) are beneficial and lead to increased autonomy during passion project work time.

Topic Challenges

Inevitably, there are a handful of children each year who assert an initial selection of something that they have no experience or knowledge about. Though we are always encouraging students to explore beyond the outer limits of their comfort zone, for the purpose of the passion project, we spend time with children defining passion as an interest and commitment beyond simply curiosity. Strong connections between teachers and students allow for open and honest conversations to support students in deciding on a topic that truly is reflective of the child.

Shortcuts

Over the years, it has been tempting to simplify the process, have students choose from a finite set of options about their content, process, and process; however, these constraints would not be in alignment with the intention of the project process. It has been tempting, when working toward a product that integrates core academic skills, to require students to write first, then build or create; however, utilizing inquiry and the creative process as a contingent reward is problematic.

Rubrics and Grades

To date, I have not seen a rubric, grade, or measurement system used that does not unintentionally create homogeneity among products and limit creativity. This is learning for the love of learning. When done well, students are holding themselves accountable and holding one another accountable. Self-reflection forms, planning sheets, and other scaffolds are beneficial in setting intentions and reflecting on performance.

Impact

Fostering changemaker student identity is an ongoing process. Passion projects can be a key part of this process. Long-term, passion projects often turn into something bigger. A number of students have turned their passion project into a larger project, summer partnership, internship, or small business. Some students sustain similar kinds of passions over time, while others look forward to the final month of the school year, planning the passion they will choose to pursue for their project throughout the school year. As a school leader, the evolution of passion project topics over years can serve as powerful artifacts that reflect the school's values and culture.

Starting Small

I began in one classroom. In the last year, two former colleagues who had moved started passion projects at two different schools as individual teachers. Though the opportunity for children to pursue a passion project each year in a K-8 or K-12 setting is ideal, one teacher in one classroom in a short time frame is a perfect place to start.

Start with what kids know, love, and can do. As changemaker educators, we often have a strong desire to push kids toward tackling big social problems. In my experience, a central challenge with this is the fact that when we tackle something huge with elementary-age children, we can unintentionally rob children of the real agency. Making signs for donations for a cause is important and useful; however, it still rests upon the idea that children are dependent on adults to provide resources to remedy a problem. Students are able to grow into tackling large social issues when they begin with problems that are close to them. While part of changemaking is about communicating and leveraging the community to take action, for very young children, it is important that we allow them to take smaller steps and that we continue to support their passions and their questions in a way that helps them develop confidence and agency. Young children *do* ask big questions and have fierce wonderings. The essence of passion projects is to allow kids to lead.

REFERENCES

World Economic Forum. (n.d.). *The future of jobs report 2020*. Retrieved November 17, 2021, from https://www.weforum.org/reports/the-future-of-jobs-report-2020/in-full/infographics-e4e69e4de7.

Chapter 8

Innovating across Multiple Dimensions in Education

Carmen Pellicer Iborra, Martín Varela Dávila, Rosa López Oliván, Marta Monserrat Salcedo, and Miguel Ignacio Garcia Morell

Spain

As a foundation concerned with achieving a model of educational excellence that responds to the needs of today's students, it is necessary to generate a transformation from the status quo to a curriculum that is both relevant and rigorous. Our model focuses on creating cycles of continuous improvement in student's academic and social development. To accomplish this, the Trilema schools focus intently on six fundamental aspects of school life at the same time: the curriculum, the methodology, the assessment, the organization, leadership, and personalization. We deeply believe that progress cannot be made if we only focus on one of these elements at a time. Like a Rubik's cube, what we have learned is that it simply is not possible to create transformational change by adjusting these elements in isolation, one at a time. Lasting change can only be achieved by moving the six sides systematically and in an integrated fashion. Furthermore, it is in the process of this kind of integrated effort that significant innovation can emerge.

CURRICULUM

One of the first things that attract the attention of visitors to Trilema schools is what we refer to as vertical projects. Students' projects are displayed in the school's hallways as a way to make visible to everyone what children are studying, learning, and doing. Each year, in their individual classrooms, students work on six projects concurrently according to a centrally organized and planned curriculum, but these projects are connected to the entire school. For example, in history the whole school engages in conversations about the same historical topics, no matter the age of the students. Topics have included technology, changes in society, improving the lives of others, and human values. A project improving the lives of others may focus on collaborating with the community businesses and council to add marked crosswalks on streets to ensure public safety. These types of projects respond to our understanding of the curriculum and focus on three main elements:

- The subject matter content and performance standards at each grade level
- The key competencies each child is to develop
- The learning and cooperative strategies and evaluation methods used to assess the first two elements are reflected in student portfolios.

This way of organizing activities for the school derives from the Trilema schools' conception of the curriculum. In particular, we aim to teach a relevant curriculum to the twenty-first-century students, which responds to the urgent and pressing environmental and social challenges facing humanity and the world. We align our curriculum with the common European framework and UNESCO's educational recommendation and guidelines and, in particular, the four pillars of education: learning to learn, learning to be, learning to do, and learning to coexist. These pillars form the foundation for inspiring students to be entrepreneurial and creative and to discover their capacities for working on teams, and build their passion for contributing to a sustainable future for everyone.

Establishing this precise curriculum helps us define *the knowledge we would like students to learn as well as the skills we want them to develop.* In order to make this possible, we select fundamental aspects from a wide range of educational materials including relevant theory, research, legal, and public policy documents to understand the disciplines and content areas in depth. We seek to enrich the objective knowledge that students possess in a creative way and to stimulate the interdisciplinary connections and understanding across different content areas and topics. In order to make this curriculum accessible and relevant to all students, we approach curricular design and redesign through a process that accounts for student learning both horizontally (i.e., in its depth at each grade level) and vertically (i.e., across grade levels).

Parallel to this real integration of curriculum, it is our aim to develop the practical and axiological competencies of students in a systematic and authentic way by carrying out routines, for example, self and group assessments as part of completing academic tasks, which let us keep track of daily progress. This approach requires that teaching methods contribute to the students' development in ways that can be evaluated at different age and grade levels.

Of course, this requires that we stay in compliance with state and national standards, yet at the same time we push for our students to experience deep learning, as we work to bring clarity to all of our assessment criteria and the grade-level learning standards. Within these constraints, teachers can select the primary content with which they want to work in each grade; therefore, they are able to integrate the content areas through collaboration with colleagues at other grade levels and in ways that help the standards be visible and appropriate to each grade level.

This integration then takes shape in assignments and *didactic units*, as well as in the *interdisciplinary projects*, which inevitably must coordinate effectively with other content areas and *work* vertically across grade levels. These didactic units may involve problem solving in mathematics that relates to application in life situations. Trilema school students have been involved in creating budgets for initiatives that benefit our school community including the purchase of ornaments and food to help underserved families celebrate the holidays. The subjects of social studies and sciences are taught 100 percent via project-based learning, and 20 percent of math and language arts use project-based as an approach.

Teachers stay in close communication in order to ensure that they have practical knowledge of the timing and rhythm needed for each integrated unit. This requires discipline and learning on the part of the teachers throughout the academic year so that the sides of the Rubik's cubes are moving in harmony toward our collective goals. What we have come to realize is that *well-structured lessons* that take into account vertical and horizontal alignment are the key to providing students with the greatest opportunities for learning and progress.

For the structured lessons, to scaffold students' acquisition of knowledge about a topic such as the Spanish civil war, teachers present content and engage students in a variety of formats that include: (a) students reading and retelling their understanding to classmates, (b) teachers using visual organizers to activate critical thinking, (c) students summarizing main concepts by using key words, and (d) using charts to arrange ideas.

TEACHING METHODOLOGIES

Trilema schools seek to provide lively and engaging classes that foster curiosity and joy combined with precision in content and in ways that instruction builds on the strengths of both teachers and students. To reach this goal, it is necessary for the instructor to know how to foster deep learning to help students cultivate strategies for learning across content areas that help each student to maximize their individual learning capacity. We aim to foster both critical and creative thinking and to support the cultivation of a dynamic metacognitive awareness among students.

At Trilema, we use the metaphor of "four drawers" that represent the four methodological/pedagogical decisions every teacher must take in order to design a good lesson plan, didactic unit, or project:

1. What actions do I need to take to encourage students to actively *collaborate and interact* with each other around course content?

We encourage teachers to experiment and use a variety of methods for grouping students in ways that connect to the student's individual work. To accomplish this, teachers need time for themselves to collaborate with each other and individually reflect on the decisions they need to make to foster a richly collaborative environment. To foster rich and meaningful interaction and collaboration, teachers use a variety of structures to bring students together in ways that support the particular content they are working on. Further, fostering this interaction requires detailed thinking regarding timing, follow-up, learning roles, and more. In the aforementioned project on creating a budget to offer holiday celebrations for underserved school families, the students are assigned different roles in their group. Roles include being the economists, marketers, or the ones in-charge of creative production.

2. What activities will best encourage students to *think*?

Providing individual or group strategies appropriate to a particular activity is not enough; the teacher must ensure that students give their complete attention and concentration to the tasks. We encourage teachers to provide a wide variety of different strategies that students can experiment with and use in various combinations in order to help students learn to think and, especially, to think about their own thinking (i.e., to develop their metacognition). We accomplish this by providing students with a variety of models, thinking routines, mind maps, graphic organizers, heuristics, and reflection questions, all with an explicit emphasis on students cultivating their meta-cogntive processes. For example, students may engage in developing a mind map on ways regarding the products they can sell to raise funds to improve their school such as buying new books for the library or a mind map for components needed to improve the systematization for library check out and return of books.

3. What should I do so that students *show* what they know, what they have been learning?

It is important to provide evidence of learning not only at the end of a process (e.g., when taking an exam) but throughout a unit, lesson, or project. We seek to do this through the use of notebooks, paper or digital, through the sharing of progress in their portfolios, through oral explanations, written expositions, formal and informal presentations, and more. Using active methodologies where students play the leading role in creating knowledge, especially through the "Aprendizaje Basado en Proyectos" (ABP), or Project-Based Learning (PBL) is the most effective way for teachers to gather evidence of learning that is focused more on the process than on the final product.

In the portfolio, students gather these multiple forms of evidence for their learning which allows students to review and remember content anytime and, at the same time, identify their own progress. Prior to gathering the learning evidence, students' works are displayed on classroom walls to remind students of the content learned in previous days and to celebrate their thinking and completion of tasks.

4. What should I do to maintain *ethical tension* to help them be better people and changemakers?

Students are encouraged to take advantage of all available resources (peers, family, teachers, resources in texts of all kinds, and the internet) and multiple strategies to develop their inquiry and investigate solutions to the problems they are working to solve. Creating ethical tension is another way to deepen students' empathy, expose them to diverse perspectives, and encourage students to consider diversity in all of its forms including linguistic and cultural diversity. All classroom projects work to encourage a healthy engagement with multiculturalism and inclusion of all perspectives. Furthermore, teachers encourage students to not only gain knowledge but to develop their empathy in order to become better people.

A key objective is developing citizens who feel responsible and are aware of the ethical impact of their choices and who also feel empowered to explore possibilities to transform the world. These kinds of outcomes are possible when students learn to look at the complexity of the world through a critical yet empathetic lens that makes room for diverse opinions but demands ethical decision making that considers the common good for all people and the planet. To help develop empathetic human beings, teachers may have students debate on "pro" and "against" perspectives about immigration in Spain. Prior to engaging in the debate, students research the topic of immigration and the benefits and issues that may emerge from people immigrating from other countries. Examples of arguments provided by the children included "pro" statements such as "They show us other ways of thinking" and against statements such as "I don't think immigrants should come here because they take jobs that Spaniards could have." Teachers add pictures of immigrants arriving on boats and guards surrounding them and ask empathy-based questions such as "What do immigrants feel in that moment?" and "what do they fear?"

We also work to provide different *settings for learning*, especially in the early grades that create opportunities for each student to develop their own unique strengths, while respecting diversity and striving for excellence. These settings include service learning, real-world projects, and collaboration with the local community. A two-way initiative consisted of kindergarteners identifying a problem (trash cans placed in the park were too high for them to reach) and collaborating on finding solutions (designing child-friendly trash cans). As an impactful outcome for the community, the city approved the children's design and adopted it, and trash cans were installed at the park closer to the ground.

Another example of community engagement, that is connected to history, involves the collaboration of teachers with an elderly resident's home, in which the children and seniors engage in two-way learning activities. During these activities children share what they have learned in school, seniors teach children how to play games from the past, and children teach seniors how to play the games they play today.

Accomplishing this type of instruction requires that teachers continually invest in their own professional development. This development prepares them to build their capacity to employ this diverse set of pedagogical approaches in ways that allow them to integrate them into the dynamics of the entire school culture. With the commitment and energy of teachers, we are able to create truly intense learning experiences that *challenge students every day*.

Finally, we must stay current with *technological innovation* and consider how it can help us to improve our teaching methods and to enhance students' learning in ways that are entirely relevant to the world in which they live. This means prioritizing digital literacies and competencies across subject matter areas. Students use technological tools to serve their community. They may use these tools to aid the process of library improvement by generating social media marketing for school students to increase their use of the library or create a digital passport to record each book read. In this way, technology is used by students, not teachers, to generate change. While technology is not a solution to the challenges of learning and teaching in itself, embracing technological change is something that our students must learn to thrive in the modern world.

EVALUATION

This comprehensive and in many ways radical type of pedagogical implementation has also required a change in our culture of evaluation. Our evaluations go far beyond measuring results through exams and multiple-choice tests, and instead teacher's evaluation *truly accompanies students' progress*. Just like in a football/soccer match, the teacher needs to be in the field, not merely as a referee who enforces the rules and acts as a judge. The teacher acts as a passionate and dedicated coach who lives and breathes each moment with the students, preparing them in the field, and considers the students' successes and failures as their own.

We believe that a singular focus on assessment systems that rely on external tests and educators' belief that these assessments are the only way to guarantee improvement miss the point of education entirely. It is not how well the referees judge the game that matters, though it is important, rather, what matters most is how the players play the game, how they learn to work together as a team, their individual skill development, and how they support each other along the way. An overemphasis on narrow forms of assessment actually destroys the possibility that teachers can change the way in which they approach their classes. Because of the negative consequences of this kind of emphasis on extremely limited assessments, we have pledged that our model of evaluation will prioritize self-assessment and metacognition and will focus on progress, not overly simplified views of success.

When assessments are integrated into the learning model, evaluation becomes a systematic and continuous process where new tools can be introduced, including self-assessments and co-evaluation. These types of assessments lead to much greater personalization of the entire learning experience and provide a much greater personalized follow-up of a student's learning progress. The student's portfolios and their projects become the primary tool for evaluation, allowing teachers and students to look at their work through multiple tools and across time in ways that respect both their individual and collaborative activities.

The stages of metacognition (initial, procedural, and final) are fundamental in this new dynamic of evaluation and assessment which involves both the energy of personality and of consciousness (elements of human psychology that defy measurement). The students' strong commitment toward their learning as evidenced in their behavior and through activities is measurable. Frequent oral presentations, records and observation scales, enriched exams which ask for the application of ideas, and localized evaluative approaches hold much greater value than that of merely reproducing that which can be easily measured. The Trilema's curricular culture includes a new vision of assessment that works seamlessly with our teaching methodologies, which are designed to promote authentic critical and creative thinking in students.

We propose a complete and broad palette of evaluation of schoolwork that accounts for the full range of student engagement—emotional, cognitive, behavioral, social, and ethical. This broad palette includes teachers facilitating evaluation sessions where they identify their students' strengths and progress, always using positive language to generate an action plan to support their academic development.

Evaluation is the side of the Rubik's cube that pushes the scope of innovation. We still have a long way to go, but we continue emphasizing that for true change to occur for the whole child and the whole school in a lasting way, we must continue to reconsider the purpose, process, and practice of evaluation.

ORGANIZATION

Revisions and adaptations to teaching methodology and curriculum also require rethinking the very nature of school itself at the most basic levels beginning with how we use, manage, and allocate space and time. As a whole school, we have to consider the implications of the structure of the school and its relationship to learning and curriculum. Rather than beginning with what has always been done, or how others have done it, we begin with the questions: How can we arrange the school and all its resources to facilitate and maximize learning in every aspect of the institution? How can we enable interconnections between content areas, grade levels, and our engagement with other educational possibilities? If indeed vertical alignment is important, and to us it is, how then do we organize ourselves to make this truly meaningful and impactful for students?

To begin with, the school and the teachers need autonomy and flexibility in deciding on and modifying teaching projects. We simply cannot afford to replicate what we see in more traditional institutions that align themselves with strict traditions. Our vision is unattainable through inflexible, homogeneous, and one size fits all approaches. Of course, we begin with many of the same raw materials (classrooms and class schedules as other schools), but we approach their organization differently. For instance, we implement allocation and use of space, the creation and implementation of schedules and timetables, and the use of resources in ways that prioritize from the beginning to the end, interdisciplinary experiences. We also prioritize collaboration, learning in vertical alignment, real-world experiences, and engagement with local community networks. The school must bring the real world into the classroom and the classroom into the real world in order to prepare students for the future real-life situations that students will face.

Some *ways of organizing* include the arrangement of thematic classrooms within the school, differentiated areas to work that enable cooperative learning, meeting points for students, layout of tables inside the classrooms, and the creative use of the playground areas. For instance, there is a math corner that presents a weekly math problem, a corner for chess games, and another corner where students practice manual arts by using recycled materials to create products.

Other arrangements include *reimagined timetables and schedules* as timetables including: (1) the core subjects that are taking place in the morning in the first and second class; (2) full block two-hour afternoon classes consisting of projects that bring together subjects like biology, technology, and language arts in ways that provide multiple perspectives on similar content. Our commitment to vertical tutorials is a decision that carries with it important organizational consequences. By allocating time and space for cooperative learning, the students of different ages co-learn and cocreate projects, inquire and investigate together, and have time to think and get involved in the ethical construction of their school, their homes, and their community.

We also strategically place a *tutorial hour* in the schedule at times when students and tutors come to the sessions with reinvigorated minds, as well as scheduling them for the whole school which enables tutorials to take place across grade levels. These kinds of strategic decisions regarding organizing time and space we consider to be essential in implementing an educational experience that is truly focused on learners rather than on tradition or what is easiest to manage logistically by the adults.

In addition, we are able to add plans, projects, strategies, and our own resources to fit within the school's educational projects (social entrepreneurship projects, interschool days, coexistence plans, environmental projects, and school garden), which also demand the rethinking of the school's organization.

Lastly, we work hard to make sure that the decisions we make regarding *meeting times, schedules, and so forth leave plenty of room for cooperative work between teachers.* If we want teachers to work on the curriculum, for instance, they need specific kinds of support and time to carry out the planning of the lessons and evaluations that need to be developed. This means, the staff room needs to function as a place where teachers not only meet but also a space and place that helps support teachers working together in large groups, small groups, or with their co-tutors and support teachers.

In the staff room, teachers also collaborate in project creation. For instance, there are important weeks in the school year when the school highlights different projects, for example music or women of science. A teacher in-charge coordinates with his/her colleagues to encourage students and families to participate in creating the curriculum and capitalize on family members' talents. It is not uncommon to witness parents that contribute their expertise or gifts during these weeks such as a mother who sang and taught gospel music for the school.

In order to accommodate the learning priorities of the school, administrators must work to relieve the bureaucratic burden. Many standard requirements do nothing to promote learning and anything that does not support the learning objectives of the school simply must be reduced to a minimum. As a result, a rigorous review and evaluation of the policy requirements are constantly necessary. In these ways we work to ensure that the teachers' main concern is their professional activity and their leadership and interaction with each other in the planning and implementation of the school's vision.

LEADERSHIP

School leaders are perhaps the most important *force of change* in the school. Without their vision and commitment and without their day-to-day decisions which encourage the continuous learning of each child and teacher, the Rubik's cube could not move in an effective way. Instead, we would be left with standard approaches that in the end will not bring the kind of change that is necessary for students in the twenty-first century.

The constant and dramatic changes in society and in the educational systems of the world require us to move on from being traditional school leaders, with managerial centralized and top-down styles, like in the industrial age, to a new style where everyone in the school can be a leader and can manage a team. Each member of the team is seen as a contributing member and potentially the most important member of the team at different times in the face of different challenges. The time has come when teachers and leaders at all levels of the school can share their vision of educational possibility and can drive decisions. This kind of leadership is not only desirable but also a requirement for educational systems that must function in this age of knowledge.

Our integrated vision asks everyone to step up and provide *clear, collaborative, and effective leadership*. To achieve this, everyone in the school, especially those leading from the middle, must have a clear vision of the ideal school, a school that they want to represent, as well as the wisdom, knowledge, and commitment that make this vision a reality.

All of these efforts require investments in *professional development, ongoing cycles of planning, and honest evaluation* of both the successes and failures. We work to build a culture where trying and failing are seen as learning and important, which invites each person, students, and teachers to give the best of themselves consistently and to share in the adventure of educating the next generation who will be responsible for the future.

It is also important that the school board leadership team provides ongoing support and clear *goals*. They must be able to transmit the vision to stakeholders at all levels inside and outside of the school and they must help to ensure that efforts are truly coordinated.

Finally, a reimagined and integrated curriculum requires real changes in the *Teachers' Professional Development models* that not only respond to the technological challenges but also that make visible ways of promoting and assessing the progress and the growth in their students in ways that respect teachers' time and autonomy. The goal is to continuously improve the culture, where reflection on teaching practices is the norm and where *the evaluation of the teacher's skills*, the development of *professional portfolios*, and intelligent uses of *classroom observations* help guide mentoring and coaching. For portfolios, teachers create their own digital documents to gather their own evidence of professional growth and successes to be shared with the director or professional development coordinator. As a whole, these comprise the core elements of our model of teacher excellence and development.

PERSONALIZATION

We understand that respecting diversity and working for equity and inclusion are crucial for our school. At the same, we understand the importance of personalization of learning for each student. Creating a schoolwide and yet individually focused learning journey for each child is a big challenge. To prepare each student as a citizen in a complex global world requires an *inclusive vision* of the educational community. We rely heavily on our tutors to help provide the personalization that students need, and we all work together to understand and provide culturally responsive instruction. We support the affective, cultural, and social environment for each student in ways that help each other find the best way for them to grow up, while considering the needs of the people around them.

To ensure success, we need an *exhaustive knowledge* of our students (their needs, learning styles, and difficulties) to be able to provide specific actions in our teaching program that gives them the response that the child requires. We need robust and ongoing knowledge of teaching methodology and pedagogy, and we need to work together to share an integrated view of subject matter knowledge and how that knowledge can work together within project-based frameworks.

We believe in being adaptable to *different challenges* for each child and in providing curricular flexibility. We seek to build a culture of evaluation based on the progress that includes the ability to detect learning disabilities. Furthermore, we seek to create opportunities in which groups of children of different ages work together and are challenged to ensure that each individual's learning needs are met in a personalized way.

We see fostering a *collaborative culture* as the real key to personalization. It is only when individuals can come together to discuss and share their perspectives on students' needs, performance, and growth, plans can be made to successfully intervene at critical points in the child's development. Everyone knows a little, but together we know a lot about strengths, weaknesses, and what we can do together to bring resources to those who need them.

The Trilema model of educating children focuses on supporting children to achieve their greatest potential no matter their physical, psychological, familiar, and socio-economic backgrounds. The goal is to make children joyful and eager to come to school where they experience an innovative and inclusive education.

Chapter 9

Changemaker Education Is for Everybody

The Sky School Model

Polly Akhurst, United Kingdom, Stuart MacAlpine, United Kingdom, and Mia Eskelund Pedersen, Denmark

WHY WE EXIST

Sky School was conceived in 2016, in response to the gap in quality education provision for displaced youth. We believe that young refugees—as all people—have a right to quality education. Yet, only 24 percent of refugees around the world have the opportunity to access secondary education. Our vision is a world in which refugees have the opportunity to build a future that they have reason to value, and our mission is therefore to use transformative education to create opportunities and inspire positive change in the life of refugees and their communities.

OUR TARGET GROUP

Our model is targeted at displaced youth between the ages of sixteen and twenty-five with few or no other educational opportunities. Most of the young people we work with would have been out of school for several years and are unable to access public or national education systems. Our curriculum is designed to be "context-proof" so it can be used with virtually any group of refugee youth around the world. To date, we have worked in Greece, Kenya, Jordan, Lebanon, Jordan, Hong Kong, and Bangladesh. We also serve youth from the host community who have few educational opportunities.

OUR GUIDING PRINCIPLES

A Belief in Altruism, Cooperation, and Relatedness

Sky School grows out of a belief in human altruism and humans' shared desire for cooperation and relatedness. When the need for feelings of autonomy, competence, and relatedness are met, people move toward thriving and wellness. We believe that together we can build leadership and capacity to thrive and create a better world.

Learning Is Both for the Individual and for Their Communities

We believe that learning is not just for the individual: learners who participate in our programs have a responsibility to share that learning among their community and to use their learning to improve the communities in which they are living.

With Not For

We work *with* learners displaced to develop learning that is valuable to them and to their communities and which can fit into their lives. Refugee learners are involved in curriculum development, facilitation, and guide the direction of Sky School

Everyone Can Be an Educational Changemaker

Our students, our facilitators, and our volunteers who develop curriculum are all educational changemakers, who share a commitment to creating a better world through education. Sky School seeks to foster this changemaking capacity across our whole community.

HOW THE MODEL WORKS

We design and develop high-quality learning, coconstructed by educators and refugee youth around the world. We partner with organizations that are serving refugee youth, providing the curriculum and training, and ongoing development for them to run our programs, using a technology-assisted delivery model.

We have two learning programs that enable youth to develop agency, create opportunities, and make the change.

- High-School Diploma Program—we have developed the first international high-school Diploma Program specifically designed to meet the needs of refugees. The program is eighteen months long and launched in 2020.
- Short programs—since 2017, we have been running short programs in specific areas to enable students to re-engage with learning. So far, 250 students in 6 countries have participated in our programs on Peacebuilding, Social Entrepreneurship, and English for Changemakers.

There are several key components of the model, both in terms of education development and delivery.

Education Development

Sky School's model of learning (see figure 9.1) puts agency for positive change at its core. In a world in which the future for our students is increasingly uncertain, the development of agency is key to enabling learners to embrace challenges and create and access opportunities. We define agency as the substantive freedoms—and capabilities—to choose a life one has reason to value.

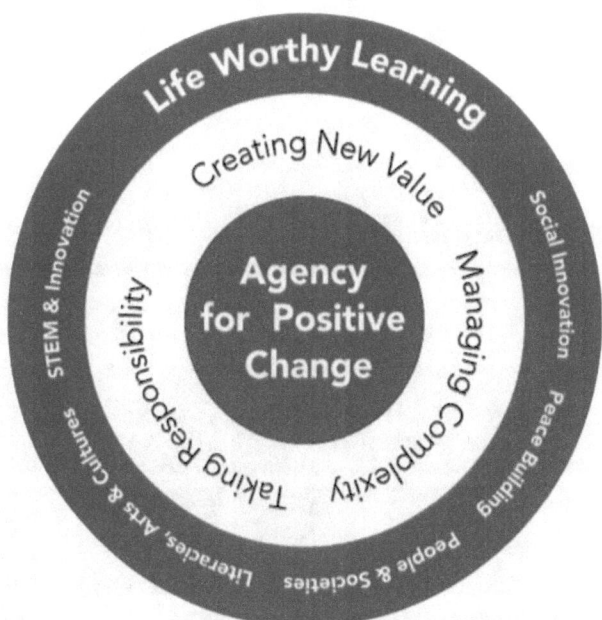

Figure 9.1 Sky School's Model of Learning.

Sky School learning develops three transformative competencies that each agency build for a positive change: the ability to create new value, take responsibility, and manage complexity. These competencies are transferable and allow learners to exercise their agency and transform their lives. Sky School measures our success according to learners being able to demonstrate these competencies.

Transformative competencies and agency are developed through "*lifeworthy learning*," a term invented by David Perkins and defined as learning that is likely to matter in the lives that our learners are likely to lead. Through our learning, students develop as active, responsible, and compassionate problem-solvers and innovators, who are able to embrace uncertainty and complexity.

Sky School provides learning in five key areas: social innovation, peacebuilding, people and societies, literacies, arts, and cultures, and STEM and innovation. All of our courses can be studied individually or as a package of ten courses that comprises the Sky School Diploma Program (see figure 9.2).

The Sky School learning model has been inspired by global education frameworks and in particular by the OECD's Education 2030 framework that speaks to the need for young people to be educated to thrive in a changing and uncertain future. Sky School's curriculum has been developed in partnership with United World College of South East Asia, one of the most well-regarded international schools in the world, who have been practicing changemaker education for decades.

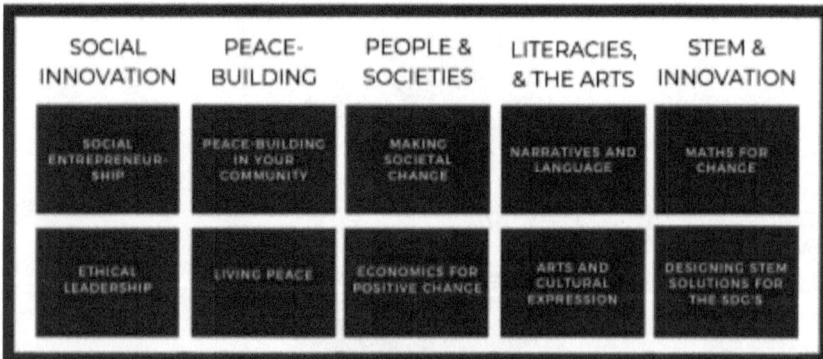

Figure 9.2 The Sky School Diploma Program.

Curriculum and Curriculum Development

Our curriculum development takes place through "curriculum hackathons," intensive weekend workshops that gather educators and young people with refugee backgrounds to develop new courses. This approach enables the participation of displaced youth and learners in the development of the curriculum itself and ensures that educators have proximity to the target group. Such events are also inspiring and engaging events for participants to engage in cocreation and improve their curriculum development and educational changemaking practice. To date, we have held eleven hackathons in schools around the world, during which 140 educators and displaced youth have developed 1,100 hours of curriculum.

To ensure that our curriculum can work in a range of contexts, we use a concept-based approach to develop learning goals and engagements that are "universal" and that are then contextualized in the environments of our learners. Contextualization takes place through the "Triple A" pedagogy, which we use to write learning engagements. Triple A comprises three stages: awareness, abstraction, and application. During the awareness stage, the learner is encouraged to reflect on their own lived experiences (which are linked to the learning goals). In the abstraction phase, conceptual understandings that these experiences relate to are introduced. In the application phase, conceptual understandings are applied to the learners' own context. For example, if learning about what a changemaker is, learners might identify someone who they consider to be a changemaker that they know, and his or her skills or abilities. They might then be presented with common traits of a changemaker and reference this against their own knowledge of the changemaker they have chosen, before forming their own definition of a changemaker (see figure 9.3).

Our curriculum is developed to be quite prescriptive in the sense that learning engagements are fully articulated so that the curriculum can be delivered by individuals who do not have subject-specific expertise.

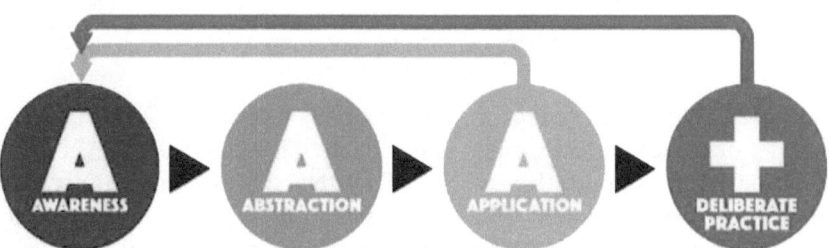

Figure 9.3 The "Triple A" Pedagogy.

Delivery

Facilitator as Educator

We work in low-resource environments where a lack of trained teachers hinders many from going to school. Sky School instead trains individuals as facilitators to run any of our programs. Our facilitators thus know how to support students to participate and deepen their learning but may not know the answers to all of the questions. We provide initial training to the facilitators in the Sky School way of learning, facilitation skills, and use of the curriculum. We then provide ongoing development and coaching opportunities for the facilitators on the ground. Many of our facilitators are themselves refugees or have previously worked with displaced youth.

Technology-Assisted Approach

One of the key reasons youth are not enrolled in education systems is that they often need to work or stay at home to support their families. The Sky School model is therefore designed to be flexible so that students can undertake other responsibilities at the same time. We, therefore, use a technology-assisted approach—where each week students study for six hours in-person and for four hours online, via our online platform "Aula." The Aula platform is designed with engagement at its heart and acts as a digital campus, enabling students to engage with each other and with content outside of class time. This learning approach is optimal as it also enables students to develop their IT skills and to effectively undertake their own research using the internet. The combination of a strong in-person community and independent work time is one of the contributors to our high retention rate.

The in-person work consists of team-based engagements such as discussions, pair sharing, and simulations, while the online work consists of independent tasks (e.g., watching YouTube videos to explore concepts), independent research (either on the internet or within their communities), and writing and assignments.

EVIDENCE THAT OUR MODEL WORKS

Two years since we started running our programs, we are seeing an increasing amount of evidence that learning is having an impact on students. In terms of outputs, our programs have a 72 percent retention rate, and 100 percent of students would recommend the programs to a friend. An internal study we conducted on graduates of our peacebuilding course in 2018 indicated that 97 percent of learners expressed that the course changed their mind on something, and 68 percent of learners referred to the course as making them think differently and critically.

In terms of outcomes, we have evidence of students changing their mindsets due to the courses: one student on our Social Entrepreneurship Course stated "Sky School made me change my way of thinking. Before I saw problems, now I see opportunities." In some cases, we see a change of identity, from being self-proclaimed "trouble makers" to "peacebuilders" or from thinking that you need to be rich to be an entrepreneur to considering yourself entrepreneur.

We see students being able to develop agency, create new value, take responsibility, and manage complexity. This differs from student to student—in some cases, it will involve students establishing their own projects and businesses, as well as supporting other initiatives and taking action to make change in the community. We also have seen alumni returning to facilitate our programs—eleven out of our twenty-two alumni from Amman last year applied to facilitate our programs, as they want to provide transformational learning experiences to others.

CONCRETE EXAMPLES OF IMPACT: FOUR EXAMPLES

Impact Story #1: Mofti

Originally from South Sudan, Mofti now lives in Kakuma Camp, Kenya. After graduating from Sky School's course on Social Entrepreneurship, he has set up a kiosk to support his brother and has started studying Business Administration at university. "I would not have thought of this idea before the course. Before joining the course I did not know what's going on [in the world]. After finishing, I know that I am needed."

Impact Story #2: Sara

Sara is from Iraq and now lives as a refugee in Amman, Jordan. She participated in Sky School's Peacebuilding course and learned about other cultures for the first time. She now feels able to respect people from other countries and backgrounds. Now Sara is a facilitator because she wants to give the "Sky School experience" to other young people.

Impact Story #3: Mousa

Mousa is from Ivort Coast and lives in Athens, Greece, as a refugee. He tools Sky School's Peacebuilding course and has since become president for the

Ivorian Community in Greece. Now, he is establishing the first restaurant in Greece that sells Ivorian food.

Impact Story #4: Zamzam

Zamzam is from Somalia and is living in Kakuma Camp, Kenya. Zamzam took Sky School's Peacebuilding course. During the course, she realized that she wanted to resolve conflicts the same way she had seen men in her community doing. Zamzam is now leading a group of young women who are participating in peacebuilding in the community.

TIMEFRAMES, COLLABORATIONS, AND RESOURCE NEEDED

Each individual course is designed to last for ten weeks and includes hundred hours of learning. Students taking our Diploma Program will study for ten courses together, which can be done in a period between one and two years—the program is modular so students can dip in and out. The resources required for Sky School for the model to work are educator time (to develop curriculum), the provision of our online platform, Aula, and time dedicated to facilitator training. The resources required by our partners are facilitator time, physical space, and devices (either computers or phones).

To develop the curriculum, we need engagement from educators and displaced youth. For delivery, we need to collaborate with partners, who could be community-based organizations, NGOs, or schools, who have a physical presence in areas where there are large numbers of refugees. While our model is designed to be context-proof and to be delivered in virtually any refugee situation, we have found that it works better in more protracted situations of displacement as it does require both infrastructure and commitment on the ground. We have run courses with partners in areas where people are on the move but in some cases have found that either students cannot commit to studying for ten weeks or that infrastructure (e.g., internet connectivity) may suddenly be shut down in the area we are working. However, we have seen that the model can work in both camp and city environments across four continents.

OUR CHALLENGES AND LESSONS LEARNED

Our greatest challenge so far has been in communicating the benefits of our learning model, which is quite different from more traditional models of education in the areas where we work. While many of our partners are aligned to our model of learning, stakeholders frequently ask why we are not focusing on "normal subjects," for example. Sometimes people do not understand that young people's challenges are not met by the local education systems and that they need to change. One lesson that we have learned is that testimonies and stories can really help to generate an understanding of the value and impact of Sky School learning on external stakeholders. It has also greatly helped us to be able to root some of the thinking around the model in work by well-respected and evidence-based organizations such as the OECD.

A further challenge is in the area of assessment, as we do not feel that an examination-based and grades-based system aligns with the learning we are providing, nor is it necessarily beneficial to the development of our learners. We are therefore looking at different ways of evidencing learning—for example, through the Mastery Transcript Consortium, which is developing a gradeless transcript.

In terms of delivery, we know that many people want this kind of education, but the fact that we use a technology-assisted learning model means that it is not possible in areas where there is a lack of internet access. One question is how we can get the model to the most vulnerable, who have the least resources but who want or need it most. This may mean being more flexible about the mode of delivery in the future.

Furthermore, the success of our model is dependent on strong partnerships, so we have learned that we need to ensure that all partnerships we develop are strong—this means collaborating with partners who are mission aligned and share an understanding of the importance of the kind of education Sky School provides.

RECOMMENDATIONS FOR OTHER EDUCATORS WHO WANT TO ADOPT OR ADAPT THIS MODEL

Through Sky School, we have seen that changemaker education is for everybody and is also hugely important for those who are underserved. Initially, we were concerned that our learners, coming from traditional systems, might not relate to our model, but we have found the opposite to be true: our learners appreciate the fact that at Sky School, their learning can be used in the "now" to improve their lives and their communities, as well as helping them to create opportunities in the future. There are key opportunities to leap frogging to changemaker education models for youth who are not being served by the current education systems they find themselves in. We encourage you to join us in this journey. If there are any educators working with displaced youth out there who are interested in becoming a partner, we would definitely be keen to talk.

REFERENCES

Dreze, J., & Sen, A. (1999). India: Economic development and social opportunity. *OUP Catalogue*.

Erickson, H. L. (Ed.). (2006). *Concept-based curriculum and instruction for the thinking classroom*. Thousand Oaks, CA: Corwin Press.

MacAlpine, S. (2018). *Triple a plus learning* (1st ed.). Singapore: Apple Books. Retrieved from https://books.apple.com/us/book/triple-a-plus/id1349112622.

OECD.org. (2019). *OECD's official website*. Retrieved from https://www.oecd.org/education/2030-project/.

Perkins, D. (2014). *Future wise: Educating our children for a changing world*. San Francisco, CA: John Wiley & Sons.

Chapter 10

A Learner-Centered Approach to Changemaker Education

Maria Isabel Valente-Pires and Luiza Nora

Portugal

Colégio de S. José in Coimbra has developed a pedagogical model called VOAR. It integrates innovative methodologies with a pedagogical vision that places the learner at the center of the educational process. Through this model, we aim to educate every learner as an active citizen in the construction of a better and more sustainable world.

We are living in a world of constant, rapid, and accelerating change. Knowledge, for example, now has a short shelf life and much of what we know today will quickly become outdated as new discoveries across all fields add to our knowledge base. These and other changes are happening so fast that it is impossible for any one individual to stay constantly updated. At the same time, we realize that today there's a strong trend to consider all values as relative, as the same values that, until very recently, were once considered untouchable are now being questioned.

All of this change coexists with a highly competitive landscape of praxis where those with the right knowledge, skills, and abilities can achieve greater success while those who do not will be left behind in a world that is ever more demanding and globally connected. These facts have led many twenty-first-century parents to desire a different kind of education for their children. They see that the acquisition of abstract knowledge and the mere storage of information are insufficient for today's world. They would rather see their children develop the abilities, skills, and process knowledge that can be put into action, transferred across contexts and domains, and used to solve problems, overcome difficulties, and face challenges.

In this shifting of desire toward higher-order "twenty-first-century skills," teachers, parents, schools, and students are contributing to the development of social progress and helping to move from a culture of dependence in schooling toward a culture of innovation and entrepreneurship. The very thing the world needs is to move forward toward sustainability and equity.

Colégio de S. José's Educational Project has aimed to address these challenges and to integrate them into an idea of a new being, a new kind of person living in a new kind of world while remaining rooted in a central core of Christian values. At the same time, they will be able to address issues and contribute to solutions both big and small in today's society.

Our school is focused on contributing to the construction of a new culture and raising reflexive, autonomous, responsible, and active citizens and engaged in the construction of a better and more sustainable world.

VOAR: A PEDAGOGICAL MODEL

Colégio de S. José is a bilingual school (from kindergarten to year 9) based in Coimbra, Portugal, which also includes a section of the American international curriculum. While the school has been in existence for over ninety-five years, it is always in a process of constant improvement, including our current work of developing a unique pedagogical model called VOAR that seeks to respond to the global dynamics of today.

The VOAR model began in 2013/2014 when the school started on a path of changing from an educational paradigm centered on teachers to one that is singularly focused on learners. The model developed as the result of an intense reflection and training process whose main concern was to adapt pedagogy to the real educational needs of students in the twenty-first century, and to our student's success after they graduated from the school.

VOAR is based on the following four pillars: attachment (Vinculações), daring/entrepreneurship (Ousadia), autonomy, and responsibility. Our main target was to educate students to be themselves, to know their strengths, to be connected to God, concerned for the common good, and willing to intervene in society and influence their culture, contributing to the construction of a better and more sustainable world (i.e., to be changemakers) (Mission of CSJ).

The integration of a pedagogical vision that centers the whole educational process on the student and, at the same time, seriously invests in effective and innovative teaching/learning methodologies (in the formal curriculum) form the core of the model. At the same time, and in a constant search for integrity and coherence across subject matter and grade levels, the school fosters different ways for learners to participate in the school's management as a mechanism for developing their tools to solve problems of the surrounding society (we think of this as the hidden curriculum).

By giving each student the main responsibility for their own education, we are also making them co-responsible for educating the rest of their community in a process of complementarity and mutual enrichment. This way the school supports them in developing their understanding of the impact of their actions on the society in which they live. By building a supportive environment (where positive emotional attachments are cultivated), with a culture of excellence, learners have a greater chance to develop their autonomy, responsibility, initiative, solidarity, creativity, and critical spirit. Under these conditions, even in the early grades students can begin to feel responsible for their community and in intervening in the world around them.

To implement the VOAR model and form young women and men who believe that it is possible to build a more just and sustainable world, who assume responsibility, understand the urgency of contributing practically to these efforts, we intentionally develop two curricula: formal and hidden. For example, many of the school spaces have been adapted with vibrant colors and comfortable furnishing where students can feel at home, while at the same time maintaining more traditional and familiar classroom spaces.

We consider each student's unique characteristics and motivations, in addition to considering dimensions of their development and learning. Each student's education is supported by a tutor—a fatherly/motherly figure who cares about the development of both their personality and their academic life. Each tutor is responsible for six to ten learners. The tutor plays an even more important role in the teen years where we work to provide male tutors as role models for the boys and women as role models for the girls, although this is not always possible.

Formal Curriculum

VOAR is a post-modern pedagogical model (Pourtois & Desmet, 2000), based on Kentenich Pedagogy (1885–1968) that integrates strands from other coherent and complementary pedagogical systems that make it more flexible, versatile, and complete but also more complex. It includes carefully chosen methodologies that place the learner at the center of the whole teaching/learning process. Collaborative project-based learning and autonomous (independent) work are our school's most common methodologies, through which the learner is able to study any knowledge field. Apart from these more general methodologies, some specific didactics allow the students to build their own knowledge in specific academic areas such as mathematics and living languages.

In these subjects we include formal lessons; however, that doesn't mean they are lectures. These periods of time are essentially interactive, allowing practical oral and written communication, according to pedagogical situations specially set up for that purpose. For example, in mathematics knowledge is created through problem solving and challenges, individually or in small groups, which are later discussed in larger groups under the supervision of the teacher. Through the discussion of the different problem-solving processes for each challenge, the teacher helps the learners build up their knowledge, structuring and systematizing it, in order to master and apply it.

The remaining subjects of the curriculum are studied, beginning in kindergarten, primarily through a project-based approach that normally involves the integration of multiple subject areas. The project-based approach has a positive impact on motivation, which is critical because the projects require a greater volume of work for the students (and their teachers) than the traditional curriculum. Our experience has demonstrated, however, that if students are deeply engaged, they work steadily and make larger learning gains. When we were reflecting and monitoring the development of the School's Educational Project, the teachers were worried about the problem of extra work and were thinking about reducing project work, but one of the teachers advocated strongly against minimizing projects, stating it would be a big mistake because children don't mind working as long as they are really interested in what they are doing.

This teacher also reported that, in her fifth grade class, more than once, after the launching of a new project, when the teachers of the subjects involved were leaving the classroom, the students asked them: So, what do we have to do? (instead of "What do we have to study?). At this age, children and teenagers are essentially "homosfaber" (solo architects). For them studying is not particularly interesting. What really matters is doing things, that is, developing projects. And, through this approach, they get ready to develop projects in real life.

In addition to the methodologies already mentioned, the school has also been using SOLE (Self Organized Learning Environment), as it has been conceived by Sugata Mitra, with the goal of increasing motivation and learning. In changing the focus of their work from an essentially transmissive function to another of leader, observer, students' learning process fosterer, the teacher puts students in the position of building their own knowledge in an active way and discovering the possibilities of taking an entrepreneurial approach to learning and their lives. The teachers themselves also develop an attitude of acceptance, promotion, and fostering difference.

The students frequently work with great pleasure, as described by a sixth-grade learner:

The thing I like best about Colégio is the learning methodology. I prefer learning through Project Work than through normal lectures. It is much more fun to study, research, clarify my doubts and do the work with my colleagues than sitting in the classroom, listening to the Teacher and . . . I, myself, can decide when I will do the two weeks' work. I can also do the work in the school and not at home, which is much less boring.

Autonomous Work

At the beginning of every fortnight, each learner plans their autonomous work in a diary (see figure 10.1), based on the suggestions that each teacher has filed in the school's Moodle platform. This plan includes the choice of both a personal effort area and a class effort area. Afterward, the plan is discussed with the tutor who refines the suggestions according to the goals and characteristics of each student.

This work plan is carried out over a two-week period, with the support of all the teachers, when they are asked, or if they consider it necessary. However, students are guided to consider the first resource for any difficulty whenever possible—their fellow students. Thus, mutual aid is fostered as a way of developing the value of solidarity, which is a good thing, both for the one who helps and for the ones who are helped (by explaining a subject, he has access to a superior level of knowledge). When the two weeks are over, each learner reflects upon the work developed, in writing, and talks to his tutor, who helps him take his reflection further (See Figure 10.2).

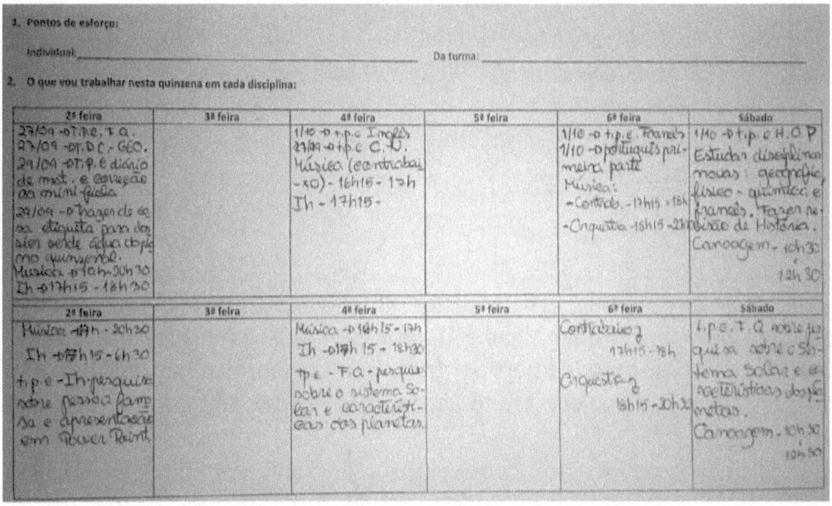

Figure 10.1 Sample Autonomous Work Diary.

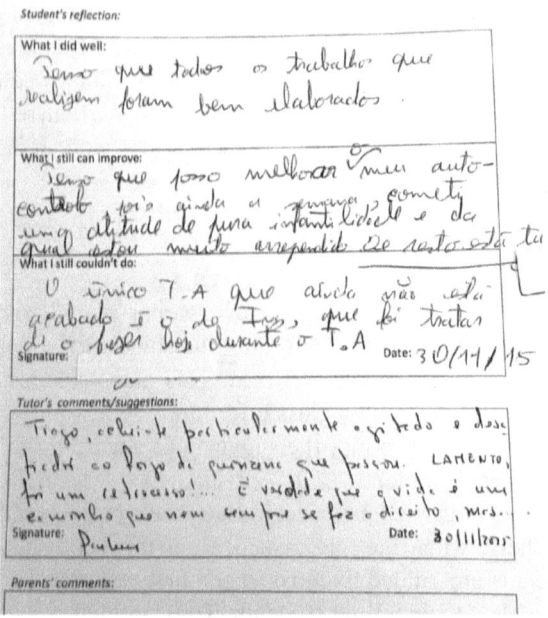

Figure 10.2 Student Reflection Log.

Finally, the parents get to know the two-week plan and its evaluation, having the possibility of including their own observations and suggestions. Below is a comment on the process from one student:

> My Colégio is special. There we learn and discover. Here we are happier than in other schools. Here we have a lot of freedom, but not to say silly things. In my school I work autonomously. We learn how to work with the Internet, we develop projects and learn from them. When we have group work, we meet at the school, during T.A. Sometimes we go to each other's houses to finish and do the projects.

Project Work

As a core methodology (with historical roots tracing back to the work of John Dewey, William Head Kilpatrick, and Célestin Freinet), project-based work positions learners at the center of the teaching and learning process, as it enables learners to actively participate in building their own knowledge.

In primary school (from years 1 to 4), we follow the "Teaching is Researching" model that shapes the whole curriculum in a project-based framework. For example, we may begin with science (experimental and social) as the doorway into the knowledge of other content areas such as Portuguese, mathematics, and art. In middle school (from years 5 to 9), we also rely on this interdisciplinary methodology. To achieve this, teachers work together to analyze at the macro level the topics that will work best. Providing teachers with autonomy and maximum amounts of choice are critical to the success of these efforts.

In Colégio de S. José, the projects are developed at three levels (Leitão et al., 1993), according to the model of the project "Teaching is Researching."

LEVEL 1: WHAT WE ALREADY KNOW ABOUT A TOPIC AND WHAT WE STILL DON'T KNOW AND ARE WILLING TO FIND OUT

We begin this work with the following assumption: "School learning never starts from zero. In fact all children's learning has a pre-history which the pedagogical action can not forget, otherwise it will fail" (Best, 1980). At level 1, pedagogical situations are created so that the learners can raise their awareness and express their knowledge and interest about the topic they are dealing with. It develops in two moments: first what we already know, and second what we want to know.

- What we already know:
  In either a spontaneous or direct way, we support the class in expressing what they already know about the topic at hand. Bringing in one's personal experience is strongly encouraged.
- What we want to know:
  Through a similar process, we surface the students' curiosities about the topic and create a list of areas that we would like to further research.

Level 1 allows the students to face the next level confidently, as they already had a first moment of reflection upon the topic and have begun activating their own prior knowledge and experience, while also learning from their peers.

LEVEL 2: PLANNING—RESEARCHING— DEVELOPING A PRODUCT—PRESENTING

Level 2 is the level at which students' autonomy reaches its fullest expression and development. Learners organize themselves into working groups and choose and negotiate with other groups and teachers what they are going to research further. They then plan their research activities that necessarily include research protocols, which they register in their diaries. Then they carry out their plan, collecting, selecting, and managing the information they have gathered and filtered. This research may include scientific experimentation, bibliographic research, and fieldwork. Many times the fieldwork is carried out outside the school, sometimes in another region of the country, or even abroad, for two to five days, in expeditions.

LEVEL 3: STRUCTURING KNOWLEDGE

At this level, the teacher has to ensure that all the learners have built their own knowledge and have developed their ability to think critically at a variety of levels of abstraction from detailed data analysis to generalization and theorizing. Concept maps are one tool teachers use to support students in working across these dimensions. In this way, level 3 helps move students toward the understanding of a variety of concepts and ideas and seeing the interrelationships between them, explicitly, which provides a common level of understanding for all.

At the end of the project, learners evaluate their own performance. Although typical project life cycles usually run around two weeks, they can be extended for longer periods based on the subject matter and student's needs.

One example of this approach comes from a group of year 5 students who had a project titled "From an Alien's Point of View." The project was launched with a short video that tells the story of five aliens who are running away from their planet that has exploded and who land on the Earth. As the earners are in year 5, they are still quite young, and so the project appeals to their imaginations and sense of fun. The place and the time where and when the aliens land on Earth is chosen according to the objectives of the contents of history and the geography of Portugal, as well as the natural sciences such as biology and geology. That is, when the fictional aliens land on Earth, they do land in the North of Portugal. That's when things get interesting as the aliens must first address survival issues, and their primary worry is to find out if the planet they have landed on is inhabitable? Is the air breathable? Do they have drinking water? What food sources exist? and so on

One of the superpowers the aliens possess is the ability to travel through time, and so the aliens visit different periods of Portuguese history until they find the right one in which to live. Below is a list of subtopics that are covered in the project:

Subtopic 1: Through the universe, running away from the war, they landed on planet Earth.

1.1. Where do the aliens come from? (NS)
- The universe
- The solar system
- The Earth
- The Earth's sustainability

Topic summaries
Level 3 (Teacher Intervention)

1.2. Is the air breathable? (NS)
- The nature of the air
- Air gases' properties
- The importance of atmospheric gases for the living beings
- Pollution
- Presentation

Level 3 (Teacher Intervention)

1.3. Where did the aliens land? (HGP—Geography)
- The location of Europe
- The Iberian Peninsula: location, borders, physical characteristics, climate

Level 3 (Teacher Intervention)
Mini test

1.4. How did they live? (HGP—History)
- Hunting/collecting communities
- The first farming communities

Expedition to the S. Lourenço settlement

In this example, learners had to study the time (pre-history) and a place (north of Portugal) where fictional aliens had landed on Earth after their planet had exploded. An expedition to S. Lourenço settlement, a beautiful and historically rich natural park, was organized so that the students were able to study early settlements and the surrounding ecosystem, which brought together the subject areas of History, Natural Science, and P.E. as well as language and art which they used in their recording of data and in their communication. Finally, each group created a final product—a poster, a PowerPoint or a Prezi presentation, a film, a text (such as a booklet)—and prepared a final presentation. These presentations were both self-assessed and peer and teacher evaluated.

The Hidden Curriculum

Educating a child involves more than academic learning. Learning to know, learning to do, and learning to live together with others are fundamental educational pillars that situate and frame each child as a whole person full of potential. This is why, beyond the academic learning, life at school extends into many different areas that aim to enrich the learners' experiences and encourage their active participation as conscious and active citizens.

Community Management

According to the subsidiarity principle, at Colégio de S. José, life is run by the learners who elect their representatives and carry out Learners' Councils (classroom-based discussions) and whole school assemblies where they discuss issues and try to find solutions.

By stimulating the creation of management boards, where the children and teenagers can debate about their needs and problems, make important decisions, regulate the school's life and make respected and supported intervention initiatives, backed by everybody, we are fostering the maturation of: (i) reflected and democratic ways of acting, (ii) respect for the others, (iii) responsibility for their own lives and for the life of the whole community, and (iv) capacity to intervene in the communities to which they belong. Both during the Students' Councils and the School Assemblies, positions and tasks are given to the learners, such as: organizing the lunch queue, tidying up the classrooms, and conducting prayer that takes place every morning.

One personal example of this activity took place at the end of a school year when the school community was saying goodbye to a group of Spanish students who had visited the school, a cyclist passing by greeted me and said:

> I would very much like to thank you . . . well, you mustn't remember me. At the beginning of the school year I asked to talk to you to tell you that your students, during their break times, threw garbage onto the street, which was wrong. I don't know what you have done, but it didn't happen again.

I thanked him and he went away, while I was thinking and I didn't remember, at all, what I had done to solve the problem. As I was returning to the school I suddenly remembered: when I got the complaint, I shared it with the president of the School's Assembly and she discussed it during the next assembly. Then it was decided to form groups of learners who would remind the others that "we shouldn't pollute the world because it belongs to everybody and deserves all our respect." And, the problem was solved.

The learners recognize the gain in having the possibility of debating and deciding about questions that are important for everybody. This school is different from the others because it has assemblies where the students can choose what's the best for the school and because it has the best teachers in the whole world.

Apart from the academic projects, our students carry out others that aim at social intervention. These are called "initiatives" because they are set up under the students' proposals. They aim at solving problems they have found inside the school or in the surrounding community. Below are some examples:

- Just in front of the school, there is an enormous apple tree that was full of wonderful fruits. As they were falling onto the ground, in huge quantities, the passing cars crushed them all. Seeing this a group of students from year 6 decided to begin collecting the apples as they fell. The apples were placed in small bags, together with sandwiches and fruit juices, which were given to the homeless, in the evening.
- During the evening distribution, the same group of students understood that the homeless people needed warm clothes. So, they organized a collection they delivered later at Christmas time when the weather was cooler.
- A group of year 5 students organized a drawing contest and another group of students with different ages set up a photo contest that had a big exhibition in one of the city shopping centers.
- In science classes, when they got to know the amount of energy spent on producing a simple T-shirt, the students of year 5 set up a stall, at school, to trade clothes. Their aim was to avoid the purchase of more clothes.
- When the school was organizing a one-week expedition to the Azores, there was a Syrian refugee at school (Colégio offered three scholarships to refugee children) who couldn't pay for her trip. So, the year 9 students, her school friends, organized a party with paid entry. The collected money was entirely given to the student.
- Wishing to make their classroom more comfortable and to buy some sofas, year 7 students asked for permission to pick oranges from the school trees. Then they made juice that they sold to the rest of the students.

These initiatives may have the form of debates about current affairs they want to talk about, as was the case of emigration.

Youngsters' Congress

Because we wanted the students and the youngsters from all over the country to have the opportunity to debate about the problems of the planet's sustainability, Colégio São José organized a congress under the topic of the UN Sustainable Development Goals. This congress, called "CidadeFora da Caixa," took place at the University of Coimbra and was attended by eighty-three teenagers from all around the country. Organized in small groups, the participants debated the problems of their cities and presented proposals for solving them.

RESULTS

In an external evaluation carried out by the Portuguese Ministry of Education, the school students demonstrated positive learning outcomes. Figure 10.3 presents a comparison between our year 2 class and the national average score of the 2017 benchmarking tests (the last ones available as of this time of this writing).

The whole educational paradigm change process of the school was investigated by a team of researchers from the Psychology and Educational Sciences Faculty of Coimbra's University. For three years, this team has researched the possible influence of the pedagogical model VOAR: (i) in the learning patterns, using the PALS Scale (Adaptive Learning Patterns Scale) that tests the orientation toward mastery (close to preference to knowledge),

REPÚBLICA PORTUGUESA
EDUCAÇÃO

IAVE

Estabelecimento de ensino: Colégio de S. José — Ano de escolaridade: 2º

	Nacional				Colégio de S. José				Turma A											
Português	C	CM	RD	NC	C	CM	RD	NC	C	CM	RD	NC	C	CM	RD	NC	C	CM	RD	NC
Compreensão do Oral	22,5	32,0	26,5	19,0	56,2	31,2	12,5	0,0	56,2	31,2	12,5	0,0								
Leitura e Iniciação à Educação Literária	23,2	39,3	29,6	7,7	81,2	18,8	0,0	0,0	81,2	18,8	0,0	0,0								
Gramática	20,5	18,4	38,3	22,6	43,8	18,8	25,0	12,5	43,8	18,8	25,0	12,5								
Escrita	13,8	14,9	37,5	24,0	75,0	0,0	12,5	6,2	75,0	0,0	12,5	6,2								
Matemática	C	CM	RD	NC	C	CM	RD	NC	C	CM	RD	NC	C	CM	RD	NC	C	CM	RD	NC
Números e Operações	42,9	26,9	22,1	8,0	75,0	25,0	0,0	0,0	75,0	25,0	0,0	0,0								
Geometria e Medida	32,1	30,2	29,1	8,5	93,8	6,2	0,0	0,0	93,8	6,2	0,0	0,0								
Organização e Tratamento de Dados	65,8	-	24,4	8,1	93,8	-	6,2	0,0	93,8	-	6,2	0,0								
Estudo do Meio	C	CM	RD	NC	C	CM	RD	NC	C	CM	RD	NC	C	CM	RD	NC	C	CM	RD	NC
À Descoberta de Si Mesmo	22,0	34,3	31,6	12,0	37,5	50,0	12,5	0,0	37,5	50,0	12,5	0,0								
À Descoberta dos Outros e das Instituições	24,0	34,6	29,9	11,0	37,5	56,2	6,2	0,0	37,5	56,2	6,2	0,0								
À Descoberta do Ambiente Natural	76,6	-	5,0	17,5	93,8	-	6,2	0,0	93,8	-	6,2	0,0								
À Descoberta das Inter-relações entre espaços	32,4	-	24,7	40,8	68,8	-	18,8	12,5	68,8	-	18,8	12,5								
À Descoberta dos Materiais e Objetos	50,6	-	-	47,5	81,2	-	-	18,8	81,2	-	-	18,8								
Expressões Artísticas	C	CM	RD	NC	C	CM	RD	NC	C	CM	RD	NC	C	CM	RD	NC	C	CM	RD	NC
Expressão e Educação Musical	30,6	31,1	25,6	12,1	68,8	18,8	6,2	0,0	68,8	18,8	6,2	0,0								
Expressão e Educação Dramática	49,0	33,3	11,8	5,6	75,0	18,8	0,0	6,2	75,0	18,8	0,0	6,2								
Expressão e Educação Plástica	62,7	24,6	10,8	1,9	81,2	18,8	0,0	0,0	81,2	18,8	0,0	0,0								
Expressões Físico-Motoras	C	CM	RD	NC	C	CM	RD	NC	C	CM	RD	NC	C	CM	RD	NC	C	CM	RD	NC
Deslocamentos e Equilíbrios	51,2	40,7	7,2	0,9	50,0	43,8	6,2	0,0	50,0	43,8	6,2	0,0								
Perícias e Manipulações	42,4	43,5	12,2	1,8	37,5	56,2	0,0	6,2	37,5	56,2	0,0	6,2								
Jogos Infantis	12,1	54,0	31,0	2,7	25,0	56,2	18,8	0,0	25,0	56,2	18,8	0,0								

Figure 10.3 Comparison between Year 2 Class and the National Average Score. *Note*: C means achieved; CM means achieved but; RD means solved poorly and NC means not achieved.

orientation toward results, self-efficacy, self-justification for failure, novelty avoidance and skepticism (regarding the school importance for life's success) and (ii) in career adaptability through the Career Adaptability Scale (CAAS) that tests concerns (about learning), control (capacity to face situations and produce changes), curiosity (for knowledge), and confidence (in their capacities).

This research involved a sample of students from Colégio de S. José (CSJ) and another one from the Polish school Gymnasium Przymierza Rodzin: Jana Pawla II. The students from CSJ got better grades than the Polish school, which implements a more traditional pedagogical model than our school. In the research report we can read: "It's possible to verify significant differences when comparing the average values of the patterns constructs in terms of learning and career adaptability in the two groups (Poland and Portugal)."

The report went on to say, "The Learning Pattern with more significant average values were Mastery Orientation, associated with the development of autonomy and adaptive learning which suggests a desire for knowledge, and is strongly associated with intrinsic motivation, self-efficacy (the belief in one's own capacities) and the importance of school for the future."

For the constructs associated with career adaptability, that is, the required characteristics for the students to face the challenges in their future, those who had the most significant values were curiosity, connected to the interest for learning; the perception of control, which indicates that these students believe in their capacity to produce change; and confidence that reflects the perception for the achievement of future success. These results point at a positive impact on learning skills and patterns when they are under the influence of an educational method based on the promotion of autonomy.

Another research study, carried out by the IDEA team from Lisbon's University, under the topic of reading speed of year 2 students, included one of our classes in a sample of fourteen groups. The results can be analyzed in the chart below (figure 10.4). The results in green belong to our school's class.

We continue to invite academic researchers to investigate the VOAR model. Currently, two Portuguese master researchers and three foreign PhD students are studying different aspects of our pedagogical model.

In several different contests, our students have also obtained excellent results, especially in mathematics. In the last few years, they have won two medals (gold and bronze) in the Math Olympiads, a first and two third-place prizes in the national competition Pmat, and also a first and two third-place prizes in the mathematics games contest.

Colégio São José has hosted a great number of visitors: teachers, educational experts from higher and lower education, Portuguese and foreign and

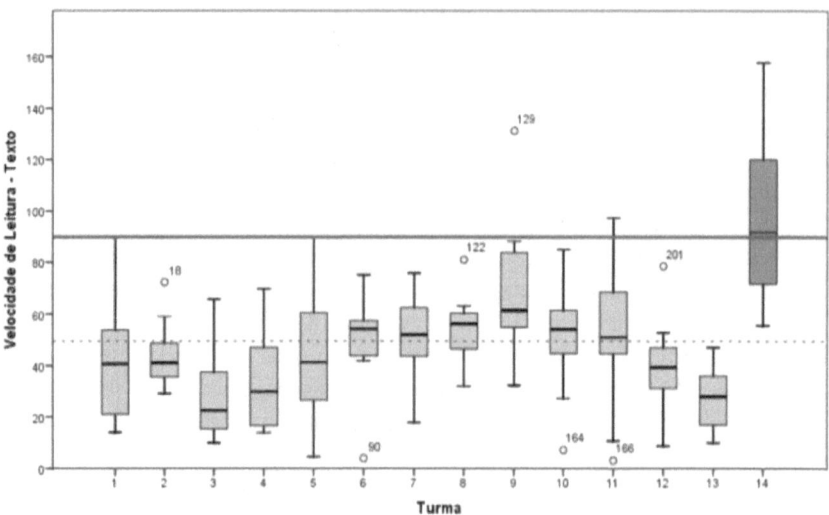

Figure 10.4 Reading Speed Comparisons.

has also been asked to supervise internships. For example, in the school year, 2018/2019, we hosted a group of Polish teachers in a two-week job shadowing experience. We have also been greatly requested to present our educational model during congresses and educational conferences and also to give teacher training sessions. In 2017/2018, we gave twenty-six presentations all around the country.

CONCLUSIONS

Through the pedagogical model VOAR, Colégio de S. José aims at raising men and women with free and strong personalities, able to build a net of deep and stable affective relationships around them. They should also relate harmoniously with life, the world around them, and with knowledge according to a set of values and ideals. We also want to educate special people: autonomous, responsible, creative, bold, entrepreneur, concerned about the common good, and able to intervene in their societies and of influencing their culture, contributing to the construction of a better and more solidary world.

Working through projects (TP) in a collaborative and autonomous way, the learners are challenged to build their own knowledge during their autonomous work (TA) sessions. By assuming the responsibility of managing a significant part of school life and carrying out several initiatives with the aim of solving problems of their community (near and far), they learn how to take an active role in their society.

The academic results our students achieve, in internal and external evaluations, and after leaving the school, show that they have acquired significant learning and developed the skills that will allow them to build their own knowledge autonomously and to carry on doing so at their subsequent educational levels and throughout their lifetime.

Throughout the process that led to the construction of the new pedagogical model, some constraints came up and had to be overcome. They are considered today as valuable lessons for the future. The most significant change concerned the teachers' involvement. The change from a transmissive attitude into another one in which the learner is in charge of his own learning has not always been an easy one. The same can be said of changing from subject-related logic to one of a global viewpoint of knowledge with intense teamwork that enables the students to develop interdisciplinary projects and actively build knowledge.

VOAR is a dynamic educational model that has been developing and continues to evolve. The team of teachers determines, at every step, the way to lead, the changes to introduce, creating new forms that demonstrate constant reflection upon the Educational Project's implementation and a truly continuous teacher training, in context, and which always aims at being inspiring.

REFERENCES

Best, F. (1980). *Por uma Pedagogia do despertar*. Biblioteca do Educador Profissional. Livros Horizonte.

Dewey, J. (1961). *Democracy and education* (paperback ed.). New York: Macmillan.

Dewey, J. (1986, September). Experience and education. In *The educational forum* (Vol. 50, No. 3, pp. 241–252). New York: Taylor & Francis Group.

Drago-Severson, E. (2012). New opportunities for principal leadership: Shaping school climates for enhanced teacher development. *Teachers College Record, 114*(3), 1–44.

Freinet, C. (1998). *Educação pelo trabalho*. São Paulo: Martins Fontes.

Gonçalves, C. Q. (2017). *Inovação pedagógica e autonomia nas escolas: o impacto de metodologias pedagógica sinovadoras em variáveis psicológicas de adaptabilidade*. Doctoral dissertation, Universidade de Coimbra.

Kentenich, J. (1951). Quesurja el hombre nuevo. *Jornada Pedagógica*.

Kentenich, J. (1993). *La educación en un cambio de época*. Santiago: Editorial Schoenstatt.

Kentenich, J. (2012). *Desafío de nuestrotiempo*. Editorial Nueva Patris SA.

Knoll, M. (2012). "I had made a mistake": William H. Kilpatrick and the project method. *Teachers College Record, 114*(2), 1–45.

Leitão, M. L., Pires, I. V., Palhais, F., & Gallino, M. J. (1993). *Da criança ao adulto: Um itinerário pedagógico, ensinar é investigar.*
Leitão, M. L., Pires, I. V., Palhais, F., & Gallino, M. J. (1994). *Eu e os outros– Um itinerário pedagógico, ensinar é investigar* (Vol. 2). Lisboa: Ministério da Educação/Instituto de Inovação Educacional.
Pires, M. I. V. (2001). *Pedagogia de vinculações e educação para os valores.*
Pourtois, J. P., & Desmet, H. (1997). *L'éducation postmoderne.* Paris: Presses universitaires de France.

Chapter 11

Design for Change

A Methodology for Young People to Change the World

Asma Hussain, India, Beatriz Alonso, Spain, and Elena Bretón, Spain

Design for Change (DFC) Global is an organization that equips children with the tools to be aware of the world around them, believe that they can play a role in shaping that world, and can take action toward a more desirable, sustainable future. The DFC core offerings and programmatic work center around the "Feel, Imagine, Do, and Share" (FIDS) framework that it has successfully implemented with young people around the world.

Now a global movement, DFC was conceptualized and founded by Kiran Bir Sethi in 2009, who is also the founder of Riverside School in Ahmedabad, India. When DFC started in India, they introduced the one-week DFC challenge in local public schools. Today they offer a curriculum about design thinking and civics education in public schools and collaborate with local education authorities in recruiting new schools to participate in their programs and in curriculum development (Harvard School of Education). Through partnerships, DFC is committed to increasing its footprint so that more children can work with the step-by-step FIDS framework and become empowered to "Be the Change." As FIDS is the most important component of DFC, the global organization works with partners to provide children and schools with access to the FIDS model in as many places as possible. These partners take responsibility for spreading the FIDS model in their own countries, cultures, and contexts and for adapting it to the lived experiences of children from all backgrounds and life situations.

This chapter tells the story of DFC drawing on the model itself and input from interviews conducted by leaders from DFC with three young people who participated in the FIDS model. We foreground their voices in this chapter as a way of highlighting the importance of listening to youth who we believe are already capable of changing the world. Specifically, we invited three members of the DFC Student Council to share their ideas, values, beliefs, and attitudes and to elaborate on their personal experience with DFC and its methodology. The questions we asked aimed to surface the ways DFC impacted each of their lives and to discover their understanding of the DFC. For DFC young people stand at the very center of the educational process, and, thus for us, the testimonies presented here provide the best way to understand how DFC empowers young people. These three members of the DFC Student Council interviewed for this chapter are Tijana Doroški DFC Serbia (sixteen-years-old), Daniel Umrou from DFC, United States (thirteen-years-old), and María Hernández from DFC, Spain (sixteen-years-old), and we have sought to include their voices and ideas in almost every section of the chapter.

PROGRAM OVERVIEW

DFC cultivates young peoples' belief that change is possible through the following program activities:

- DFC provides a free, flexible toolkit of a four-step design process of FIDS. (A link to a toolkit can be found at this url: https://globaled.gse.harvard.edu/files/geii/files/toolkit_global.pdf)
- Teachers receive professional development services and use the toolkit with children in their classrooms to author projects to create change.
- DFC curriculum: This is a yearlong curriculum that extends the weeklong experience. The curriculum is delivered through sixty minutes, once per week sessions at schools. It has been piloted in sixty-four schools in India since 2014. Through activities such as hands-on projects, scenario-based role plays, and design thinking, children develop FIDS competencies.
- The one-week "Be the Change Conference" brings together young people from across the world to showcase their stories of success. In the most recent event, 500 young people from 22 countries participated.

DESIGN FOR CHANGE'S TARGET POPULATION

DFC has impacted over two million children between the ages of eight and eighteen across sixty-five countries in the past decade. The children come from different cultures, socioeconomic backgrounds, religious, and ethnic identities. From the children in Benin to the children in Copenhagen, DFC places equal importance on the abilities of each child to be an agent of change.

The Members of the Student Council know that young people are clearly the primary target group for DFC: Daniel Umrou remarked: "I do believe that DFC targets mostly children and teens and encourages them to use their voice." Tijana Doroški remarked similarly: "DFC is specially targeted at young people in schools, ergo-youth up to 18 years of age." And, María Hernández noted that: "DFC is targeted at every public, but it is specially oriented to youngsters. It allows them to experience and squeeze their creativity."

From the beginning of DFC, and in many ways for the first time at scale, adults consistently ask children for their opinions, what changes they would like to see, and how they think adults can help them bring it about. What seems like a simple shift actually represents a dynamic shift in power that can make adults extremely uncomfortable, but, once the initial ground of self-doubt is broken through with the youth and they are given freedom to discuss the problems they face along with their peers, creativity begins to emerge.

This fundamental insight remains core to all of DFC's work around the world. In 2009, when DFC was founded, there were very few people looking at design thinking as a method for empowering students as agents of change. But, the methodology pioneered by DFC has spread, and today there are many other programs placing young people at the center of movements for social change, such as The Teachers Guild (2016), Designathon Works (2014), Design and Invention Pedagogy (2016), and The Biz Nation (2017). Members of the Student Council echoed the importance of putting the youth in charge of the movement. Tijana Doroški from DFC Serbia noted that the "DFC was created not only to encourage children to think for themselves and to share their ideas, but also to help them make their ideas come true." And, María Hernández, from DFC Spain, said similarly: "In my opinion, DFC was created to show children and young people that it is possible to change and improve the world." Daniel Umrou, from DFC United States added: "DFC was created to share children's ideas and to let children motivate each other to be the change they want."

GUIDING PRINCIPLES AND PHILOSOPHIES

Promoted by M. K. Gandhi, DFC's guiding philosophy is "Be the change you wish to see in the world." Inspired by this principle, DFC has an annual "Be the Change Festival" where every country shares its stories of change and problem solving with the world, including addressing identity crisis, gender inequality, providing educational resources during the pandemic, alcoholism, child labor, environmental challenges, and suicide.

Children themselves form the cornerstone of DFC. In DFC, we say that children naturally gravitate toward free thinking, and our work is to remove barriers that stand in the way of them using their natural ability to make the world a better place. For DFC, treating children as if they must wait to change the world is a fundamentally flawed view, which becomes evident when hundreds of examples of young changemakers from around the world emerge.

> For the longest time, educators has believed that children are the future, that "ONE day" they will grow up and make the world a better place. And in waiting for that "One day," educators have deferred the promise that it made to its children to help them become creative, proactive, empathetic and responsible citizens. This resulted in children graduating saying "I CAN'T." (Design for Change, 2014)

But, what if educational leaders believed their mission was to empower every child to say "I CAN" and that children are not helpless, that change is possible, and that young people can drive it. What if adults, teachers, and leaders helped to promote a positive belief in children's ability to lead change right now? Young people get it, and they are looking at each other and saying *If not us, then who? If not now, then when?* What is needed is for young people to see in themselves their own power to make change, to find the role models among their peers, and to give themselves permission to channel their optimistic mind-set, empathy, and compassion and drive positive change and to contribute to solving the challenges in their community and the world. As Daniel Umrou from DFC United States said, "The philosophy of 'Be The Change' guides Design for Change. If children are allowed to be changemakers and to participate in decision-making processes at an early age, they can learn and build a better world."

HOW DOES THE MODEL WORK?

The founders of DFC developed it to change the idea that children are a future asset and a current liability to the world and to eliminate the idea that children must always be told what and how to do things. Children have a great deal of social awareness, yet, they frequently lack the self-efficacy and belief that they already have the agency to act upon their own ideas. While the entrenched educational systems of the world promise children that one day young people will lead positive change, DFC believes they can guide important and significant change right now.

With this fundamental premise of children's ability to lead change now, DFC established its course methodology on four principles rooted in the

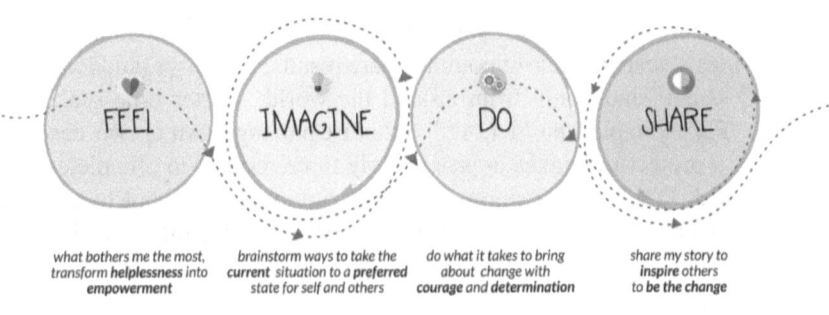

Figure 11.1 The DFC Methodology.

design thinking model: Feel, Imagine, Do, and Share (FIDS) (See Figure 11.1). This methodology provides young people with a simple, accessible, actionable framework through which children can act on their ideas to solve the problems and address the challenges they face through a lens of empathy, enabling them to participate as active citizens of society.

THE IMPORTANCE OF COLLABORATION IN THE FIDS MODEL

Collaboration is an intrinsic aspect of the FIDS model. It gives us the freedom to be able to articulate our thoughts and feel more confident about them, but at the same time we engage in debate and walk a mile in another's shoes, thus developing our compassion through the FIDS process and sharing these values with our community. This development, from self-doubt to change in the community, really highlights how FIDS makes us "aware of our agency and helps us feel empowered and enabled to act as changemakers."

Daniel Umrou elaborated further:

> I feel empowered when using the FIDS method. It was a very effective method that enabled me and my friends to brainstorm ideas, imagine a perfect world while facing many challenges. We came up with lots of ideas and solutions on how to stop the spread of viruses. At that time the flu virus was affecting many of our peers at school. We had to choose a solution that children our age would understand, remember easily, and that was not too costly.

THE ROLE AND IMPORTANCE OF TIME

It takes time to make a change, and the FIDS model has been adapted successfully to a variety of time scales. While "Be the Change" event occurs annually and provides a yearly check-in point to share results, successes, and learnings for DFC leaders and youth from around the world, shorter time scales are possible. For example, the "I CAN" School Challenge (which we describe below) is a project that takes approximately three months to complete from start to finish. The process starts with an invitation to a school to tackle a challenge which—as an example—can broadly be divided into five phases.

Phase 1: Sample Survey

Step 1: Do a survey of both public and private schools in your country. Collect data of the school holidays/timeline, national holidays of the country to see when the students are more relaxed and freer to do the challenge. Once the survey is completed, analyze the data and make a timeline for the country's "I Can School Challenge."

If possible, given the feedback of users, it is a good idea to choose dates of "national significance" that are easy to remember. For example, in India we choose the following:

- August 15 (India's Independence Day) as the registration deadline
- October 2 (Gandhi Ji's Birthday) as the submission deadline
- November 14 (Children's Day) as the results announcement deadline

Phase 2: Announce the challenge digitally via email, social media, the internet, and so on.

Make sure there are exciting incentives to motivate young changemakers to participate. Start distributing the toolkits and lesson plans to all the partners and schools in their preferred language in your country. Send guidelines to all the schools for easy registration and submission. Make follow-up calls to your complete data for the registration and submission of the "I Can School Challenge."

Phase 3: Select your jury and create an online jury platform to start the judging process.

Select the topmost inspiring stories that have enabled or created change in their environment. Send congratulation emails to the topmost inspiring stories and gratitude emails to all the participants.

Phase 4: Announce the topmost inspiring stories and invite them to celebrate and collaborate with the other participants.

You can conduct workshops/presentations/camps/festivals, and so on. Also, give the topmost inspiring stories their certificate of appreciation and incentives if any.

Phase 5: Send gratitude emails to all the participants along with participation certificates, incentives, videos, or a glimpse of the celebration to motivate the schools to participate in the coming years.

Other projects work on longer timescales as Daniel Umrou noted,

> The time frame for DFC to work varies according to the social issue or problem. It takes a few months to do a project and create an impact. In my case, it took close to a school year for our stop the spread of campaign research and impact.

RESOURCES REQUIRED FOR IMPLEMENTATION

As a program designed to scale around the world, the DFC model is both low tech and low cost, that is, it can be done with very little additional resources for a school or children. For example, a study done in Tamil Nadu in India concluded that for USD 10, a DFC teacher can be trained and enabled. With that investment, at least ten students can be impacted through the DFC challenge using conservative estimates. Thus, for an investment of USD 1 per student per year, DFC addresses the need for learning transferable skills and creating a long-term impact on students. If the impact on teachers and community is considered, the DFC program is arguably one of the most cost-effective means of instilling agency, attitudes, values, and skills most needed for the twenty-first century.

PROGRAM CONTENT

Through fostering design thinking and the "I can" mind-set, DFC encourages children to become change agents and take initiative. It targets the interpersonal competencies of ethical behavior, responsibility, self-direction, and citizenship. The "Feel" and "Share" component of the FIDS toolkit and curriculum invites children to empathize with people who are affected by the problem they try to solve. Children also develop the interpersonal competencies of collaboration, leadership, and communication in the process of solving problems. Cognitive competencies that develop include problem solving, critical thinking, and creativity skills during the process of creating change. DFC and FIDS also foster positive attitudes and values, most notably the "I can" mind-set, community engagement, responsibility, and active citizenship.

The program engages students through actionable thinking routines and starts from issues in students' immediate surroundings in daily life. The key pedagogical features are hands-on activities and collaboration with others.

EVIDENCE OF IMPACT

DFC has been committed to assess its model and has taken part in rigorous research to test its effectiveness. Some of these evaluations are listed below:

- In collaboration with The Good Project, an initiative under Project Zero at the Harvard Graduate School of Education, research was conducted to test the impact of DFC. The study found DFC to be the most inclusive initiative with 56 percent of students' participation from rural and semi-urban schools, with equal participation from girls and boys and solving problems in sixteen diverse sectors from education to drug abuse, traffic problems, inclusion, disability, and many more. Furthermore, students developed positive attitudes toward studies with over 80 percent saying they were now highly motivated.
- INSEAD in collaboration with Stanford University conducted an in-depth analysis and wrote a research paper studying the impact of the FIDS methodology on children's creativity. The study concluded that children showed a significant improvement in ideational fluency and divergent thinking. Additionally, the students reported a boost in confidence especially among the female students.
- An educational research consulting firm "Eval Design" studied the effects of the DFC program in Tamil Nadu, India, on multiple stakeholders such as the students, teachers, and parents. The students had been observed to have developed greater creativity and twenty-first-century skills and attitudes. Within a short time frame, there was a 28 percent increase in confidence and an 11 percent increase in social consciousness. The teacher involvement improved, and parents developed a positive attitude toward their child's education. Overall, the DFC program was deemed cost-effective, that is, it takes USD 10 to train a teacher, with at least ten students being impacted by a teacher thus a child can increase their creativity, confidence, critical thinking, and leadership skills for as little as USD 1. The program was found easy to replicate, sustainable, and with long-term positive changes.
- Terpel Foundation in partnership with DFC Colombia ran a comparative study on the development of children's skills using the DFC frameworks. A significant increase in empathy, creativity, problem solving, planning, collaboration, and critical thinking was observed.

- In 2018, DFC France conducted a study with 159 students to see the effects of the FIDS process on student's confidence and ability to succeed at school. It was concluded that the children had developed a strong sense of resilience with an 11 percent increase in self-efficacy.
- In 2020, Universidad Complutense de Madrid in collaboration with DFC Spain started a study focused on the analysis of the empowerment of students from two schools in Madrid that use the DFC methodology. The research is still ongoing, and the outcomes are yet to be seen. The research design includes two schools of Madrid with children and teenagers between ten and fourteen years old. The group of students includes both K-12 and high school levels. The schools are located in different socioeconomic areas of Madrid. The expected sample size will be about 150 students to research the concept of empowerment used in DFC methodology.

Beyond these evaluations are stories of change and impact. One such story took place in 2011, in a school in Pune, India, where the female students noticed the lack of girls in their school due to low female birth rates in their village. They used the FIDS model to start a campaign to spread awareness through rallies, door-to-door campaigns, and street plays. Through this, the FIDS model wasn't just about how the students pioneering the project felt but how the entire school and their village felt the excitement of the change the young girls wanted to drive. The model helped the entire village feel the ambition of the girls, and it moved the *gram panchayat* (the local village governing institute) to start a program where a mother who gives birth to a girl child would receive Rs. 100 every month till the girl turned eighteen years old.

The Student Council Members also shared their views on the impact of DFC. Tijana Doroški, from Serbia, says:

> During the many years of DFC's work, many successful projects have been created. Just from the fact that it works and has partners in over 65 countries, we can say that the impact is huge. At our Annual Celebration in November, many projects were presented, including my school's project about improving our town's tourism, while bringing the whole community together.

Daniel Umrou, from the United States, said:

> I know DFC works because I did a project in my school community that focused on stopping the spreading of viruses that cause the flu that made a massive impact in the world. It was successful because we made organic soaps for children at our school to wash their hands. We conducted surveys in the beginning of the project that showed many students didn't wash hands with soap and

water, however, after our project the surveys showed a real increase in students hand washing with soap and water. The outcome of this project is that many children and adults started to care about their health and decided to spread the message, and we believe less people got sick too. Personally, the DFC project helped with my self-confidence, problem solving, public speaking, and teamwork. I became confident and was able to speak publicly at a school in another state about my project and how children can make a change.

THE ROLE OF COLLABORATION AND PARTNERSHIP

The most unique feature of DFC is that it is not only simple but also open source, contextual, and inclusive. The framework encourages children to "Feel" about an issue that bothers them, "Imagine" ways to make it better, "Do" take action, and "Share" their story of change with the world to inspire others!

DFC introduced design thinking for children when it was not a part of the mainstream to build a mind-set of optimism and collaboration. Also, unlike the teacher-driven method of project-based learning, DFC encourages teachers to step back, listen, and trust the child. This approach, though common sense, was not common practice and that was disruptive and unique. Children as young as six years of age are solving day-to-day problems they face as individuals, as a family, or as a community. Daniel Umrou, member of the Student Council, shared his thoughts:

> From my experience, I wish that more schools, teachers would collaborate with DFC and allow children to use this method besides the standard way of learning. More parents should learn about the DFC way too, and push for this type of teaching in schools for their children because through the process students develop many different skills that will definitely help them in the future.

THE CONTEXTS IN WHICH THE MODEL WORKS BEST

DFC has adopted a flexible and decentralized model to spread the impact and scale of the movement. Through a partnership model, like-minded people from different countries are provided with tools, strategies, and support to implement DFC. Every partner raises funds, translates the toolkit (there are over seventeen versions of the toolkit), reaches out to schools, trains teachers, and grows the impact of DFC. The global team supports the partners with resources, social media, and networking through both online and offline touchpoints. As a movement, DFC engages and stays connected through several activities throughout the year—partners offering skill workshops, a Student Council representation, buddy program for new partners, an annual global gathering and celebration of students, and their solutions and a global partner meet. The website is also a rich repository of material, stories, content, and inspiration. The global team reaches out to the partners formally and informally to provide assistance and advice—as well as actively seeks opportunities to increase the footprint of the partner—either through grants or network organizations. In 2018, DFC was created as a 501C3 nonprofit organization in the United States. Until then, DFC was supported by Riverside Education Foundation since it began in 2009.

CHALLENGES AND RISKS

In the beginning, it can be intimidating because we are moving from a passive education to an active education. Unfortunately many schools continue to deliver outdated forms of pedagogy, content-heavy curriculum, and competition that strips away opportunities that promote thinking, communication, innovation, and collaboration.

What DFC does is to provide young people with opportunities for authentic and consequential collaboration, real-world contexts in which they can apply critical and creative thinking and problem solving, while developing their empathy and interpersonal communication and interaction abilities and skills. Bringing the methodology of design thinking to schools changes the focus from teaching to active participation in learning by students. In particular, the yearlong immersive DFC Curriculum develops and nurtures changemaker behaviors and skills, both in students and in teachers. When teachers and students come together to create solutions in the classroom, transformation can also take place in the school and in the community.

Many schools espouse the idea to children that failure is not an option. Tests, exams, marks, and grades bring fear instead of confidence, anxiety instead of anticipation, and rote learning instead of role modeling. But, what DFC does is to give responsibility to children to identify problems, choose optimum, viable solutions, implement solutions, and then share with their wider community. This heightens children's confidence, sense of ownership, and their feelings of accomplishment which can further unleash their "I CAN" super power.

All too frequently teachers and parents believe and tell children that they are too young to change something around them. What DFC does is to help change the mind-set of adults to believe that "age has nothing to do with competency." Children as young as six years of age are solving day-to-day problems they face as individuals, as a family, or as a community. When they see it in action, teachers start seeing the power that children possess to lead change. And, while we want our children to graduate as responsible citizens, our pedagogy does not give them an opportunity for empathy, ethics, excellence, and elevation.

Given the exponential growth of knowledge on the internet, teachers are no longer needed to simply deliver content or information; instead, they are needed to facilitate problem solving, enable students with strategies to negotiate and communicate well with others, and to create an environment where they can discover their own power to become citizen leaders of the world. What DFC does is that it brings design thinking into classrooms, gradually making the way to approach a more user-centric (human-centered) and work on what is more relevant for them and their immediate environment. Applying Design Thinking in Education has helped schools reimagine their curriculum to integrate Design Thinking Guide (DTG) so that children can do good and do well and graduate with both passion and compassion. Today, we live in a world where children know fictional superheroes. This made-up world does not prepare children to handle unprecedented levels of stress and uncertainty in real life. We are cultivating in children a sense of helplessness and apathy concerning taking ownership for and tackling the challenges faced by the world today.

Inviting children to become equal participants in shaping their world sends a clear message that their voices and imaginations matter right now and that children are not the future, they are the present. DFC promotes creative confidence in children to take on challenges as opportunities and find the superhero inside themselves.

According to the World Economic Forum, the job market in 2025 will see an increased demand for twenty-first-century skills, like empathy, critical thinking, and leadership. With the pandemic, new emerging skills like active learning, resilience, stress tolerance, flexibility will be critical for thriving in a rapidly changing world. These twenty-first-century skills are currently not being adequately addressed by traditional school curricula whether offline or online.

Given that the engagement of a student with the DFC program is approximately only ten to twelve hours over the course of three months; the impact emerges as very significant that leads to a further improvement in outcomes and learning goals including the following:

- Children demonstrate higher creative skills
- Children learn twenty-first-century skills and attitudes
- Teacher involvement also improves as facilitators
- Students' self-efficacy increases significantly
- Children become more collaborative.

DFC has so far impacted 2 million children from approximately 21,000+ schools, 76000+ teachers, 31,000 stories of change in over 65+ counties and regions. Children have addressed fifteen of the seventeen SDGs and addressed more than forty-five causes proving that children have what it takes to "design" a future that is desired by them. Tijana Doroški, from DFC Serbia, put:

> The main lesson is that everything is possible. Nothing is far-fetched if you have the right idea. Also, it is important that you are never too young, and you shouldn't give up on your ideas because of your age. That's what the other members and coordinators are here to help with.

FINAL RECOMMENDATIONS

If you observe a problem and want to change it, the recommendation is to rely on your life experience and intuition to carry out the change you desire. Authenticity is the most disruptive quality you can bring to the table. The DFC FIDS model not only helps you bring your ideas to fruition, but it will bring you one step closer to your most authentic self. You CAN have the agency to change the world and you CAN have the agency to Be the Change yourself. Below are the recommendations that the Members of the Student Council have for other children and young people wanting to adopt or adapt to DFC:

> Daniel Umrou: "DFC is a great program for children to share their ideas, make an impact, make their voice be heard, and find your power at a young age by doing activities that make our communities better. It doesn't matter how young you are, you should feel you can make a difference. I felt like I have the power to make a change since I did a DFC project in 2018. With patience and persistence, the project, our stop the spread campaign is even more powerful now during the COVID-19 pandemic."

Tijana Doroški stated: "Go for it! DFC is good and functioning as it is, but it has to change over the years, just like everything else. It can only get better from this point on." And, in the words of María Hernández, "I think that it is worthy to fight for changing the world. The best thing is that I can find people that look for new challenges every day and support me, so we all fight together. I CAN, YOU CAN, WE CAN!"

REFERENCES

Design for Change. (2014). *If not us then who? If not now then when?* Retrieved from https://www.dfcworld.org/SITE/dfcstory.

Chapter 12

The Ecosystemic Pedagogy of Vila Schools

A Brazilian Educational Proposal for Social and Environmental Transformation

Patricia Limaverde

Brasil

According to Paulo Freire (1979), human beings cannot actively take part in history, society, or in the transformation of reality, if not assisted, while developing the consciousness of their potential to change the world.

Education, culture, society, and the environment are aspects of the same autopoietic cycle (Maturana & Varela, 2001), that is, the cyclical property of a living system to maintain and renew itself by regulating its composition and conserving its boundaries. The interactions of human beings with their social and natural environment, as they are lived and passed on across generations, characterize our culture and value systems and form the educational base of a society. Quality education, therefore, comes from the perception and contextualization of those interactions.

Brazil, a country with continental proportions, is rich in cultural and biological diversity, including more than 11,000 animal species, over 40,000 plants and fungus in 6 land biomes, along with an extended sea biome. Brazilian cultural diversity has been shaped along a historical complex of interactions among many different peoples. Today, Brazil has more than 250 peoples of indigenous ethnicity and native communities who speak more than 150 languages. Through colonization, more than 2 million Africans from 9 other ethnicities were brought to Brazil to perform forced labor. Besides the Portuguese, native peoples, and the Africans, many other people have migrated to Brazil, such as the Spanish, Jews, Germans, Italians, Arabs, and the Japanese, giving birth to descendants and building true communities.

However, all this cultural and biological diversity remains invisible to most Brazilians. The ability to coexist within this rich diversity is lacking and poorly developed, which prevents a holistic and authentic view of the nation. Many conflicts arise from this lack of cultural awareness which hinders the resolution of social and environmental problems that Brazilian communities face, as well as the possibility of constructing a more just and sane world.

Several aspects contribute to this situation, including a specific educational paradigm that is widely spread and valued in the country, which only aims at reproducing concepts and ways of existing in the world. This massive targeting of education does not take into account the importance of learning contextualization nor the development of coexistence skills within diversity and acting concerning the transformation of socio-environmental realities.

The Ecosystemic Pedagogy proposed by Vila School places the highest value on relationships between people, their community, and the environment. We emphasize individual critical reflection and social and environmental responsibility. We promote acting in constructive and transformative ways in the situations and contexts in which we live. The main objective of Ecosystemic Pedagogy is to develop the understanding that human beings are responsible for their relationships with themselves, their communities, and their environment, and, as a consequence, they are co-responsible for the reality of the world in which they live. Our perspective agrees with Paulo Freire's (2000), who indicated that while education alone cannot change society, without the right education society will not change.

AN ECOSYSTEMIC PARADIGM

Our ecosystemic paradigm begins with the assumption that all life is interconnected, and, therefore, we as human beings are not independent, rather we are interdependent. Further, human actions and relationships with other people and the natural environment have deep consequences on our lived experience and the world in which we live. Through our educational work, we aim to stimulate the development of young people who are eager to take responsibility for co-constructing reality, fostering positive relationships, living together within a context of rich cultural and biological diversity, and bringing a transformative praxis to the world.

The Vila School's motto *Building a Better World* highlights the main goal of our Ecosystemic Pedagogy toward which we have been working for over three decades. This vision of education as capable of enabling social and environmental changes is a result of a paradigmatic shift, one that considers students, teachers, extended family, and indeed all members of the school community as changemakers who are able to bring about systems change and can help shape what we call a transformative ecosystem (i.e., a healthy and sustainable permaculture).

We promote change within the scope of the systems in which we live—social and environmental. This belief in one's ability to change the world rests at the core of the Ecosystemic Pedagogy curriculum, which foregrounds active engagement in cultural and ecological diversity, critical self-reflection, and collaborative learning. The development of these abilities is not restricted to students but extends to everyone within the school community: teachers and other professionals, students, relatives, community partners, and more. We believe that through developing each individual's understanding of their mutual interconnection and interdependence, they are able to reflect upon their choices and lifestyles and the impact of those choices on those around us. Coexistence is the very essence of the symbiotic movement of our everyday lives that we must come to embrace if we are to survive and thrive. These ideas form the basis for our educational vision.

Traditional schools however tend toward reinforcing existing social structures based on limited points of view of causal and linear sequenced order, mechanistic, determinant rationalism, content fragmentation, unidimensional view of culture, the decontextualization of lived experience, and the devaluation of corporeality and emotions. Such traditional assumptions compose a shared reality domain among the majority of educational social systems as well as in many academic and scientific systems. These paradigms and ways of thought focus efforts on the reproduction and conservation of fragmentary, mechanistic, and Cartesian dualistic ways of knowing rather than holistic views of life.

Maturana (1999) argues that, if we wish children to learn human values, they cannot merely be taught about values. They have to be experienced in daily school life. We cannot simply teach cooperation; rather, children must learn it "through living, for it is by living with mutual respect for others that mutual respect will come" (p. 66).

ORIGIN OF ECOSYSTEMIC PEDAGOGY

The innovative praxis of Vila School emerges from observing the need to create a new society, starting from the education of new individuals. In the beginning of the 1980s, in Fortaleza, capital of Ceará, a favorable condition emerged for making changes to the local educational landscape. Specifically, mothers and fathers were earnestly searching for an alternative to traditional education, while at the same time a new paradigm based upon interconnections between different fields of knowledge, between theory and praxis, and between thinking, feelings, and bodily awareness was gaining momentum. An education in which the body, the arts, and coexistence with nature could have a legitimate space in curriculum and in teaching and learning.

Within this milieu, a group of families gathered up to start what would be the embryo of Vila School: a nonformal space of learning through the intermingling of artistic activity, handcrafting, theater and drama, music, bodily expression, planting, and other educational activities. A space where children and "guides" established their goals together and accomplished specific learning projects. These projects included cultivating plants and gardens and watching them grow, harvesting the fruit and creating meals to eat and share; building toys and other crafts out of *junk*, wood and other recycled and reused materials; regular engagement in artistic performance (a new activity every week); hosting social and environmental awareness campaigns and public gatherings which involved all the families; and do physical exercise and meditation to promote physical and mental well-being and health.

This new proposal, which some considered to be extremely ambitious, while others took it as a natural progression, began attracting the attention of many individuals from all parts of the city, including university professors, journalists, artists, ecologists, and civic leaders. Soon dozens of city children began spending their afternoons in this shared space—the Backyard of Fatima Limaverde, the founder of this project.

At this time, in October of 1981, the project was called the *Backyard*. Soon the activities at the Backyard attracted the attention of a researcher who helped create a formal project proposal, which was the beginning of the Vila School and the formalization of this innovative pedagogical experiment. The idea to create a rich, diverse, multidisciplinary learning environment based on the cultivation of empathy, respect, and appreciation for cultural and biodiversity, which was rooted at the most fundamental levels on individual critical reflection began to impact the further development of what is now referred to as Ecosystemic Pedagogy.

PEDAGOGICAL ELEMENTS OF THE VILA SCHOOL

The educational practice of Vila School aims to bring knowledge together across disciplinary boundaries; to reintegrate body, feeling, emotion, intuition and thinking; and to link individuals to nature, as well as their individual and interpersonal social environment. Below are the basic elements of Vila's Ecosystemic Pedagogy, from kindergarten through ninth grade.

Curricular Web

Based on a critical reflection on traditional curriculum, we observed that the fragmented arrangement of content into different disciplines, isolated from their respective contexts, although familiar, does not contribute to the most productive and meaningful learning of these subjects, and even less to the development of empowered socially and environmentally aware citizens capable of taking action for change. The disciplinary and decontextualized curriculum, in fact, focuses on some restrictive ways of thinking and acting in the world, such as constant reinforcement of certain mental operations based on differences rather than on building understandings of relationships between ideas, knowledge, contexts, experiences, and people.

Thus, Vila's Ecosystemic Curriculum (Nascimento, 2008) is arranged in a web form, which facilitates the visualization of the interconnection of disciplines and content areas across areas of knowledge, which is operationalized within various projects and learning scenarios. According to Heilman (2011),

> At the center of Escola Vila's curriculum stand three conceptual pillars: (1) the individual's relationship with oneself, (2) the relationship between human beings and their environment, and (3) the relationship between human beings and society. These three pillars are incorporated into lessons, discussions, homework, and art projects to reinforce the importance of each of these relationships. (p. 11)

The Curricular Web, therefore, brings together the goals of Ecosystemic Pedagogy and arranges the content along three interconnected axes: Caring for Oneself, Caring for the Social Environment, and Caring for Nature. From this new way of thinking about the curriculum, it becomes much easier for young people to work in groups, create different learning scenarios, and work with projects. Moreover, the web links the content of different courses and enables a much richer engagement and contextualization of current issues faced by the community with what young people are doing in school and in ways that help students begin to recognize and value different kinds of expertise and cultural approaches to problem solving.

Group Organization: Microsystems in Action

Vila's students are always organized in groups. The work developed in the different learning scenarios of the school is based on the development of collaborative learning skills. Each week students are organized by teachers into a variety of groups, which ensures that all students learn to interact with as many individuals as possible throughout the school year. Notably, the school takes special efforts to promote diversity among the families and students who attend the school, including different nationalities, cultures, religions, and social classes (about 20 percent of students have scholarships) and individual special needs.

Activities proposed by the teachers and students are developed in these groups, which promotes an active and authentic classroom space for the development of important living skills, such as:

- respect and appreciation for the diversity of opinions
- team spirit
- collaborative learning
- distribution of tasks
- group self-regulation
- conflict mediation

Rocha (2007) notes that in the Ecosystemic Pedagogical model, whenever possible, the teacher

> [. . .] proposes activities to the group and not just to students individually, thus favoring the development of social skills such as cooperation, tolerance, communication, and mutual help. In group work, students find the possibility of highlighting differences and learning to live with them: different ways of solving situations, thinking, expressing oneself, overcoming particular limitations and skills, and engaging with divergent opinions, etc. Valuing and respecting human diversity are major challenges of new education and also elements of environmental education. (p. 164)

Just as every organ in a living system has its functions, each group of students has its responsibilities in order to ensure the organization and functioning of a particular aspect in the classroom. There is, for example, a group responsible for distributing, storing, and ensuring the organization of all the collective material provided in the learning scenario. There is also a group responsible for nutrition, which must organize the collective natural foods provided by the school. There is also a group responsible for keeping the room organized and a group responsible for project management and execution. Learning to take responsibility helps shift the balance of power from the teacher to the students and helps them to seek out and develop creative and effective means of collective organization and cooperative management.

Learning Scenarios

With the aim of promoting transdisciplinary activity, classes are arranged differently based on different projects and learning scenarios. These arrangements cater to the needs of the students, and the nature of the projects they are working on are designed according to the research activities, key concepts, and skills applications that students will need to be successful in the learning scenarios.

Vila's Ecosystemic Pedagogy recognizes two types of learning scenarios: structured and unstructured. Structured learning scenarios are environments organized to contain tools of all kinds that directly support the research, exploration, and construction of cooperative work products. Unstructured learning scenarios, on the other hand, comprise shared working spaces in which there is no predefined structure. In this cases, projects can be connected to what's happening in the school or in external spaces, such as a town square, villages of indigenous communities, the neighborhood around the school, or institutions that care for the elderly. Limaverde and Moraes (2008) point out that

> activities that constitute the daily school life of Vila's students are not "extracurricular" activities, developed as something complementary to the privileged content in the classroom. In fact, these activities constitute the classes themselves. [. . .] It is a lived transdisciplinarity that presents itself not only as a theoretical-epistemological principle of the process of knowledge construction, but is present in daily actions, social coexistence, coexistence with nature, and the learner with oneself. (p. 265)

Among the structured learning scenarios, Vila has eight "laboratories." These laboratories take up the original meaning of the Latin word *laboratorium*, which means "place of work." The eight Vila's laboratories are learning scenarios where teachers and students work together with a common goal, involving knowledge from different areas, and which are interconnected in a transdisciplinary way. They are:

- *Fauna*: transdisciplinary scenarios that have a nursery of animals of different species. In this learning environment, students are motivated to develop conviviality skills with animals, as well as the ability to observe and contemplate. They are encouraged to research about the organic systems of each group of vertebrates and invertebrates, witnessing aspects such as locomotion, reproduction, feeding, and other typical characteristics of each species.
- *Vegetable Garden*: transdisciplinary scenarios with vegetable beds in horizontal or vertical planting systems. In this learning environment students are encouraged to choose a type of vegetable to be planted in groups, observe the entire process of vegetable development. They also research planting procedures, the time of development, and the soil and climate conditions that are favorable to the chosen species. They also study the nutritional value of each species of plants, as well as its use in cooking, as well as in preparing a variety of dishes.

- *Living Pharmacy*: Scenarios where there is a diversity of medicinal herb species commonly used to treat a variety of symptoms. Students are encouraged to value folk and traditional medicines, which are sometimes centuries old. They research the active ingredients of the various herbs and their correct use as medicines. In addition, they make ointments, syrups, creams, and cosmetics with cultivated herbs, as well as teas, patches, and compresses.
- *Orchard*: The fruit trees of Vila School spread in different environments and are often used by students. They study the different methods of tree propagation, such as cutting, layering, and grafting, among others. They also study the nutritional value of fruits and the different ways of using them in food and health maintenance.
- *Garden*: In this learning environment, students learn the importance of creating aesthetically pleasant and balanced environments in the composition of natural landscapes. They research ornamental plants, their use, and propagation, as well as the best way to arrange them in order to bring beauty and aesthetic balance to different living environments. Thus, students are encouraged to value the contemplation of nature in its harmony of colors, aromas, and other possible expressions.
- *Alternative Technologies*: This scenario fosters a creative environment, which includes the use of all kinds of equipment and small building construction materials, which are rooted in ideas of sustainability and eco-design that have in their conceptions the idea of sustainability and eco-design. In this scenario, students get to know alternative technologies aimed at harnessing solar energy for water heating, drying fruits, and herbs, cooking food; rainwater collection and utilization; water reuse in urban construction; paper recycling; and the reuse of scrap materials in the manufacture of household objects. In addition to researching these materials, they design and execute the construction of a wide variety of products.
- *Maintenance*: keeping the environment clean, pleasant and conserved is the main objective of this learning scenario. Students learn conservation techniques in electrical and plumbing installation, furniture restoration, household appliances, and the repair of a variety of objects.
- *Health and Eating*: a learning scenario which involves working in an experimental kitchen where students make natural and healthy recipes. They research and elaborate recipes of typical dishes from different regions of the country and the world, including experimental, vegetarian, and organic recipes, among others. In addition, they study the nutritional values of foods and the different ways of balancing a menu.

During the development of these activities in the laboratories, research is also carried out to complement the knowledge necessary for their execution, which provides a space for the application of traditional disciplinary content and also for the interconnection between content areas and disciplines. These activities also take into account the desires and motivations of the students and the teachers, as well as the cultural contexts and the relationship of the learning scenarios and laboratories to urgent and nontrivial social and environmental issues.

In addition to the laboratories, there are five workshops that are also structured learning scenarios:

- *Visual Arts*: workshop where the student learns many art techniques, such as the various styles of painting, sculpture, woodcut, collage, and so on. The ultimate goal is to go beyond technique. This workshop promotes the possibility of using symbols, language, and other media for concrete expression, with the help of different materials, and internal factors, such as emotions, thoughts, opinions, and impressions. Ideas of balance and aesthetic diversity are also explored.
- *Handicraft*: workshop for creating handicrafts with various techniques such as crochet, knitting, sewing, macrame, papier-mache, and so on. Willpower and discipline are very well-developed skills in these spaces, as well as improvement and dexterity. Notions such as workmanship and durability are also explored, as is the reuse of items that would otherwise be thrown away, such as packaging and other disposable goods.
- *Theater*: theatrical expression in the most different genres, including mime and clowning. Using the body, voice, gestures, costumes, masks, and settings, students are encouraged to represent situations and transpose themselves to unlived experiences, experiencing different personalities and reflecting on the roles they play.
- *Music*: music is a kind of subtle expression, not visible but quite touching, that reverberates in feelings and impressions. Singing and playing instruments have been fundamental to human beings since early times. Developing musical ability and instruments reconnects us to the ancestral human being, who was able to put into practice the Brazilian saying "those who sing put their sorrow away" in the most essential way.
- *Body*: *yoga*, meditation, *tai chi chuan*, *do-in*, and massage techniques are part of the curriculum of this workshop. Self-knowledge and the health of the body and mind are the main goals of these classes.

Projects, Research, and Transdisciplinary Teaching Material

Projects are the basic tool for connecting all the work in the daily routines of Vila School. Each class develops their projects based on particular demands and interests, but at the same time in dialogue with other classes, who also develop their projects, typically with a common theme. These themes involve social activities, interaction with nature, critical reflections, different examples of artistic expression, and appreciation of popular traditions.

With the objective of providing pedagogical resources to facilitate work processes with inter/transdisciplinary projects, Vila School developed teaching materials that promote the integration of formal subjects (math, reading, writing, etc.) and projects developed in the classroom, interconnecting knowledge of different fields within the same activity. Vilas' didactic material also stimulates group work, research, and the appropriation and the active construction of knowledge.

Evaluation

Typically school assessments, measurements, and evaluations are instituted only as control mechanisms, moving away from their real value which is to promote and create a feedback loop into the learning process and to be a tool for teachers to reflect upon her/his own pedagogical practices in order to improve them. The meaning of evaluation, indeed, should provide information to the teacher and to the student which helps them both to develop and learn.

Evaluation should not exclude students' multidimensional and holistic development, by trying to measure each student's knowledge in discrete areas. Rather, students' development should be taken into account as a whole, enhancing multiple aspects of their growth. Evaluation should attempt to integrate and involve all areas of learning. Moreover, in a dialogical process, students' evaluation cannot have only one perspective. The mix between teacher and peer-evaluation, self-evaluation, and eco-evaluation is necessary, in order to attend to multidimensional kinds of development. With these principles in mind, Ecosystemic Pedagogy generated its own evaluation system, which involves multiple criteria and attends to a wide variety of skill development. It includes a self-evaluation process, group evaluation, and the evaluation of different teachers.

Professional Development

Vila School teachers take part in continuous professional development involving an intensive workshop system three weeks a year, besides one Saturday per month and evaluation and planning meetings concerning the projects every two weeks. Continued professional development is essential for teachers' ability to deliver a meaningful pedagogical experience that impacts the students and the teachers themselves. Further, due to particularities of Vila School's Ecosystemic Pedagogy, with group works, inter/transdisciplinary projects, and different learning scenarios, without a substantial focus on developing teachers, the successful implementation and coordination of activities could not be achieved.

Professional learning and development focus on more than theory. It also includes somatics, the arts, debate, and discussion, all of which work to help integrate knowledge, empower teachers, and to transform thinking and action. We know that a good curriculum is no substitute for a great teacher. This means professional development is an extremely important tool at the very foundation of the work of the school. This activity has helped to build a teaching community that is deeply committed to the principles developed at the school.

RESEARCH AND EVIDENCE

Vila School's work has become the focus of study and research in different universities in Brazil and in other countries. The reach of its pedagogical practice, beyond the significant and citizenship formation of the students, mobilizes change of attitudes and behaviors in the lives of the students, teachers and families in the school.

Research carried out at this school and beyond has sought out former students who are now adults, workers, and many who are already fathers or mothers and has demonstrated that the educational activities implemented at the Vila School for more than three decades of work have contributed to effectively developing more autonomous, socially active individuals who are concerned about environmental causes. In addition, these former students know the importance of developing their self-awareness, bodies, emotions, and artistic skills.

We can, through conscious and creative educational practices, build educational processes that reveal the skills of each human being rather than forcing them into a standard mold imposed by society. The global market too is asking for a new worker profile: someone who is creative, communicative, and able to cooperate and work in teams.

In her research, Rocha (2007) perceives some of the results of group work at Vila School:

> Children work very well in groups, they have autonomy to overcome small impasses, there is "respect" for decisions made by the group. It is very common, for example, for them to decide who will give a particular answer, such as the "such" puzzle answer. Sometimes, I witnessed some mistakes made by this one and did not see, once, one of them criticize, or want to respond by running over his classmate. This happens normally, without the teacher's interference. There

is a culture of "dialogue" installed in the school, there is respect for each other's differences and limits. (p. 165)

Regarding the Curriculum Web of Vila School, Bezerra (2012) comments from her research:

> I consider this school curriculum organization to be evidence of itscommitment to a more comprehensive education and not just content based. This extension of the curriculum, through laboratory activities and complementary classes, is developed within the perspective of project pedagogy and transdisciplinarity. This model represents a confrontation with the fragmented and disconnected curricular model, with which knowledge is traditionally produced and transmitted and imposes on us, as educators, aspointed out by Morin (1999, p. 11), the need to rethink the school curriculum with the purpose of building a comprehensive view of knowledge, recognizing its complexity. (p. 156)

Heilman (2011) points out that, regarding evaluation, Vila School:

> At the end of each quarter, the children evaluate their work in the class and give themselves grades based on personal reflection on their work over the quarter. The children also assign their peers grades based on their perception of the student in class and information on participation, attendance and homework provided by the teachers. This type of evaluation teaches children to evaluate themselves and others honestly and justly. (p. 11)

Moreira (2014) states that:

> Vila School, by proposing to work with principles of ecology, brings the work around the social with great force, showing they understand that social and environmental conflicts are intrinsically related to social problems of great complexity, adhering to the sense of building a better world to everything that man raises in the world. Thus, it goes beyond talking about the environment, or working with recycling, building vegetable gardens or other consensual themes, but it seeks taking a stand in relation to what is elaborated socially, politically, economically, scientifically, culturally, etc., and with that, reveals its understanding that there is no separation between environment, man and society. (p. 140)

In her research on teacher education at Escola Vila, Sotero (2018) concludes:

> Intuitively, the statement that teacher education at VILA not only subsidizes teaching pedagogical practices but also transforms people was revealed in a kind way by the research subjects. The speeches of these subjects revealed the

courage to open up to experience the unknown, which may suggest an answer to the paradigmatic problem of the divergence between the knowledge learned in the initial teacher education and the knowledge necessary for effective teaching practice at Vila School. (p. 114)

These and other research activities have addressed different actors in the Vila School Ecosystem: students, alumni, family, teachers, and staff. This research has brought some visibility in the national academic field, including research from other countries, such as Spain, Peru, and the United States.

DISSEMINATION AND OVERCOMING CHALLENGES

The Ecosystemic Pedagogy called attention to other schools that sought to implement this proposal with the help of the Vila School team, both in private and public education. Adherence to Ecosystemic Pedagogy requires openness and willingness to face challenges, starting with the paradigmatic change necessary not only for teaching practice but above all for understanding the purpose of education. In this way, an ecosystemic network is established among all partner schools so that mutual support is possible, always with the systematic support of the Vila School team itself. With the intention of providing better support, Vila School prepared teacher and management team training resources, both online and face-to-face courses, and offered as well a schedule of online meetings, in which it is possible to discuss the demands of challenges that occur and to help generate solutions collaboratively.

While collectively facing the initial difficulties that had been discovered, it was found that, during the first year of implementation, partner schools had already incorporated the main characteristics of Ecosystemic Pedagogy in a structural way, causing changes beyond the school, involving the surrounding community and families of the students. According to the experience of implementing Ecosystemic Pedagogy, it was observed that both the private and public school contexts are successful during the first year, but there are some particularities between these two spheres. Private schools that start implementing Ecosystemic Pedagogy have a tendency to endure, while public schools cannot keep up the proposal for more than one management term or cycle. This is due to successions in the political contexts of many cities, where the elected management must undo the policies implemented by the previous management, always proposing new approaches.

This characteristic, which is present not only in the Brazilian context but also in many countries, makes fruitful long-term results impossible, although it generates excellent short-term results during implementation, such as the reality-transforming action through the numerous projects developed by each class in a single year. Generally, each class develops at least six projects throughout the school year, often culminating in intervention actions in different social and environmental contexts of the community.

Thus, we think that Ecosystemic Pedagogy still has a long way to go, always in the perspective of reaching new partnerships in the most different contexts of the planet, always seeking to achieve its goal of building through education a better, more supportive, humane world, a world open to coexistence in diversity.

REFERENCES

Bezerra, A. C. G. (2012). Escola Vivência Infantil, Lazer e Aprendizagem (Vila): experiência de educação integral. *Em Aberto, Brasília*, 25(88), 151–162.
Freire, P. (1979). *Conscientização: teoria e prática da libertação*. São Paulo: Cortez & Moraes.
Freire, P. (2000). *Pedagogia da indignação: cartas pedagógicas e outros escritos*. São Paulo: Editora UNESP.
Heilman, I. A. (2011). Feeling, experiencing, learning: Environmental education at Escola Vila. *Independent Study Project (ISP) Collection*. Paper 1173.
Limaverde, P., & Moraes, M. C. (2008). É possível reinventar a escola e reencantar a educação? In M. C. Moraes (Ed.), *Ecologia dos saberes complexidade, transdisciplinaridade e educação: novos fundamentos para iluminar novas práticas educacionais* (pp. 263–291). São Paulo: Antakarana/WHH.
Maturana, H. (1999). *Transformación en la convivencia*. Santiago: Dolmen Ediciones.
Maturana, H., & Varela, F. (2001). *A árvore do conhecimento: as bases biológicas da compreensão humana*. São Paulo: Palas Athena.
Moreira, L. L. (2014). *O pensamento ecológico na formação cidadã: a formação humana na Escola Vila*. 156 f. Dissertation (Master). Rio de Janeiro: UFRJ.
Nascimento, P. L. (2008). *Currículo ecossistêmico e mutações de sistemas sociais*. Thesis. Brasília: UCB.
Rocha, I. M. Z. (2007). *Escola VILA: Pedagogia da Sustentabilidade*. Dissertation (Master). Fortaleza: Universidade de Fortaleza.
Sotero, M. C. L. (2018). *Dos saberes docentes à prática pedagógica na Escola Vila: contribuição para a formação de professores*. 146 f. Dissertation (Master). Fortaleza: UECE.

Chapter 13

Educators as Changemakers
A Model for Infusing Social-Emotional Learning during Educational Transitions to Increase Readiness and Address Intergenerational Poverty

Seth Sampson, Nancy Lewin, and Paul Rogers

United States

This chapter tells the story of a collaborative project in Laredo, Texas, focused on addressing intergenerational poverty and preparing the next generation of teachers. Based on interviews and participant observation, this chapter shares the work of a wide range of stakeholders and centers who are committed to integrating community-based (and other) resources in ways that amplify and reinforce the local knowledge and wisdom (known as the dichos) and that establish culturally responsive pathways supporting the long-term development of youth in Laredo.

El que no escucha consejo, no llega a viejo.

The dicho above, shared by Valencia one of the aspiring teachers at the center of our work, translates as "the individual who does not heed advice, will not survive to see old age." Dichos, like this one, have been and will continue to be an integral part of life in the Latino community. In Spanish, the word dicho means an adage or a refrain; however, the depth of the meaning goes beyond the simple translation of the word. Dichos are authentic expressions of truth that transmit wisdom in the face of life's challenges, trials, and tribulations. These dichos help contextualize and inform everyday life experiences, and they also serve as a form of guidance aimed to support an individual's forward progress. The value of the dichos extends, however, beyond the individual, to the community, and, in the case of the work described here, to the school systems, as well as to all of us working to support the community in achieving systemic change. Searching for and honoring the dichos, that is, the hard-earned, experience-based wisdom passed down from generation to generation is a key methodology of the collaborative approach we have taken to reimagine the development of teachers, addressing the teacher shortage, and engaging the community of Laredo, especially its youth.

VALENCIA'S STORY: STUDENTS AT THE CENTER

Valencia, a nineteen-year-old aspiring future educator and student at Texas A&M International University (TAMIU) is excited to have the opportunity to make a difference in children's lives as a teacher. Meeting Valencia, one soon discovers her unwavering determination to see her dream of becoming a teacher come to fruition. To achieve her dream, however, Valencia faced many of the common trip wires and barriers associated with seeking a college degree, especially in the field of education.

The term "trip wire" comes from the Prichard Committee for Academic Excellence (2015) who conducted a Post-Secondary Project which sought to highlight the "inequities that thwart students from making successful post-secondary transitions" (p. 4). They define a trip wire as "little-discussed, powerful obstacles that tend to sabotage students on the way to a self-sufficient, thriving life after high school." In their report, the Prichard Committee identified three major trip wires, all of which impacted Valencia:

- The Birthright Lottery
- Veiled College Costs
- College and Career Unreadiness

For Valencia these challenges, especially the financial burden, were overwhelming. When she received the tuition information for attending college to become a teacher, she "felt that it was impossible. The amount was impossible for my parents to complete and pay it off." However, because of community support the challenge served to add fuel to the fire of the determination burning inside of her to become the teacher that she knew she could be. And, her dream would not be deferred. In the face of this challenge, her family rallied together to assist her on her educational journey. When we asked her about how she set out to address this challenge, she described the outpouring of support she received from her family,

> So, I think that as a family, what we did was my mom got a side job repairing apartments and cleaning houses. We would go and help her. My dad would

mow lawns. Me and my brother would go and help them mow lawns, anything that was offered to us, like we would all take it and help each other out. So, then my college expenses could be paid for with prayers and everything.

The experience of working hard for what she wanted and seeing, not only her family, but the community support her in this endeavor, created an appreciation for the sense of connection that exists within this tight-knit community. As Valencia went on to explain:

My parents are also there to help me. We're a community. We're family. We're not the only ones struggling. And for other people to also be willing to give you that opportunity, like, you know what, you need the money. I have this little job. I have something else for you to do. It's also appreciated because as a community, you want to see each other succeed.

Valencia is just one example of a young person pursuing the dream of becoming a teacher. She is a trailblazing changemaker, in that she is one of the founding members of the first-ever Texas Association of Future Educators (TAFE) TAMIU Chapter. Valencia, along with her peers, is a driving force in changing the narrative of educator preparation programs. They are shining a light on how shifting and adapting existing support systems can clear the pathway for others to becoming educators and in ways that can contribute to long-term sustainable change within the community and beyond.

Valencia is a resident of Laredo, Texas, a predominately Hispanic community located on the southern border of the United States and Mexico a few steps away from the Rio Grande River. Founded in 1755, Laredo is the largest inland port of entry on the border of Mexico and the United States. Laredo prides itself as a community that has retained its resilience throughout its complex history.

According to the Center Square "The Laredo metro area's share of extreme poverty—neighborhoods where at least 40 percent of residents live below the poverty level—is the highest in Texas. One out of every 3 of Laredo's 265,761 residents live in poverty. Over 17 percent of the population has less than a ninth-grade education with 14 percent attaining only some education in grades 9–12. Twenty-five percent are high-school graduates and over 16 percent have some college education attainment. Only 14 percent (13.99 percent) have obtained a college degree."

Laredo's citizens also face serious economic challenges. For those individuals with less than a ninth-grade education, the average yearly income is USD 24,405 for males and USD 14,275 for females. Those with high-school diplomas earned more, where males earned USD 31,694 while females earned USD 19, 192 per year. The earnings of individuals with a bachelor's degree are USD 52,233 for males and USD 46,965 for females. If our group increases the number of individuals that successfully earn a bachelor's degree, they will be earning an income above the poverty threshold.

THE LAREDO LEGACY PROJECT

Laredo has become the site of a unique collaboration of educators and community members working to address two seemingly intractable problems, which Valencia's story illustrates: the teacher shortage, which is at once a global, national, state, and local problem; and, intergenerational poverty, which is the cycle of poverty that is faced disproportionately by underserved and poor communities wherein system-wide barriers trap families in poverty for multiple generations. At the heart of this collaboration is the specific context of the Laredo community and a vision of community-based resources, including local knowledge, like the dichos, as well as the bringing together of financial, cultural, social, and emotional supports, which when mobilized and utilized can generate positive culturally responsive sustainable change.

The collaboration, which is called by some as the Laredo Legacy Project (LLP), seeks to identify, celebrate, and integrate over the long term the existing assets that Laredo's citizens (especially the youth) and families possess. Indeed, it is these community-based resources that are viewed by the members of the LLP as the most critical levers to create and sustain systemic multigenerational transformation. As a part of this co-creation effort, the collaborators of the LLP represent a diverse group of stakeholders (footnote) who have been brought together through the vision and leadership of the TAMIU's College of Education's Dean, James O'Meara.

The College of Education at TAMIU is mission-aligned with TAMIU's overall vision in that it aims to provide a comprehensive and coherent professional development system for educators which link all aspects of the education profession. Through educational experiences provided by the professional development system, the TAMIU College of Education prepares teachers to provide learner-centered instructional experiences that will promote excellence and equity for all students.

One way the leadership within the College of Education has sought to pursue its mission is to take responsibility for moving families out of multigenerational cycles of poverty by increasing levels of "readiness" among families living in Laredo with one or more children who are aspiring teacher candidates. O'Meara envisioned the formation of a collaborative group from a multidimensional lens, which would work to enhance and incorporate four categories of "readiness" for future educators:

- family member readiness-preparing all family members to support young people who are aspiring to be teachers throughout their educational journey
- financial readiness-assisting families in covering the cost of post-secondary education
- college readiness-providing accessible and effective support that help candidates develop the knowledge, skills, abilities, and competencies required to succeed academically at every stage of their college journey
- social and emotional readiness-fostering resilience, purpose, and well-being in teacher candidates by building their capacity for establishing and maintaining high levels of self and social awareness, in addition to responsible decision making and relationship building skills

Including family members in the process of building readiness is a crucial step in developing culturally responsive and sustainable pathways for young people to reach their full potential as a classroom teacher. Through a stronger focus on parents and families, the educator pipeline can be continuously refreshed and a broader base of community support can be established for the future generations of teachers within the community. The vision of increasing levels of readiness in order to address intergenerational cycles of poverty set the stage for the establishment of a collaborative group (or network improvement community) whose central purpose was to illuminate the tremendous community resources in Laredo, including the hidden treasures of knowledge (the dichos) that have been passed down from one generation to the next in ways that bring a new vision to the community for what it means to be an educator.

Built around both the needs of the community and the incredible depth of human resources within the community, this group of visionary organizations led by the College of Education at TAMIU and the Laredo Independent School District has worked to create a sustainable and replicable model of a more vibrant teacher pipeline and educational ecosystem (what O'Meara refers to as permaculture) whose long-term goal is to eliminate intergenerational poverty within Laredo.

The LLP's vision of addressing the teacher shortage and intergenerational poverty is both aspirational and practical and aimed at multiple generations of community impact while also supporting the journey of individuals like Valencia who are on their way to becoming classroom teachers. In our interview with him, O' Meara described the vision this way:

> The mission here is the increase of access and success for the students in the teacher pipeline, which in this case is the Laredo Independent School District, and the specific goal here is to increase the representation of teacher candidates from the underserved and underrepresented high schools in Laredo. We're

saying, look at this idea of preparing teachers from the neighborhood for their neighborhood. In other words, new teachers coming back to where they are now [Laredo] and where they came from in terms of the local high schools, the local middle schools, and preparing them to be the changemakers in that context.

This vision provided the foundation for the formation of an integral partnership to be established with Raise Your Hand Texas (RYHT), a nonprofit organization that supports programmatic initiatives structured to identify, pilot, and scale systemic improvements in public education. Thea Ulrich-Lewis is a program director at RYHT, and in our interview with her she shared that RYHT itself was established with the belief that the future of the state and the nation is sitting in our schools right now. In the early stages of the LLP, Thea and Dean O'Meara began developing the team that would become the Laredo Legacy Project and began looking for ways to strengthen the educator pathway during the process.

Raising Texas Teachers is one of the initiatives within the RYHT that is designed to support teacher preparation programs in addressing the needs of twenty-first-century students and encourage individuals to pursue teaching as an important and fulfilling profession. Thea explains that "Raising Texas Teachers is really about elevating the teaching profession." She continued to describe "the initiative's primary focus is on university-based teacher preparation programs because the faculty within these programs have a chance to spend more time developing their future teachers." The universities working with the Raising Texas Teachers initiative are being provided with outside evaluations and guidelines for some areas of improvement, in addition to funding for creating continuous improvement plans over a period of three years.

Cody Huie, the vice president of programs at RYHT, described the theory of action approach that is at the core of RYHT's mission:

> For us to ensure that all students meet their full potential, we need a strong principal at the helm of every school, and we need an effective teacher in every classroom. So, we design our programs around that theory of action. Within our Raising Texas Teachers program, we really do believe that every student in every classroom, in every year deserves an effective teacher. And unfortunately, that's not true right now. The quality of your teacher in Texas largely depends on, in many cases, the color of your skin or your family's income. So, we want to do our part to ensure that that's no longer the case. We don't want your demography to be your destiny.

An additional component of the work RYHT does is advocating for more effective educational policies, while also meeting the direct needs of the community and including school district representatives in the cycle of improvement of the teacher preparation programs. Huie notes that

> while typically, the universities usually bring in their faculty and discuss steps they can take to improve their existing program after receiving guidelines for improvement. Dean O'Meara, has thought totally out of the box about who he brings together . . . and is on a totally different level, bringing in so many outside organizations looking even to staff, . . . both for expertise across the university and just out there in the world. All while keeping the needs of the school district in the city at the forefront.

Indeed, the central partnership in the LLP is the one between the TAMIU College of Education and the Laredo Independent School District which has a yearly average of 25,000 enrolled students and over 4,500 employees striving for academic excellence. The district is made up of twenty elementary schools, four middle schools, and three high schools. Laredo ISD is home to eight United States Department of Education Blue Ribbon Schools and eight Educational Research Partnership (ERP) Honor Roll Schools. The district plays a crucial role in preparing students to meet the challenges and demands of today's high-tech and multicultural workplace. Establishing and maintaining an active collaborative relationship with the local school districts is at the core of the LLP and serves as a critical starting point for others who are seeking to create a similar impact.

Israel Castilla, the director of Secondary Education for the Laredo Independent School District and member of the LLP, frames it this way, "I work with such a very special community that drives me to make a difference. I want the work we are doing to create a better system for generations to come, rather than just a fad." Preparation and readiness are key themes in Israel's collaboration and approach in working toward a long-term solution to the challenges of intergenerational poverty and the teacher shortage. Castilla notes,

> We want to make sure that we have at least those foundational skills embedded in the students through their experiences so that we align what the university is expecting, regardless of the university you attend. We want students to have the type of experience that when you work for something and you really struggle through the challenge you appreciate it, but you also make that experience something that is going to be very valuable for you in your near future.

Dean O'Meara agrees:

As we transform from an educator preparation program to an educator preparation learning community including learners like Israel is essential for ensuring we co-design an experience characterized by meaningful preparation opportunities, access to high-quality teacher educators, as well as timely and relevant support. Spending time in community with our external partners, including Israel, has helped us build a culture of high expectations, trust, and shared responsibility for ensuring access, success and mobility for all of our candidates.

The connection of the group's work to addressing the teacher shortage with new teachers who can deliver culturally responsive educational experiences to future students is clear and greatly needed in Texas where the teacher shortage is an ongoing and serious challenge. The connection to addressing intergenerational poverty, while less obvious on the surface is, however, equally as vital. As Michelle Accardi, director of Policy and Partnerships for the National Board and long-time member of the Laredo Legacy collaboration, explains:

> Education is an onramp, if you will, to increased opportunity and the opportunity for communities to benefit from the work that their teachers are doing. And one of the reasons that we are perpetually seeking out opportunity for projects and why we are focused in different areas of the country [including Laredo] is that we know that we can leverage the expertise of Board-Certified Teachers to enhance the opportunities that in many cases have been denied to various communities of people, and we have seen just tremendous results in those ways.

Specifically on the issue of addressing intergenerational poverty, Accardi notes,

> There have been studies that show that having just one board certified math teacher will increase a student's lifetime income by forty-eight thousand dollars (citation). That's significant! And imagine if we're able to stack those benefits on top of not just one board certified teacher, but four or five, 12 over the course of a lifetime. And when we look at population trends that traditionally have not had these opportunities for economic advancement, just having these board-certified teachers can break that cycle of perpetual poverty by in a variety of ways.

Indeed the vision for the Laredo Legacy Project includes a finely detailed elaboration of the timeline of teacher development that extends across the many pivotal moments in the growth of a new teacher, from generating interest in the teaching profession during the middle schools years, to the providing of practical and formative experiences for future teachers in the high school and college years, and continuing through their years in the College of Education including student teaching, through their placement as a teacher in their first classroom through their development as a national board-certified teacher. One of the most critical links for the young people in Laredo moving across this timeline is the Texas Association of Future Educators or TAFE [pronounced taf- eee] whose mission, according to Donita Garza, member of the LLP and the director of TAFE, is to encourage students to learn about careers in education and assist them in "exploring the teaching profession while promoting character, service and leadership skills necessary for becoming an effective educator." TAFE provides its members with the opportunity to develop effective teaching skills, through competitions at the regional, state, and national levels, starting in middle school.

Garza served as the main liaison for the TAFE organization and each educational region in the entire state of Texas. She collaborated with TAFE Teacher Leaders around the state and provided resources and support to help establish and enhance the TAFE presence within schools to nurture the next generation of teachers. Garza believed that the collaborative group is aiming to address inequities within the community by encouraging them to

> understand that anyone can be successful if they just persevere [and] put their mind to it. And, don't listen to the outside negative forces that keep them from doing things, so long as we're providing them the opportunities and encouraging them along the way, I think we can close some of those gaps that are in the community.

TAFE is doing the work to help close the gaps by providing personal and professional development in ways that truly support the preparedness of individual students and the families and community members who support them as they aspire and work to become effective teachers. TAFE's work calls to mind the dicho "El que a buen árbol se arrima, buena sombra le cobija," which literally means "If you position yourself under a good tree, good shade will provide protection." TAFE works to support students' needs in ways that complement the assets students already possess in ways that powerfully enhance and support their desire to become quality teachers.

As one of the undergraduate students in the TAMIU College of Education and TAFE officer Leigh recounted,

> I was in elementary school, and I remember there was this organization called TAFE, it was built in the elementary level and I remember I was part of it. I felt like I wanted to be a teacher. Middle school came along, and I was also part of TAFE [then]. I remember all of my elementary and middle school [years] going to this [TAFE] mini conference that was held. And this has been

something I've done for a while for the love of education, because of organizations like TAFE.

Indeed, all of the student members/TAFE officers we interviewed said if they were to advise a young person who was considering being a teacher but did not feel ready to make the commitment, becoming a member of TAFE would be the first place to start. One of the officers explained that she "would advise them to search for programs and organizations [like TAFE] that could help them in any way to get experiences with children or any type of career in the educational field." Another student officer stated that she "would advise individuals to join organizations that have to do a lot with kids or volunteer at a school to just get a little taste of it and see if they actually enjoy it or talk to teachers." In this way, students exploring the teaching profession can discover the qualities of service, character, leadership skills, and the collegiality necessary to become effective educators.

Being active members of TAFE and other organizations that are designed to build upon individuals' content knowledge and enhance their exposure to educational and leadership experiences helps to lay a foundation of preparedness at an early age to enter the teaching profession and to develop their identity as a teacher. A crucial ingredient in creating one's professional identity as an effective educator is to participate in experiences and events that provide ideas and opportunities to network and to view a variety of perspectives on how to teach different levels of content and material. These are some of the things that TAFE provides. Specifically, at the middle school level, students exercise their goal-setting abilities as they begin honestly considering the teaching profession. At the high school level, TAFE sponsors competitive events that include differentiated lessons, professional development, and impromptu lesson competitions, where students are prompted to create a lesson on a specific topic and are given a set amount of time and resources to create an effective lesson, with measurable outcomes. At the high school and collegiate levels, students create portfolios that include resumes, teaching experiences, and examples of lessons and projects they have worked on that have enhanced their professional growth and prepared them for entering the field of education with a readiness which is a core focus of the LLP (TAFE Appendix B).

Implicitly in TAFE and more explicitly in the College of Education at TAMIU, these future teachers are given opportunities to develop their social-emotional competence in ways that align specifically with TAMIU's education preparation program and ultimately the needs of the schools and classrooms of Laredo. Donahue-Keegan et al. (2019) argued that "supporting teachers to develop emotional awareness and agility during preservice education can help to increase their capacities for handling the normative yet complex challenges of classroom teaching" (p. 152). The intentionality of incorporating social-emotional learning into the education preparation program at TAMIU stems from the charge to address intergenerational poverty and existing factors that lend themselves to "college and career unreadiness" as the Prichard Committee (2015) identified. Indeed, while subject matter expertise, knowledge of pedagogy, and knowledge of student development are core components of teacher education and teacher effectiveness (Darling Hammond, Preparing Teachers for a Changing World), the integration of social-emotional learning into teacher education programs is equally as important if teachers are to succeed in today's classroom. As Donahue-Keegan et al. (2019) suggest:

> Socially, emotionally, and culturally competent teachers are better equipped to reach and equitably teach students with a broad range of backgrounds (e.g., socio-economic) and social identities (in terms of culture, race, etc.). Social-emotional competencies are critical to authentic, culturally relevant and responsive teaching and learning in schools. (p. 154)

As members of TAFE, students can enhance their individual capacity for what the Collaborative for Academic, Social, and Emotional Learning (CASEL, 2013) has identified as the five core competencies of SEL:

- Self-awareness
- Self-management
- Social awareness
- Responsible decision making
- Relationship skills

Providing examples of and training for students as part of their growth as future educators give them opportunities to integrate social-emotional learning into their lessons during their field experience (i.e., their student teaching experiences). Further, socially emotionally intelligent teachers will inevitably pass on at least some of these skills and qualities to their own students, who, in turn, can be examples and advocates in advancing positive youth development and showing the power of empathy in the community. Bringing social-emotional learning to young people really must begin at an early age, with not only the mandated academic content and material but crucial life-long skills that can be employed throughout adulthood and increase the probability of success, which is why family and community involvement is so critical.

An integral component of preparing future educators to become effective and empathetic teachers is to ensure they are well equipped to serve the diverse student population needs they will encounter as they enter the workforce. Incorporating social-emotional learning, trauma-informed and culturally responsive pedagogical practices into a teacher preparation program can enhance each individual's capacities for inclusivity and provide a platform of diversity, equity, and justice to be established and sustained within a classroom setting. One way SEL has been incorporated into the educator preparation program at TAMIU has been to provide workshops for teachers candidates, focusing on social-emotional daily lessons they can use to enhance their students' empathy when they enter the classroom.

BUILDING DIVERSITY, EQUITY, AND INCLUSION INTO THE MODEL

Another key partner in the collaborative is ACT: the Center for Equity and Learning (CEL). As part of ACT's mission of improving opportunity and achievement for all, the (CEL) supports research that focuses on closing gaps in equity and achievement. Their goal is to produce actionable evidence to guide thought leadership and inform changes in policy and practice that will lead to improved learning and achievement. ACT "exists to fight for fairness in education and create a world where everyone can discover and fulfill their potential." ACT's "North Star" or central belief is "the knowledge that Education has power that changes lives forever. It serves to create opportunities to lift up individuals and create societal change that echoes through generations to come."

ACT enthusiastically joined the Laredo Legacy Project in part because the work aligns so closely with ACT research-based recommendations (Croft et al., 2018) that suggest a key lever in addressing the teacher shortage is "facilitating recruitment and training among teacher candidates already residing in the school district," as well as with the LLP's intentional efforts to engage students beginning in middle and high school. CEL works actively to reduce trip wires and increase readiness in very practical ways for students entering the College of Education at TAMIU. CEL's presence in the community is about much more than bringing the tools/products of ACT, rather it is about advancing equity and connecting with the individuals in the community in authentic ways.

Dr. Nancy Lewin, senior director for CEL, describes the center's mission as "closing the gaps in equity, opportunity and achievement for underserved populations and helping people achieve education and workplace success." A first-generation college student, former principal, and teacher herself, Lewin understands deeply the ways in which local knowledge serves as a call to action to open the pathways for access to educational equity. Her position affords her the latitude to build relationships outside of her organization to create larger, positive circles of influence aimed at increasing access to opportunity and advancing equity by addressing the challenges that come with intergenerational poverty and the lack of equity that exists within the educational system.

Dr. Lewin's work focuses on the imperative of helping future teachers in "seeing people's true values and strengths and setting the stage for them to be able to highlight and show the skills that are going to open up the path for them in accomplishing big things and helping other people." A strength-based approach is central to Dr. Lewin's work on the Laredo Legacy Project, she says, "we're helping to create and set the climate and the foundation for future teachers to be able to empower themselves and then to continue that empowerment for other people in ways that can potentially extend well beyond the Laredo community." As ACT CEO Janet Godwin said in recent remarks regarding the importance of building the teaching power within the Latino community:

> "Each of us has a piece of the puzzle. Alone, we're not going to make a difference. Locking arms, we can provide more cohesive services and insights and make a real difference in people's lives." On a tactical level, ACT's Center for Equity in Learning provides ACT resources for future teachers to meet the entry requirements for the College of Education at TAMIU. From ACT's view, success for high school and college of education students as they progress through the horizontal stages and gates at each grade level also requires a vertical alignment and solutions as students move across grade levels. One of the main tools in supporting the readiness of future teachers is the Pre-ACT test and the data it provides, which helps support students in the four main subject areas of math, English, social studies, and science. Using the Pre-ACT also helps support students and families financially through providing post Pre-ACT 8/9 and ACT Test data so that students can work on skills that will reduce the need for taking remedial courses. Students also gain experience with the types of content and the mental tasks required by the ACT tests. In addition, with the help of ACT's Center for Equity in Learning and the Pre-ACT resources:

- students, parents, and educators understand relative strengths and weaknesses in four subject areas;
- readiness improves as students prepare for the ACT, and, more importantly, for college and careers;
- students and parents become aware of free online learning and test preparation resources;
- schools and districts gain important insights about curriculum and program effectiveness;

- educators more accurately identify students who are ready for advanced high school coursework;
- students become more informed about and engaged in college and career exploration and planning.

Lewin says,

> If I'd have had the advantage of Pre-ACT 8/9 testing data as a student, I would have had the benefit of knowing my strengths and skills as it pertained to college readiness. Having the knowledge of your own data allows for the opportunity to empower oneself into taking action toward solidifying and identifying skills for improvement. As I interacted with my peers and many other students, I realized some were placed into remedial courses which extended the time that it took to complete courses toward their degree. They also had larger amounts of debt as they had to pay for these remedial courses in addition to courses required to complete their degrees.

The decades of research behind ACT's assessment provide reliable data for educators, students, and their families to make timely and informed decisions that affect their future. In addition to the practical benefit of time and dollars, the ultimate outcome of the assessment is the pathway that is opened as the trip wire is removed.

Because readiness and mitigating intergenerational poverty are a priority for the LLC in the Laredo community and are core to ACT's nonprofit mission, ACT is using resources for this collaboration to provide students and educators with metrics that can be used to make informed decisions and to take timely action to help ensure student success. It is often too difficult to retroactively make changes when time is of the essence. As the teacher pipeline is strengthened, the entire Laredo community advances in not only preparation with readiness but also in moving the economic development of the community forward toward parity. In thinking about what success looks like, LLP's efforts to create systemic, sustainable, positive change in the community are a success. Lewin says we need to look no further than the students who become teachers themselves to see if they possess a philosophy of "it is a privilege and my moral imperative to go back into my community and create pathways of success for children."

BUILDING EDUCATOR DIVERSITY

Another partner in the LLP is the organization Branch Alliance which stresses the educator diversity gap that exists within the United States by articulating that 51 percent of America's public-school children are children of color and 20 percent of their teachers are from those same racial and ethnic groups, 48 percent of whom are prepared by our nation's minority-serving institutions. Branch Alliance's vision is to strengthen, grow, and amplify the impact of educator preparation programs at minority-serving institutions, with the broader goals of both diversifying the teaching profession and intentionally championing educational equity for all students.

Branch Alliance suggests that having diverse educators in our nation's classrooms benefits all students and helps prepare them to succeed in our heterogeneous society. The lack of educator diversity in classrooms around the United States continues to perpetuate inequity and undermines student learning. Students of color have higher test scores, high-school completion rates, college matriculation rates, and school attendance rates when taught by teachers from their own racial/ethnic groups (Branch Alliance, 2020).

To address this lack of educator diversity, TAMIU, along with two other educator preparation programs around the country, has been charged with developing a rubric for inclusive instruction by Branch Alliance. The intentionality behind the construction of the Inclusive Instruction Rubric is multifaceted. First and foremost, the aim is to address the diversity gap in education by placing the onus on teacher educators to hold themselves accountable for the robustness of their educator preparation programs. Examples of the kinds of actions teachers are holding themselves accountable for include:

- Providing opportunities to explore identity including intersections of identity.
- Encouraging praxis through informed action, advocacy, and/or activism.
- Involving collaboration and community building with stakeholders in k-12 education, including schools, families, and communities.
- Including representation of cultural, ethnic, language, gender, ability, sexuality, and religious diversity in its materials and among those who develop and deliver the instruction.
- Utilizing aspects of Universal Design for Learning (UDL) to ensure engagement, access, and needed support for every student.
- Providing flexibility, variety, choice, and differentiation in learning and assessment.
- Developing critical perspectives in teacher candidates that result in accurate critiques of the system.
- Developing and integrating asset-based pedagogies of care.

Ultimately, however, the implementation of the rubric aims to address issues of equity and poverty that exist within the community through the future generations of teachers. The rubric will serve as a guide for faculty at

TAMIU to ensure they are integrating the culturally responsive pedagogical practices they will model for the teacher candidates, so the students can create lessons and practice using the methodology prior to their field experience and as they enter the profession. When the rubric is incorporated into a teacher preparation program, it is intended to be used as an evaluative tool in the cycle of improvement and is designed for sustainability and collaborative relationships with local school districts which is a vital part of this process. Representatives from the teacher preparation programs should collaborate with school district administrators to discuss specific areas of teacher shortages, preparedness of first-year teachers, mentor or supervising teacher expectations, and, most importantly, how best can the higher education institution support their community's school districts.

RESULTS SO FAR

The members of the LLP take seriously a commitment to the long-term impact. While the work is still early stage, several streams of work have emerged from the collaborative that are serving to reinforce what O'Meara refers to as the permaculture, that is, an ultimately self-sustaining ecosystem where being a teacher in Laredo is a desirable pathway, where future teachers are cultivated from early ages, where families and the community help support the profession of teaching seeing its value for the community, and where resources are reinvested into the community to contribute to the common good.

TAFE Growth

With assistance from teacher leaders across the state and the TAFE Board of Directors, Donita Garza developed a new TAFE Chapter Guide for others to initiate the process of building the TAFE organizations at their respective campuses. A collegiate TAFE Chapter Guide is now being developed and the input from the TAFE TAMIU Chapter will serve as the framework to establish TAFE student organizations at college and university campuses around the state and also create a model for other states and even countries to use to create similar resources for aspiring teachers.

In addition, members of the LLP are working with TAFE leaders to reimagine the portfolio project for aspiring teachers to make it more closely aligned with the admissions process of the TAMIU College of Education (and other Colleges of Education). Being exposed to a variety of teaching methods and networking with current educators as well as future teachers, is at the core of TAFE's mission. As stated previously, TAFE holds an annual area conference, each including several counties throughout the state. The TAFE Area One Conference, which consists of Region One & Region Two Education Services Centers and the school districts within 18 counties in the state, will be held at TAMIU this year. The Director of TAFE Ms. Donita Garza asked that the TAFE Officers at TAMIU be a part of the conference planning process. The officers, along with their faculty advisor, Dr. Seth Sampson, who also serves on the TAFE board of directors, as well as the area coordinator, and teacher leaders from the area, had to make the decision to hold the area conference virtually due to the COVID–19 pandemic. However, many areas on the TAMIU campus will still be used for hosting judges for the competitive video events that students will submit online. The conference will serve as an invaluable leadership experience for the officers and the TAFE TAMIU Chapter members involved in the planning of the annual event. The conference is designed to provide opportunities for future educators at both the secondary and collegiate levels, to construct a variety of innovative lessons they can use in the field as they grow personally and professionally. Additional opportunities for the TAFE TAMIU Chapter to provide services to the community are also taking shape.

Working with Parents in the Colonias

Families are a particular area of focus for the LLP, and one important area of the work involves engaging with a large area surrounding Laredo, which is divided into four precincts known as the Colonias. Many of the students that attend TAMIU and are even members of the TAFE TAMIU-Chapter come from the Colonias. The Webb County Parent Education Program stemmed from TexProtects, which is an organization that engages in research, advocacy, and education, promotes social reform and appropriate increases in federal, state, and local funding for three priority areas:

- Prevention: Increasing investment in proven child abuse prevention programs.
- Protection: Strengthening and reforming the CPS system.
- Healing: Ensuring victims receive adequate and accessible treatment.

An integral part of the organization is the Texas Prenatal to Three Collaborative which has the vision that all Texas children are born healthy and have equitable access to health and early learning support in their homes and their communities. TAMIU faculty are beginning to establish relationships with promotores or trusted individuals within the four precincts' education centers. The aim is to listen to the successes the members of the community are already experiencing and provide services in the areas they share that are hindering families from reaching their full potential. One way this can occur is for students who have been through the transition from their community to higher education to work with the promotores at each education center within the Colonias and the families who reside there, to assist them with navigating through common trip wires that have historically inhibited members of the community from reaching their goals.

The faculty at TAMIU's College of Education and the TAFE TAMIU. Chapter members will strive to strengthen this collaboration for future generations. An additional project the TAFE TAMIU Chapter is working on is establishing Imagi-Nation University on the TAMIU campus. Imagi-Nation University is a nontraditional conglomerate of educational networks coming together to train and organize individuals to end educational inequity and create a fairer world. The launch of Imagi-Nation University at TAMIU took place on World Teacher's Day 2021. Dean O'Meara suggested that TAFE TAMIU-Chapter members can serve as co-founders of Imagi-Nation University. Dean O'Meara also explained,

> The co-founders of IMAGI-NATION University will be mobilizing 100 other students to become mentors and, in turn, inspire 100 local high school students to nurture a new, transformative mindset that's focusing on addressing educational inequity through ongoing engagement and action.

The TAFE TAMIU-Chapter officers and members serve as the catalyst for changemaker education to occur in the Laredo community. They are blazing a trail for younger generations to follow in their footsteps and build more equitable opportunities for future agents of positive educational change.

First-Ever National Board Cohort in Laredo

Another huge step forward in establishing O'Meara's permaculture is building a pathway to National Board Certification for teachers in Laredo. LLP member Michelle Accardi and our NBCT peers have provided feedback on five course descriptions that will form a specialization available to our C&I Graduates and most likely our MAT students. The launch date for the first cohort will be fall 2022.

The LLP as a Model of Changemaker Education

Another member of the Laredo LLP, Dr. Paul Rogers, a long-time consultant with Ashoka, innovators for public and an associate professor at UC Santa Barbara, notes,

What is perhaps most remarkable about the Laredo Legacy Project are the ways in which members of the LLP have found ways to integrate their own organizational missions in a way that contributes to something much larger than what any one group could do on their own. There is a very obvious practical and collective commitment to work together for empowerment and equity, but another remarkable aspect of the LLP is that each of the members are all passionate changemakers themselves. It's not just a curriculum. It's not just a program. It's not even just a project. The LLP embodies one of the core principles of Ashoka, namely that "changemakers identify resources where others only see problems. They view the community as the solution, not a passive beneficiary. They begin with an assumption of competence and see themselves primarily as unleashing already existing resources in the communities they're serving (Bornstein, 2004)." It's not just the individual efforts, it's the collective commitment to taking action which has brought this vision to life.

The work of LLP and its focus on a self-sustaining changemaker ecosystem that is anchored by culturally responsive activity is a work in progress. As the group's vision continues to evolve and the network of participants continues to grow, O'Meara remains steadfast in his commitment to readiness and addressing intergenerational poverty, noting that for every child in Laredo to have had access to a classroom-ready educator we must:

- Recruit teacher candidates who represent La Cultura (culturally based leaders) by celebrating their culture and modeling "Respect, Integrity, Service, and Excellence (RISE)" as described in the dichos of their abuelos.
- Prepare educators and leaders who can model Juntos (which means "together") community leaders by sharing the vision of "a quality teacher for all" and recognizing the importance of a paso a paso (step-by-step) approach when realizing this vision.
- Provide international opportunities for educators to develop Adelante (globally minded leaders) by forming the international connections required to prepare graduates for leadership roles with local, state, national, and global settings.
- Support our Alumni to be Si Se Puede (which means "It is possible") social justice leaders who RISE above their daily challenges and connect with local groups to make a difference in the communities they serve.

CONCLUSION

The model outlined within this chapter is designed to serve as a blueprint for communities around the globe to glean existing knowledge and wisdom from local families, while incorporating educational resources designed to support and propel future generations of educators out of intergenerational poverty by increasing levels of readiness during educational transitions. The professional collaborative group was established on the foundation of cooperation, mutual respect, reflection, and shared goals. The successful functionality of the LLP is characterized by constantly evaluating the efficiency of educational pathways, effective communication, the sharing of new perspectives, inspiration, innovation, coordinating actions, and the willingness for continued mutual learning to occur. Constructing a collaborative group to meet the needs of your respective communities begins with the shared vision of enhancing educational equity and elevating educational opportunities of the community in which you live and the ability and commitment to build trusting relationships with supportive entities, while listening and heeding to the words of wisdom that have been passed down from one generation to the next.

REFERENCES

Bornstein, D. (2007). *How to change the world: Social entrepreneurs and the power of new ideas*. New York: Oxford University Press.

Bridges, C. A. (n.d.). *A guide to the core SEL competencies [activities included]*. A Guide to the Core SEL Competencies. Retrieved November 23, 2021, from https://www.panoramaed.com/blog/guide-to-core-sel-competencies.

Donahue-Keegan, D., Villegas-Reimers, E., & Cressey, J. M. (2019). Integrating social-emotional learning and culturally responsive teaching in teacher education preparation programs. *Teacher Education Quarterly*, *46*(4), 150–168.

Uncovering the Tripwires to Postsecondary Success. Prichard Committee for Academic Excellence, 2015. Retrieved from prichardcommittee.org/wp-content/uploads/2015/06/2015-SVT-Postsecondary-Project-Report-full.pdf.

Chapter 14

Changemaking in Teacher Education
A Journey from Inspiration to Action
Viviana Alexandrowicz
United States

The "Starfish Story" is about a boy who picks up starfish one at a time and gently throws them back into the ocean, so they do not die. A man tells him he will not make a difference since there are hundreds of starfish along the miles and miles of beach. The boy picks up another starfish and throws it back into the surf and responds, "I made a difference to that one." This chapter tells the story of teacher educators who are making a difference in the lives of future teachers, so these teachers make a difference in the lives of each of their students. It is the story of what may be necessary to help develop changemaker teachers, children, and youth so they can see themselves as agents of change.

    The main purpose of this chapter is to provide insight into the process followed by a teacher education department in its journey to integrate changemaking (CM) into their one-year and two-year duration programs. The initiative was a pilot for Ashoka, an organization that believes, "The world is defined by change and requires a new mindset . . . Ashoka envisions a world in which everyone is a changemaker . . . a world where all citizens are powerful and contribute to change in positive ways" (Ashoka, 2018). The chapter defines and explains changemaking in the K-12 educational context (mind-set, culture, curriculum, and leadership) and makes a case for CM in teacher education. The chapter reviews educational theories that support CM in education and shows the alignment of CM principles to the California Teaching Performance Expectations or TPEs for teacher preparation. It also includes examples of coursework integration aimed to equip changemaker teachers and highlights research findings based on pre- and post-surveys of students' perceptions of their preparation in becoming changemaker educators. The chapter concludes by making recommendations for integrating CM into teacher education programs around the world.

WHAT IS CHANGEMAKING?

> By actively tackling a social problem, changemakers demonstrate they are motivated to act. It is not enough to have the intention to do something good, intentions must be translated into action. This begins by having empathy for others, identifying a specific problem or opportunity to tackle, and giving oneself permission to do something about it. It doesn't stop there. Changemakers keep trying until they have made a difference. (Changemakers Learning Lab, 2016, p. 2)

Changemaking in K-12 supports and guides all children in making a positive impact for the common good of their families, their schools, their communities, their cities, their states, their country, and the world. It supports young people, especially those traditionally marginalized in educational systems (e.g., culturally and linguistically diverse learners and students with disabilities), to participate fully and take the lead in transforming their world. Changes may range from children learning how to interact respectfully with peers who are different from them to planning and implementing a campaign to address pollution.

Changemaking and Changemaker Educators in K-12 Educational Contexts

One of the first steps to prepare teachers to understand and implement changemaking with their students is to draw on the examples of schools that have ascribed to the CM philosophy. Ashoka set out to identify "changemaker schools" around the world. In 2010, Ashoka launched the Changemaker Schools network, with the first elections coming in the United States. Between 2010 and 2016 (when Ashoka closed its Changemaker Schools selections), the Changemaker Schools network in the United States grew to include more than 85 schools across all 50 states and approximately 400 schools around the world. Hay (2018) described the schools this way:

> The curriculum, culture and physical environment are used as opportunities for students to connect to their passions, collaborate, lead, problem-solve, analyze, synthesize, create and contribute to their community. Changemaker educators aim to foster both the will and skill to make the world a better place. They emphasize values, attitudes and behaviours as much as academics. Students are encouraged to be entrepreneurial, creative, empathetic, and community-oriented leaders no matter what career path they choose to follow. It is a combination of a deep understanding of what is, and the ability to imagine and bring about what could be. It is as much about how to be than who to be.

Changemaker educators (in and beyond the changemaker designated schools) prepare students for a world that does not yet exist. They facilitate experiences to support students in cultivating attributes that will help them strive in unknown future relationships and jobs. Surviving and succeeding in these constantly changing societies require twenty-first-century skills, "a new kind of skills and qualities like collaboration, creativity, and willingness to innovate. Unfortunately our education system seems to be one of the last paces to grasp the reality and urgency of this shift" (Start Empathy, 2016).

Changemaking skills align with what has been identified as twenty-first-century skills. According to Ashoka (2015), changemaker skills are identified as being empathetic, being thoughtful, being creative, taking action, leading the way, and being a collaborator. Similarly, Rivers et al. (2015) listed specific changemaker attributes that (although drawn from a higher education context) include self-confidence, perseverance, internal locus of control, self-awareness, action orientation, creativity, critical thinking, being reflective, communicating clearly, emotional and social intelligence, problem solving, leadership, and empathy. In addition, among the skills that Khan and Jakel (2017) list in their book on developing leadership and changemaking in Pakistani youth are: (a) initiating things and creating from nothing; (b) serving people from different backgrounds, faiths, ages, and races; (c) imagining, dreaming, and bringing future in their hands; (d) making decisions, choose between good and bad; (e) altering circumstances or direction to improve their lives and inspiring others with thoughts and actions; (f) collaborating by working together toward common goals through sharing responsibility; (g) caring by genuinely helping others and paying attention to their needs; and (h) feeling and empathizing, walking in someone else's shoes.

Although changemaker administrators and teachers hold diverse interpretations and establish different avenues for helping students cultivate these skills, in one way or another, they have transformed their school stakeholders' mind-set, culture, curriculum and instruction, and systems to be supportive of the attributes listed above. An example of the mind-set of changemaker K-12 schools is the belief that "Everyone a Changemaker" (Drayton, 2012) is possible and that critical thinking and problem solving are key to developing well-rounded, engaged citizens. In changemaker education, teachers validate students' voices and students take ownership of their learning. Changemaker skills may take the form of students surveying peers about recess and later submitting a proposal to the principal about modifying recess allotment during the day or creating a plan to address global warming.

Changemaker schools cultivate cultures of equanimity and collaboration where teachers allow a shift in power from themselves to the students. Thus, students have the opportunity to be equal participants in their learning, and they feel included, respected, and a part of the decision-making process.

Students decide what "hurts their heart" such as bullying, and they choose a format to present solutions to real audiences on issues that matter to them. In the changemaker curriculum and instruction, core subjects such as math and science drive learning about life. One sees students using statistics to learn about food scarcity in their country and learning about the causes of the problem. Teachers create spaces and activities on a daily or weekly basis that support the development of socio-emotional learning and empathy. The systems in these schools are led by administrators who provide spaces and financial support for dialogue and professional development to prepare teachers and staff as changemakers themselves. These professional development opportunities may focus on social-emotional learning, project-based learning, social justice issues, and technological applications.

Like their K-12 counterparts, changemaker teacher education programs ground themselves on philosophies and theoretical frameworks that are aligned with the values of CM and which help to guide the pedagogies, curriculum, and field experiences of the teacher candidates. At the University of San Diego's Learning and Teaching Department in the School of Leadership and Education Sciences, faculty members believe in and use a variety of theories that are aligned to the principles of changemaking. They utilize curriculum and instruction grounded in theories on social-emotional and empathy development (Levine, 2013), on self-efficacy (Bandura, 1997), on culturally relevant and culturally responsive pedagogy (Gay, 2010; Ladson Billings, 1995; Winkleman, 2005), inquiry and constructivism (Brunner, 1961; Dewey, 1997; Vygotsky, 1962), critical pedagogy (Freire, 1984), and inclusion (Annamma et al., 2018; Baglieri, 2016).

When integrating changemaking into teacher preparation, leaders, administrators, and educators must consider these theoretical frameworks to strengthen the validity for the implementation of changemaking work, particularly in academia. Alignment of practice to the theory that is conducive to transformation is critical for scholars. The challenge associated with not doing the alignment promotes a lack of credibility for CM conceptualization and for implementation. Furthermore, theories of experiential education and inclusion provide a sound foundation for introducing changemaking in the context of highly regulated teacher education programs.

Beyond validation at the program level, teacher candidates themselves must make the connections between these theories and the implementation of changemaking into their classrooms. A critical question for teacher candidates to reflect on is "How is a particular theory reflected in my practice?" For example, when implementing theories of inclusion which refer to the placement of students with special educational needs in mainstream settings, along with other students without disabilities (Al-Shammari et al., 2019; Artiles et al., 2006), teacher candidates reflect on their effectiveness to address the needs of students with disabilities. One example of what inclusion looks like in a changemaker classroom involves students with and without identified learning disabilities work together to create brochures on the subject of personal hygiene. Classmates are aware of the social and academic goals set for themselves, and for their special needs peers and they collaborate to achieve these goals under the guidance of a resource teacher. The goals may include using appropriate language for interacting with others or academic language to explain what the brochure is about. This approach to addressing the needs and capitalizing on the assets of students with disabilities creates an environment where everyone contributes to the final product and where no one is considered less important in this "asset-based" process. Changemaker students see that everyone has strengths and capitalize on those strengths through positive interactions. This ability to recognize other individuals' strengths and contributions and collaborate for a common goal to address the needs of others are important skills for the twenty-first century.

CHANGEMAKING INTEGRATION INTO USD'S TEACHER EDUCATION PROGRAMS: AN ORGANIC PROCESS

In 2008, Ashoka launched a program called AshokaU, which identified and designated universities as changemaker campuses. In 2011, the University of San Diego became a changemaker campus. The university describes its vision as "The University of San Diego sets the standard for an engaged, contemporary Catholic university where innovative changemakers confront humanity's urgent challenges." Since receiving the designation, USD has nurtured many different initiatives focused on social innovation, community engagement, and social change.

In 2017, two faculty members attended the annual Ashoka Exchange Conference and were inspired by the ideas presented in a two-day education track on how CM could be brought to fruition in K-12 education. By participating in the sessions, they learned how two school districts were implementing CM in elementary and secondary schools (Ashoka Changemaker Communities, 2017). In this meeting, connecting with Ashoka members was instrumental because Ashoka leaders invited the lead faculty to visit the sites and to attend training for teachers and parents in one of the school districts. In these trainings, the faculty member had the opportunity to interview teachers and administrators informally to better understand the elements of CM, and how they would apply in teacher preparation.

These initial conversations served as the basis for planning CM integration into USD's teacher education programs. Although at the time AshokaU had designated forty-two changemaker campuses in the United States (AshokaU Campuses, 2021), no other teacher education program had committed themselves to integrate changemaking into their work, though a number of colleges of education were in conversation with Ashoka on issues of youth and changemaking. The Department of Learning and Teaching in the School of Leadership and Education Sciences at USD took the opportunity to become the first CM teacher preparation program in the United States and set about to integrate Ashoka changemaker philosophy into the preparation of their teacher candidates as changemakers.

Eventually, the faculty member was designated as an Ashoka Change Leader for teacher education and was tasked with forming a team that would be passionate about the initiative at USD. Together with another faculty member who attended the exchange and the support of the department chair, a team was formed at USD that began moving forward conversations regarding the integration of CM into the teacher education program. The lead faculty member used her courses to provide the foundation for teacher candidates to understand CM; a second faculty member brought CM to two curriculum methods courses. During the first year, these courses provided initial opportunities for candidates to create lessons and units that integrated CM across different subject areas. The incoming department chair was instrumental in making CM a priority in the programs, and as a visible centerpiece at national and international organizations and conferences in teacher education.

The following sections outline the seven steps used to integrate CM into the USD teacher education programs.

Step 1: Engaging Faculty in Introspection and Initial Ideas

At the beginning of first-year implementation, one goal was to conduct meetings with small groups of faculty members who were open to exploring CM frameworks and practice. In this phase, faculties were encouraged to engage in introspection on how they were changemakers. The concept behind the dialogue was that one cannot teach CM without walking the talk and practicing what we teach. The process of reflection for faculty began with a focus on the inner life and an exploration of identity and purpose by asking questions such as "Why did I become an educator?" and "How do I see myself as a changemaker?" The faculty then shared responses to these questions. Several faculty members said their inspiration was to help children or college students acquire the skills needed to achieve their passions and goals in life. Surprisingly, one faculty member who helped build a school in Africa had a difficult time identifying herself as a changemaker. This type of response was an indication that faculty members needed a better understanding of the concept and the practice of CM, as well as an understanding of the importance of owning one's changemaker journey, because our students will need to do the same. Humility is a virtue to be sure, but we serve no one by playing small, and young changemakers will also face challenges in identifying themselves as changemakers. These sharing times were critical to the process of creating a common understanding of CM within the teacher education program, and the ways in which CM could serve as a framework that encompassed a broad range of educational philosophies, and theoretical perspectives, as well as pedagogical principles and practices. Through this process, individual faculty members came to see that they were at least in some measure changemakers.

Following the small group meetings, the faculty lead met one-on-one with faculty who had expressed interest in being a part of implementing changemaking in USD's teacher preparation work. She also delivered a presentation to the faculty at large on CM principles and provided ideas of ways that CM could be implemented in language arts, science, math, and social studies/history. Together in these conversations faculty brainstormed further possibilities for integrating CM activities into specific teacher credential and master's degree level coursework. For example, for the literacy methodology course, the faculty discussed including lessons on critical literacy that would be based on authentic children's books and young adult literature as a means to promote higher-level thinking and empathy development related to the characters' experiences. In these initial group and one-on-one meetings, it became clear that to succeed faculty and students would need many more specific examples of CM instruction in the K-12 classroom to build on. Additionally, faculty participants repeatedly brought up the question of the ways in which CM educational principles and practice differed from philosophies and approaches already used by faculty in courses and research (e.g., social justice education, SEL, and project-based learning). As an outcome of these discussions, faculty members came to realize that changemaking could serve as a useful unifying umbrella term for theories and practice already used, as long as it was coupled with a strong emphasis on taking action.

Step 2: Expanding the Knowledge about Changemaking

As a designated changemaker campus, USD became a laboratory for exploring what CM could look like in teacher education. Vipin Thekk, Paul Rogers, and Ross Hall, leaders from Ashoka, visited USD and facilitated forums on CM education for all students and faculty (during scheduled class time). During these events, the Ashoka partners explored the possible roles for CM in the context of current educational practice and the relevance of CM education to the challenges schools and children face now and in the future. These events were critical in providing a common understanding among everyone in

SOLES for changemaking and the ways in which it was relevant and indeed necessary.

One compelling argument which Ashoka leaders presented for CM-based education was the ways in which CM education could help prepare young people to thrive in highly volatile and uncertain future in a rapidly and constantly changing world and to prepare them for jobs that do not yet exist. Another core argument centered around how all citizens need to contribute to addressing societies' many difficult problems in such a way that one-day solutions would outpace problems. These solutions would require each person to work effectively on teams and would also involve the ability for those teams to work together as a fluid "team-of-teams," where each player is a powerful contributor and leader. This kind of effective collaboration in a team-of-teams environment can only work when individuals possess high degrees of empathy, that is, the ability to understand and respond to the feelings of others. In Ashoka's view, in an "Everyone a Changemaker" world, empathy is as fundamental as reading and math.

This philosophy creates a new social imperative to ensure that every child fully develops their own innate capacity for empathy (Ashoka, 2018). In later years, the lead faculty member served as the primary source of inspiration and knowledge for sharing the vision of CM education by visiting courses every semester, sharing up–to-date knowledge, facilitating conversations, and conducting short activities in faculty meetings and elsewhere to ensure all students had the basis for understanding CM in K-12 classrooms and schools.

Step 3: Sharing Resources

One challenge experienced during presentations and meetings with faculty and students in the first year of implementation was the scarcity of materials about CM. The department provided funds to acquire the book *Changemakers: Educating with a Purpose*, written by the Start Empathy group at Ashoka and provided a copy to all faculty. Other pieces were available internally or as online documents, also published by Ashoka, such as "The Changemaker Journey" (2016) and "More simply than doing good" (2016). Unfortunately, not many examples existed of K-12 CM curriculum in the form of lessons or activities or school and classroom descriptions in the literature or websites. As a result, candidates had a difficult time visualizing instruction and CM environments. To address the need for more resources, the lead faculty created a center that compiled many resources such as articles, websites, and videos (Changemaking Center for K-12 Education, 2020).

These materials have been instrumental in helping teachers, teacher educators, teacher candidates, and families to understand theory and practice. The center's website includes: (a) articles on learning theories and academic research (e.g., constructivism) and resources on (b) CM education, teaching, and learning; (c) social-emotional learning and empathy development; (d) community engagement and service learning; (e) social entrepreneurship; (f) English learners and CM; (g) culturally responsive teaching and inclusion; (h) CM organizations; (i) books and publications; and (j) videos on CM. The center's website also includes a section on implementation that features written lessons, curriculum outlines and project-based learning units, and video lessons. Other activities planned for the center include workshops on well-being, PBL, Design Thinking, and standard-based lesson planning in the different subject areas.

Step 4: Connecting Theory and Practice

One key development in this stage was understanding many topics and activities that faculty already incorporated in their courses which were highly aligned with CM work. For instance, in the Methods for Language Arts course, instructors used cross-cultural literature and books to represent the various ethnicities and cultural experiences of the K-12 student population. In the one-on-one brainstorming meetings, faculty figured out alternative activity extensions such as analyzing stories examining the characters' perspectives and feelings about conflict. They asked teacher candidates to engage in reflecting on their own positionality regarding those perspectives. In the math and science curriculum methods course, project-based learning was already used in building lesson units, so candidates just needed to tweak their planning to have a focus on CM by solving community, environmental, and social justice problems. For the various courses, it was critical to conceptualize CM broadly by acknowledging that some CM components were already incorporated in the department's curriculum, instruction, and scholarship.

To explore CM connections to the courses they were teaching, some faculty members met with the lead CM faculty to examine possibilities for integration. It is important to note that integrating CM into courses was always optional. This decision was supported by the theory of diffusion that maintains that when an idea is to be spread and adopted, there will be different categories of adopters: innovators (2.5 percent), early adopters (13.5 percent), early majority (34 percent), late majority (34 percent), and laggards (16 percent; Rogers, 1962). Based on this theory, the four faculties who integrated CM into their courses consisted of 45 percent of the full-time non-tenured and tenured faculty. Unfortunately, part-time adjunct faculty who taught approximately 50 percent of the courses did not participate in meetings the first year and, as a result, did not integrate CM into their courses. As a result of this challenge, one objective for the second year was to include adjunct faculty in meetings in the different activities on CM.

Step 5: Aligning to Teacher Performance Expectations (TPEs) and Integrating into Coursework

Given the nature of the standards, values, and experiences inherent in California's teacher preparation programs, it was easy to make an explicit connection between outcomes outlined by the California Commission on Teacher Credentialing (CCTC, 2016) with the CM philosophy. For example, TPE 1 *Engaging and supporting all students in learning* requires that candidates be able to "Connect subject matter to real-life contexts (and community-based instruction) and provide active learning experiences to engage student interest, support student motivation, and allow students to extend their learning." The standards also require to "Promote students' critical and creative thinking and analysis through activities that provide opportunities for inquiry, problem solving, responding to and framing meaningful questions, and reflection." As mentioned earlier, connecting material and experiences and engaging students in critical thinking and problem solving are key to CM in real-world contexts.

Faculty had freedom in terms of adoption, so CM activities in courses were not planned and delivered in an articulated manner. Students had unequal exposure to CM, dependent upon courses taken. Some examples of CM integration aligned with TPEs in courses include the following:

- In a Psychological Foundations required course, candidates created a toolkit of classroom strategies that used learning theories discussed throughout the course. For instance, for critical pedagogy, a teacher candidate planned to engage her class in discussions about their community where candidates were asked what they believed were the greatest needs of their community. After an acceptable amount of time had been given to discuss, understand, and find consensus about community needs, the teacher proposed students to get involved in solving one of these needs. Another activity that exemplified CM was discussing B.F. Skinner and behaviorism theories of positive and negative reinforcement and punishment and "time out" as a classroom strategy. Candidates were assigned "problem students" and were charged with designing a "time out" chair for that particular student that was supportive and constructive rather than punitive.
- In a Methods for English learners required course, candidates explored the principles of CM in depth by reading the *Changemakers: Educating with a Purpose* book (Start Empathy, 2016), articles, and by watching videos. Students created a poster explaining the core CM skills (e.g., empathy, collaboration, problem solving, and leadership) and what these skills might look like in practice. Teacher candidates also developed lessons for English learners that promoted English language development, equal access to the

curriculum, and engagement activities for taking positive action. One lesson example for this class was teaching about the history of immigration in student-centered ways. The teacher planned to capitalize on the students' individual, family, cultural experiences, and "funds of knowledge" (Moll, 2019). This lesson supported students in language expansion and usage to explain their ideas (e.g., using sentence frames).

- In an Equity and Advocacy in Education Systems required course, candidates developed grants to be submitted to the California Department of Education-Teacher Initiated Equity Grant Program. In developing these grants to address social justice challenges, students contextualized equity issues learned in the course and applied asset-based frameworks in advocacy situations. The most common goals for proposals submitted were to seek funds to provide K-12 training, resources, and programs to support students' health and social-emotional and academic growth (e.g., STEM and mathematics). The majority of proposals were directed at multilingual and culturally diverse students and students with disabilities. Other grants sought to increase inclusion in history education, expand counseling services to address mental illness, and establish mentorship courses for high schoolers with elementary students. Moreover, one grant planned to generate funding for training on restorative justice to reduce minority students' suspensions and expulsions.
- In a Methods for Curriculum and Instruction required course, candidates used Design Thinking to develop a PBL unit and individual lessons aligned to the Common Core Standards. Most projects sought to identify and find solutions for community and environmental problems involving science and math. Examples of PBL units include units on sustainability for planting and caring for vegetation during drought times and a unit on protecting butterflies. One exemplary unit focused on reducing carbon footprint addressing the questions such as, "How can we reduce our carbon footprint?" and "How can we be more responsible and conscious when helping the environment?" Lessons included an activity where children calculated their personal carbon footprint, graphed the results, and had them postulate how they can personally make a positive impact on climate change. The same course also engaged candidates in a STEM night with families in a public school that was created based on teacher candidates' desire to encourage traditionally marginalized groups of students such as Latino youth to go into the STEM field.
- In an elective course on CM and K-12: National and International Perspectives, candidates examined CM theory and practice in the context of schools in the United States and Spain. Candidates interacted and collaborated with teachers and administrators in both countries to discuss and develop implementation using the diverse methodologies that supported children and youth's development of twenty-first-century skills. Furthermore, candidates

examined the schools and classroom mind-set, culture, curriculum, and systems in both countries conducive to CM. They created CM lessons and units in different content areas for secondary instruction and in all areas for elementary instruction. The learning objectives for some lessons created by candidates for K-12 students were: (a) understanding and analyzing different types of fuel used to generate energy and engineering a renewable energy device, (b) learning about probability and relating it to real-life issues such as COVID–19 and creating an educational campaign, and (c) learning about water scarcity and water contamination within the Navajo community located in Church Rock, New Mexico.
- In an elective course in South Africa, students were provided with the opportunity to learn more about local and global perspectives on educating diverse learners. Students were asked to complete a changemaker project in collaboration with African educators from universities and schools. Additionally, students attended and presented at the International Association of Special Education 16th Biennial Conference in 2019 in Magamba, Tanzania, and made a pledge to share their experience in a local community event in California.

These examples of integration of CM in coursework reflect the faculty's intentionality to teach CM to teacher candidates at different levels:

- In level 1, provide exposure to the principles, models, and effective instruction for CM;
- In level 2, practice for integration of CM in planning lessons and activities;
- In level 3, offer opportunities for teacher candidates to take action by themselves (e.g., writing grants for social justice causes).

Step 6: Developing a Changemaker School Partnership

To provide candidates with opportunities for creating CM environments, lessons, and units, the USD CM team and Ashoka staff developed an experimental CM partnership with a k-8 school. The goal was to offer a minimum of two workshops on CM theory and practice to support teachers and several student teachers completing their placements in the school. The workshops were attended by school staff, administrators, student teachers, and a few learning and teaching department faculty. The second workshop attracted some of USD's learning and teaching department full-time faculty and adjunct faculty. There were also representative teachers from other schools in the district (one or two teachers from each grade level at participating schools). The partner school and school district provided substitute teachers for teachers who attended, as the administrators were highly committed to the training. As a result of the partnership, and with their cooperating teachers' guidance and support, student teachers developed CM units or lessons. Their lesson plans focused on empathy, social and environmental issues awareness, and on becoming engaged in action in the school, community, or world. It was exciting to see how children learned about litter and recycling in two kindergarten classrooms and took action by educating others through posters and by picking up litter around the school. In first-grade classrooms, children learned about ocean pollution and brainstormed ways to help. In upper grades, three classrooms collaborated on a unit that intended to increase understanding of CM and what citizens can do to improve the community.

Step 7: Assessment of Impact

A key component of implementing CM education into the teacher education program was collecting data and measuring the impact on teacher candidates. The main goal of the research was to assess the candidates' growth in their knowledge of and ability to put CM into practice. The summary results presented next are drawn from a larger 3-year study of the integration of changemaking into the USD Teacher Education Program and focuses on year-1 results and the impact on year-2. The full details of the study and its methodology are forthcoming as of the time of this publication.

The research we conducted during the first year of implementation consisted of a thirty-two-item pre- and post-survey that included twenty-six statements on a five-point Likert scale (1 = *strongly disagree* to 5 = *strongly agree*) and six open-ended questions. The statements were intended to capture the respondents' understanding of CM, awareness of the skills required, familiarity with implementing CM in the classroom, curriculum, and field experiences, and use of strategies to help students CM initiatives and projects. Additional statements focused on the availability of resources and receiving a foundation from the teacher education program to be a beginner changemaker teacher. These results were used to make improvements in the programs and to support teacher candidates more effectively.

Results on Candidates' Growth

Data collected showed several areas of growth and some areas for the pre- to post-survey where integration did not have much impact. Some highlights and brief analysis of the results follow:

- Survey Statement: "I have a good understanding of changemaking."
  Data indicated 15 percent of candidates thought they understood less about CM, 27 percent remained the same, and 57 percent grew one or

more levels. The fact that candidates felt they knew less about changemaking may be an example of the belief that "the more we learn or know, the less we feel we know." The results show a high number of students were impacted by the new learnings.

- Survey Statement: "I am aware of the skills required to be a changemaker."

  Data indicated 63 percent of the candidates grew one or more levels (18 percent grew three levels), 21 percent stayed the same, and 15 percent regressed two levels. These results may reflect that workshops and forums conducted by Ashoka and the changemaking lead faculty effectively explained changemaker attributes, such as being empathetic, collaborative, a problem solver, and a leader.

- Survey Statement: "I am familiar with a variety of ways that changemaking can be implemented into the K-12 curriculum."

  Data indicated 70 percent of candidates grew one or more levels, 24 percent stayed the same, and the regression percentage was minimal at 6 percent. These results may indicate that discussions on creating environments and developing activities, lessons, and units in different courses helped candidates feel confident about integrating changemaking into curriculum and instruction.

- Survey Statement: "I know how I will implement changemaking in my field experiences."

  Data indicated 24 percent of candidates' responses stayed the same, 24 percent grew one level, and 31 percent grew two or more levels. These data reflect the few opportunities to integrate their learning into practice in their placements. Fifty-five percent of the respondents grew in their ability to implement actual lessons. This number may reflect the nature of the classroom and teachers that the department uses for placements that may be aligned with the programs' philosophies.

- Survey Statement: "I know how to implement a variety of strategies that will help my students carry out changemaking initiatives/projects in K-12 settings."

  Data indicated 18 percent of candidates' responses stayed the same and 66 percent grew one or more levels. These results may indicate that student teachers were able to implement instruction beyond individual activities or lessons in the form of longer-term projects. Projects usually provide opportunities for student engagement in addressing real-life issues for the common good. The following quotes reflect the types of projects and lessons that were implemented by two elementary education teacher candidates:

> Yes! I had my students use recycled materials to create a model of Earth for Earth Day. We are also doing an ocean unit so I had speakers from

environmental agencies come and speak to my class. They provided examples to help us protect the environment so my class is making reusable bags and posters for the lunch area to remind students to pick up their trash.

Yes, I have students investigate the 17 UN world problems that need to be solved by 2030. They use the design process to ideate ways to solve.

- Survey Statement: "I have access to resources on changemaking such as videos, articles, and so on."

Data indicate that 27 percent of candidates' responses stayed the same, 54 percent grew one level or more. These data were particularly surprising given some comments in the open questions spoke to the lack of sufficient resources and materials, such as model lessons candidates could use as a reference.

What Candidates Said about Successes and Challenges for K-12 Implementation

In the open question responses, the successes candidates mentioned reflected their ability to implement units and projects in their placements. According to a single subject candidate:

Yes, we did social innovation challenges around pollution. (Single subject candidate)

Two elementary education teacher candidates shared the following:

We talked a lot about community issues and worldwide issues, and how to make a change (recycling, emotions, etc.).

Yes. though I was not able to get to the project level, I have implemented change making activities and lessons in the classroom. One activity/lesson was focused on what students can do to slow down climate change. Another activity/ lesson was focused on what students can do to create a more positive and happy learning environment in the classroom/at school.

Analysis: The fact that several candidates had opportunities to implement changemaking instruction may speak to the nature of placements in terms of alignment to USD's CM philosophy. It may also reflect the candidates' freedom in creating lessons in multiple subject areas that sought to develop students' awareness of real-life issues, empathy, and their ability to do something about them.

Regarding the challenges encountered in implementing CM instruction, a few respondents felt it was not difficult to implement CM in their placements. Two elementary education teacher candidates explained the following:

> I think it's really easy because it's all about giving the students a reason to care about the curriculum. It helps them make real world decisions.
>
> I did not experience any challenges instituting change maker activities last semester, but in this semester, the school site already had a lot of their planning finished before I arrived.

On the other hand, candidates also experienced many challenges when implementing CM lessons, activities, and strategies. These included time constraints, foundational knowledge, cooperating teacher support, pacing lessons, and giving students freedom to develop their perspectives. The following comments reflect some of these challenges:

- "Foundational knowledge and where to get started with them, time constraints involved in planning, commitment and support from cooperating teacher, and grade-level teams." Elementary education teacher candidate
- "Difficulty incorporating this with math" Secondary education teacher candidate
- "Not enough time, as a result of the workload required of a student and teacher simultaneously." Secondary education teacher
- "Having students believe that they can be changemakers." Elementary education candidate
- "For me, it was hard to be very hands-off and let the students come up with the ideas/implementation plan all by themselves. I always caught myself providing them with my input/opinion, which I tried really hard not to do!" Elementary education candidate

Analysis: These challenges suggest there must be stronger preparation throughout different courses at the elementary and secondary levels on how to take students through the stages of becoming a changemaker. Candidates must be better prepared to use critical inquiry and student-centered pedagogies in the context of changemaking goals and outcomes. Teacher educators may explicitly show candidates how to engage their students in problem-based learning in more than one course, align CM outcomes to state address standards, and integrate CM goals in the different subject areas.

Teacher Candidates' Preparation to Be Changemaker Teachers

Only a few respondents mentioned sufficient preparation regarding the candidates' preparation to implement changemaker education in the classroom. Most comments focused on insufficient reinforcement throughout the program and the need for having more concrete practice integrating CM into the curriculum:

- "Yes! I attended two changemaking seminars and I think it sets USD apart from other credentialing programs." Elementary education teacher candidate
- "No, I think there should be more help with designing curriculum for changemaking in all classes, especially in math because everyone shies away from math." Single subject candidate
- "Somewhat. More practical activities during class would be helpful. It would be nice to implement more applicable material in classes. Possibly planning lessons in USD classes that promote change making." Secondary education teacher candidate
- "I don't think the program taught us many ways to implement Changemaking sufficiently in our curriculum. I understand the character traits it promotes and the importance of it, but am unsure on how to create efficient curriculum, especially for a 1st and 2nd grade level." Elementary education teacher candidate
- "I think that in my program we did not have much curriculum on change making. In Dr. A's class on ELL instruction, we had an introduction to change making. However, there was no other class that really discussed change making. I think that having an entire class on change making would be very beneficial to future USD students. I also think that incorporating change making into every class, in some way, shape, or form, would be beneficial as well." Elementary education teacher candidate

Analysis: These candidates' perceptions about first-year implementation guided the decision for improvement for the second year. The responses suggested the need for a consistent articulation of theories and activities used in courses across the programs for single subject and multiple subjects credential candidates. Teacher candidate's skills must develop at four levels: (a) theoretical and knowledge base level in more than one course, (b) engagement level (e.g., experiential activities they can later use), (c) a hands-on planning level where candidates engage in developing instruction with a focus on changemaking, and (d) implementation level, where candidates have the opportunity to put in practice CM instruction. This last area is dependent on finding teachers who have experience with CM or are open to integrating it into their curriculum and instruction.

Success Path for Changemaking in Teacher Education

In addition to the impact on teacher candidates, there were five critical outcomes from the process of integrating the changemaking process at the programmatic level into the USD Teacher Education Program. The first successful outcome was adopting Making Change for a More Just World/CM as one of the four departmental meta values (USD/SOLES Department of

Learning and Teaching). Other departmental meta values include Diversity and Inclusion, Critical Enquiry, and International and Global Citizenship. These values permeate the programs' coursework and experiences. As a result, all course syllabi now reflect these values explicitly by identifying outcomes, incorporating activities, and requiring assignments that address the values, including CM. In defining changemaking, the faculty decided *by the end of the program, students will:*

- Be empathetic and relevant
- Transform themselves, students, classrooms, and environment
- Make a difference—innovate, lead, take action to improve the world
- Problem-solve
- Build and use relationships, teamwork, collaborate.

A second outcome was including adjunct faculty in the one-on-one e-meetings to learn about changemaking, explore resources, and consider pedagogical and curricular options for integration of CM in their courses.

A third outcome was disseminating the knowledge gained on integrating CM into teacher education programs in the first year. The faculty team presented at numerous national and international education conferences (Alexandrowicz, 2018, 2021; Alexandrowicz & Hansen, 2018, 2019; Alexandrowicz & Quezada, 2018; Alexandrowicz et al., 2020). The faculty lead presented to deans of schools of education and was invited to the Global Change Leaders meeting that brought together over 200 world change leaders in Lyon, France (2018).

The fourth outcome was publications by department faculty on CM. The lead faculty published an article on using CM and adult ESL (Alexandrowicz et al., 2018) and a second one on CM and K-12 English learners (Alexandrowicz, 2019). A second team member published a chapter specific to CM and experiential education in the book *The Heart of Teaching* (Hansen, 2019). In addition, a faculty member whose area is special education presented at national and international conferences in collaboration with doctoral and master's students (Jez, 2019). A second faculty member whose specialization in disability studies published a chapter in *Changemakers! Practitioners Advance Equity and Access in Out-of-School Time Programs* (Stolz, 2019).

A fifth outcome was the development of a CM center for K-12 education directed by the lead faculty Viviana Alexandrowicz and co-directed by Bobbi Hansen, the second team member. This center took two years to create and offers resources that include: (a) CM education, teaching, and learning, (b) community engagement and service learning, (c) culturally responsive teaching and CM, (d) English language learners and CM, (e) social-emotional learning and empathy development, (f) social entrepreneurship and changemakers, and (g) social justice and equity. The center will offer workshops and modules for pre- and in-service teachers in the aforementioned areas.

Challenges and Recommendations: Success Paths for Integrating the Changemaking Process

It is important to understand the miscellaneous challenges and roadblocks that one might encounter when implementing this concept to integrate the changemaking process successfully. These challenges may include:

- Faculty members have limited time to read and watch CM resources and to attend small meetings.
  - Potential solution: Provide short readings on main concepts. Use meeting time to explore resources. Hold online meetings.
- Faculty members' interests and scholarly research may not directly relate to CM.
  - Potential solutions: Help faculty members connect their research interests to CM. Often, their research is already a form of CM, so it is generally not difficult to tie it to CM.
- Resources are limited for professional development in CM.
  - Potential solutions: Involve school or departments' decision makers (e.g., chairs, deans, and committee leads) in the CM process. Invite them to meetings and forums. Conduct short presentations to explain the benefits of becoming a CM teacher education program.
- Part-time faculties have limited participation due to schedules and insufficient efforts to include them.
  - Potential solutions: Offer alternative times and days for remote groups and one-on-one e-meetings. Use hands-on approaches, for example, brainstorming how to tweak their grade-level content to have a CM focus.

General Recommendations and Implications for Teacher Education

- Identify a team of faculty champions.
- Ensure faculties, including teacher candidates, understand that it is possible to integrate CM in their own classroom and not just as a whole school.
- Demonstrate to teacher candidates how CM instruction and learning can be implemented by modifying their lessons and daily activities.
- Show many examples of curriculum and implementation in schools, which is key for teachers to learn how to "intentionally" help all students develop CM skills in the K-12 classroom.
- Demonstrate how CM implementation is aligned to state or country K-12 educational standards.

- Provide many resources candidates may use for background information or as examples of how CM is implemented.

The USD's pioneering CM initiative provides the field with valuable information and insights about the process and components that need to be considered for effective CM integration into teacher preparation programs. Having a faculty leader who is passionate and spearheads the initiative is paramount. Coupled with this, the team must include at least two other faculty members interested or passionate about CM. This lead faculty and the team should be willing to coordinate professional development, articulate activities, conduct follow up with school partners, organize small meetings, share resources, and research the impact on candidates' preparation. Schools of education or department administrators (systems) should consider providing financial support or time for professional development and activities. A culture that includes constructivist and experiential methodology for social change is also necessary. Integration of the CM philosophy, engagement, practice, and implementation across the curriculum and field placement in an intentional way will [support the success of this program].

Another critical component our program has not yet fully developed is engaging candidates in developing CM action plans based on what students learned in courses. For example, when learning about English learners' experiences in schools, candidates created an action plan to provide students with equal access to the curriculum they teach in their current teaching placement. This objective may be accomplished by teacher candidates modifying their attitudes, instructional strategies, and their environments. Classrooms should be welcoming, inclusive, culturally responsive, and linguistically comprehensible to address children and youth academic and social needs. Moreover, teacher educators must guide candidates in developing a mind-set that places students at the center of learning and helps students empower themselves to act to better their lives and the lives of others. Future teachers need to help students see themselves as leaders and collaborators, no matter their linguistic and cultural background, ability levels, gender, or socioeconomic status. One major difference of the CM curriculum is going beyond philosophizing and discussing topics and issues and taking action that will bring about change.

A major implication is the potential benefits that CM initiatives may generate. CM-oriented programs will attract candidates who are empathetic and passionate about social justice, equity, and other societal issues critical to current education and the world. Schools of education must keep up with the times and prepare educators with twenty-first-century skills. Our responsibility as teacher preparation leaders is to predict what do we need to teach children who can act to find solutions for all kinds of problems and to be prepared to work in an unpredictable workforce, thus, making "Everyone a Changemaker" a reality.

REFERENCES

Alexandrowicz, V. (2018, April). *A journey of changemaker teacher education.* Presented at the Ashoka Exchange Conference, Boston.

Alexandrowicz, V. (2020). Changemaking and English Learners (ELS): Language, content, and skill development through experiential education. *English Language Teaching, 14*(1), 107.

Alexandrowicz, V. (2021, March). *Changemaking, language, and ELS: Integrating lessons on solving community problems during COVID and normal times.* Presented at the California Association for Bilingual Education Conference, Online.

Alexandrowicz, V., Andres, A., Danaher, C., & Valdivia, P. (2019, December). Supporting community leadership development through ESL classes: A changemaking initiative. *The Catesol Journal, 31*(1), 151.

Alexandrowicz, V., Boedicker, N., Dykson, C., & Ye, V. (2020, February). *Everyone a changemaker.* Presented at the Ashoka Exchange Conference, Online.

Alexandrowicz, V., & Hansen, B. (2018, February). *Changemaking in teacher education: A journey from inspiration to action.* Presented at the Association for Teacher Educators Conference, Las Vegas.

Alexandrowicz, V., & Hansen, B. (2019). *Changing the world: One classroom at a time.* Presented at the *EDInnovate Live 2019*, The Jacobs Institute for Innovation in Education Conference, US, San Diego, CA.

Alexandrowicz, V., & Hansen, B. (2018, October). *Developing a changemaker teacher education program: The first year.* Presented at the California Council for Teacher Education Conference, San Diego, CA.

Alexandrowicz, V., & Hansen, B. (2019, February 19). *What theories drive our changemaking work anyways?* Presented at the Ashoka Exchange Conference, San Diego.

Alexandrowicz, V., Quezada, R., & Raman, V. (2018, July). *Changemaker education.* Presented at the International Council on Education for Teaching World Assembly, Laredo Texas, July.

Ashoka. (2015). *Every young person becoming a changemaker.* Retrieved from https://issuu.com/ashokaspain/docs/every_young_person_becoming_a_chan.

Ashoka Changemaker Communities. *Changemaker school districts.* Retrieved from https://www.changemakercommunities.org/changemaker-school-district.

Ashoka U Campuses. https://ashokau.org/changemakercampus/campuses/.

Ashoka Youth Ventures. (2016). Changemaker journey. PDF publication.

Bandura, A. (1997). *Self-efficacy: The exercise of control.* New York: Freeman.

Bruner, J. S. (1961). The act of discovery. *Harvard Educational Review, 31*(1), 21–32.

California Commission on Teacher Credentialing. (2016). *Teacher performance expectations (TPE's)*. Retrieved from https://www.ctc.ca.gov/docs/default-source/educator-prep/standards/adopted-tpes-2016.pdf.

Changemakers Learning Lab. (2016). *More than simply "doing good": A definition of a changemaker*. Retrieved from https://www.evansville.edu/changemaker/downloads/more-than-simply-doing-good-defining-changemaker.pdf.

Changemaking Center for K-12 education. Retrieved from https://www.sandiego.edu/mccasa/changemaking-center/.

Dewey, J. (1997). *How we think*. New York: Dover Publications.

Drayton, B. (2012). *Everyone a changemaker*. Retrieved from https://www.youtube.com/watch?v=V0w_o5PAzPQ.

Freire, P. (1984). *Pedagogy of the oppressed*. New York: Continuum Publishing Company.

Gay, G. (2010). *Culturally responsive teaching: Theory, research, and practice*. New York: Teachers College.

Global Change Leaders Meeting. Lyon, France. (2018). Retrieved from https://www.sandiego.edu/news/soles/detail.php?_focus=66542.

Hansen, C. B. (2019). *The heart and science of teaching*. New York: Teachers College Press.

Hay, L. (2018a). *A school culture of Changemaking*. Retrieved from https://laura-c-hay.medium.com/a-school-culture-of-changemaking-e9996e79269f.

Hay, L. (2018b). *Changemaker students*. Retrieved from https://medium.com/@laura.c.hay/changemaker-students-7f658491f0d3.

Jez, R. J., Campisano, M., Burciaga, D., Torres, D., & Murphy, K. (2019). *Changemaking education: A collaboration between Tanzania and the United States*. Paper presented at a meeting of the International Association of Special Education, Mgamba, Tanzania.

Jez, R. J., Hauth, C., & Ramers, L. (2019). *Decolonizing global education TK-12: Using changemaking to ignite teacher education in the United States and South Africa*. Paper presented at a meeting of the National Association of Multicultural Education, Tucson, AZ.

Ladson Billings, G. (1995). But that's just good teaching! The case for culturally relevant pedagogy. *Theory into Practice, 34*(3), 159.

Levine, D. A. (2013). *Teaching empathy: A blueprint for caring, compassion, and community*. Bloomington, IN: Solution Tree Press.

Moll, L. (2019). *Elaborating funds of knowledge: Community oriented practices in international contexts*. Retrieved from https://journals.sagepub.com/doi/10.1177/2381336919870805.

Raza Khan, A., & Jakel, T. (2017). *Yes! Youth-led Changemaking: A game changer in the field of youth development*. Berlin, Germany: YES Founders Foundation gUG.

Rivers, B., Armellini, A., & Nie, M. (2015). Embedding social innovation and social impact across the disciplines identifying "changemaker" attributes. *Higher Education Skills and Work Based Learning, 5*(3), 11.

Rogers, Everett M. (1962). *Diffusion of innovations* (1st ed.). New York: Free Press of Glencoe. OCLC 254636.

Shammari, Z., Faulkner, P., & Forlin, C. (2019). Artiles, Dorn, & Christensen. (2006). *Theories-based inclusive education practices.* Retrieved from https://www.researchgate.net/publication/333817006_Theories-based_Inclusive_Education_Practices.

Start Empathy. (2016). *Changemakers: Educating with a purpose.* Arlington, VA: Ashoka.

Stolz, S. (2019). What does it take to provide disabled youth access to out-of-school time programs? In F. Vance & S. Hill (Eds), *Changemakers! Practitioners advance equity and access in out-of-school time programs.* Charlotte, NC: Information Age Publishing.

University of San Diego Changemaker Hub. Retrieved from https://www.sandiego.edu/changemaker/about/.

USD/SOLES' Department of Learning and Teaching. Retrieved from https://www.sandiego.edu/soles/learning-and-teaching/.

Vygotsky, L. S. (1962). *Thought and language.* Cambridge, MA: MIT Press.

Winkelman, M. (2005). *Cultural awareness, sensitivity, & competence.* Peosta, IA: Eddie Bowers Publishing Co., Inc.

Afterword: Schooling and the Development of Changemakers

An Interview with Ashoka Young Changemaker Victor Ye

Viviana Alexandrowicz and Paul Rogers

United States

This afterword captures the experiences of the main protagonists of the change-making journey: young changemakers. Youth and children around the world are transforming society in multiple ways, individually and with peers and adults. They put empathy, collaboration, leadership, and problem solving into practice in their homes, neighborhood, cities, states, countries, and the world. They are designing social enterprises to increase water access, provide girls with education, offer tutoring to children, and a wide variety of technological and non-technological ways to improve the living conditions of their communities.

The chapter delves deeply into the experiences and wisdom of one such changemaker Victor Ye and the path he followed to bring his dreams into fruition. Victor was elected as an Ashoka Young Changemaker in 2019. He is an avid reader of current events and often finds himself scrolling through Google News to keep up with the world. Increasingly eager to be a global citizen, Victor wondered why the news, or even global issues, weren't a priority in his school's curriculum. Victor saw the importance of both understanding the world and feeling capable of creating positive change, but he felt this changemaker education was missing in his school. Taking action, Victor and his classmate started InnovaYouth, a youth-led organization to encourage young people to become active and passionate lifelong learners and global citizens through developing their skills in research, collaboration, and communication. Through workshops, conferences, and digital media, InnovaYouth challenges students to tackle real-world issues in their local communities through a changemaker mind-set.

The afterword presents Victor's views of how young changemakers can be supported by their local ecosystem including teachers, adult mentors, and peers and presents his suggestions for adults and youth alike about how to be resilient and to persevere as a changemaker. Victor's responses invite reflection for those committed to developing young changemakers on how they can encourage and guide students' development as conscious citizens who are intentional at noticing what is going on around them and learning to take action.

This interview with Victor occurred as part of a changemaking elective course titled *K-12 Education: National and International Perspectives* offered in the Teacher Education Program in the School of Leadership and Education Sciences at the University of San Diego. During the interview, most of the questions were posed by graduate students who are also teacher education candidates. The interview began with the professor stating that "If we didn't have the voice of actual youth when learning about Changemaking, it would be kind of cheating," and it is in the same spirit we present this final section on models of changemaker education.

Q: Do you think that youth get enough opportunities to become changemakers?

Victor: In my experience, many students who wanted to study environmental sustainability were in the classroom memorizing cell structures and models when they really, really wanted to do big things like eliminating single use of plastic bags in stores, or they actually wanted to look into more of the particular problems that plague our current generation. For me, it was seeing the lack of social mobility and also creativity around me that really enabled me to start on my changemaking journey, and which led to the founding of InnovaYouth when I was fifteen years old. Starting then and over the next three years, we saw a lot of impacts originally in Los Angeles, where I am from, to ultimately hosting conferences in over a dozen countries. Also, we were a part of launching more than hundred community impact projects from mental health awareness to students working on banning plastic bags and plastic water bottles in their cities and also in different grocery stores. Now, there are students who are working on storytelling, cultural communications, creating podcasts, and interviewing authors and historians. Through these experiences, I have learned that students really have the power to change the world.

Q: What is one thing that you wish teachers did for you or how they could have supported you more when you were starting to get into this journey?

Victor: The first thing that I would really, really give advice on, especially for teachers and educators, is to go a step further than just teaching knowledge. If teachers could reflect on the way in which their lessons and classroom teaching, and this applies to all subjects whether it's humanities or the sciences, can really help us understand, not only the world around us with a global perspective but also the major crises going on around the world, as well as the ways in which different problems are being resolved. I also wish, teachers had asked

Afterword: Schooling and the Development of Changemakers 249

more about how and in what ways *we can engage with our communities*, and, actually, if we're learning about history or English literature, to put that community connection into the lessons so that we're able to put that knowledge to use and to make the classroom more than a static place for us to just learn information.

Q: How would you describe or explain the importance of balancing academic success with being empathetic and a changemaker?

Victor: First off, being a changemaker already encompasses what most of us believe to be important: resilience, persevering, and also being empathetic. Changemakers not only see the problems and gaps in particular systems but actually work to change the status quo in a way that provides more opportunities for those who need it the most. I think when we have this changemaking mind-set; we see academics as an important way to understand how things work and as a way of developing expertise as well. So, having the changemaking mind-set means getting the information that we need first and then seeing; step two is how it relates to the particular issues and community problems we can see in our cities, and also maybe nationwide, or even globally, and understanding how that knowledge could potentially have an impact on a young person really working to bring about change. That's something that is super important in that we're not just learning through school, and then maybe graduating and having a degree, and then getting a job which is definitely what most people are doing, but what the changemaking mind-set does is to provide students with a broader subject matter knowledge and a mind-set to think about ways in which they can positively impact communities, while, of course, also learning as much as possible, not only just in the classroom but also by participating and having other involvements outside of their classroom experiences.

Q: What advice would you give teachers to be able to engage students in social entrepreneurship?

Victor: I would love to tell teachers to bring up the role models, because the first thing that I started was to look for other young people who had started to work before me to catalyze that first motivation I had, and to see that, wow, this is actually possible! I am sure that there are ways to access many different tools and resources, specifically in the realm of social entrepreneurship that teachers can provide as well. A really good example I think for many is Forbes which every year releases a list for those under thirty years who are working in the realm of social entrepreneurship: the Thirty under Thirty list. The list includes people from all walks of life from education to the sciences and who are from ages eighteen all the way to age twenty-nine. Even though these individuals are far beyond the beginning stages of their changemaking journey, the list at least provides teachers and students with the resources to show that changing the world is possible and that in the beginning everyone starts from ground zero. It also shows this it is not too far away from where we are in terms of our own educational status or in terms of our age, because at the end of the day, most students are going to be at fourteen to eighteen years of age if they are in high school or eleven to fourteen year of age if they are in middle school, and this means they are almost in the same generation as those that are making the biggest changes. I think finding role models to provide students allows them to feel that there is a chance within themselves that they can also bring about the same change as those that are outside of their communities who are leading change. It is also important that teachers recognize young people for their work and social impact. *Teen Vogue* every year releases what is called 20 under 21 and that list is actually geared toward women and young females who are trailblazers in the world of social impact.

Q: How did you access resources or funds to help you produce and disseminate services that support your cause?

Victor: I think the first thing to know is that all of the conferences that we led were developed with zero budget. We did zero fundraising, zero grants, and it all came from partnerships and work alongside adults who believed that young people could potentially work in the same areas that adults were working on. The first thing that I did was to look for venues that would particularly not only partner with nonprofits but specifically geared their work toward prioritizing young people as a forefront of leading workshops and conferences. So, I actually went to my local community center and, as you know, there were a lot of tries and rejections. It took time to convince people that we were going to be really good at leading and facilitating different workshops and experiences. So, the first thing that young people should do when working to lead change is to find allies and to start building a support network of not only just educators who can provide spaces such as their classroom as a first catalyst experience but also to look outward toward adult community members who have access to places like the senior centers, libraries, community centers, concert venues, and auditorium spaces in their community, which can serve as venues for events that aren't going to necessarily need to be costly.

Q: Did you have to upskill or re-skill in any way to be able to educate others about causes that you care about?

Victor: I definitely had to because a lot of the subjects that I needed to really come up to speed on things like the United Nations Sustainable Development Goals and corporate social responsibility. These are subjects that are typically not mentioned in the classroom experience so we needed to understand them really well to actually present them to others in a digestible way. When we talked about these things, we gave a lot of examples. We didn't just talk about the definition, but we actually used all kinds of different models and examples, whether that was companies that are being more corporately socially responsible or enterprises that are actually working on ways in which they are producing better impact toward society. So, for me, re-skilling really meant learning

Afterword: Schooling and the Development of Changemakers 251

deeply so I could provide information and give real-world examples in a way that would actually be helpful to teenagers, so that they can understand the information and see ways in which these particular examples would apply to students on a daily basis.

Q: In this line of work, how do you tend to your mental health and/or prevent burnout?

Victor: A lot of the time, I believe that it requires a team, instead of just an individual, effort to make this happen. I do realize that a lot of times I do receive the feeling and the emotion of burning out and the only way to continue forward is to have the allies in the support network that continue to motivate and tell you that your work is impacting a lot of people. What I take into consideration is that every single workshop that we have or conference or whenever someone creates a tangible project that becomes impactful, I simply ask the participants for their experiences or their reflections. After compiling a lot of those, it is actually quite heartwarming to see the impact that one can see from someone just attending a workshop and then creating a huge project that is impacting hundreds and thousands of students. What prevents me from continuously burning out is stepping back to recharge my batteries and also getting to read the stories of other young people, who, because of the work that we've been able to make happen at these small conferences and workshops, have impacted lives, from 5 people to 100 people to 1000 people. This helps me to keep fighting the good fight and helping others to do the same.

Q: What were the most helpful experiences or teachings that helped you discover your passion for changemaking?.

Victor: The most helpful experience that helped me discover my passion for changemaking was when adults or people in positions of power prioritized providing young people with a seat at the table to provide insights and advice in ways that actually impact the decision-making process. This truly made a big impact on the way that I have been working as well. I know that my experience at Ashoka has definitely been much more than a fellowship experience or an experience of mentoring. It has been more of getting to work alongside adults who believe that young people, as much as adults, have the same expertise, or the same experiences, to be able to provide the same level of insight, while we're all working together as one team. So my helpful experiences have been, when I am speaking at conferences or having speaking engagements at summits, that I am not only heard within those experiences and also within the school community where I present my own ideas but also that the teachers and other leaders acknowledge the value of the ideas we are sharing. It is helpful when the teacher provides further input by pushing and motivating students to think bigger and outside of the box and that is not only creating ideas but also helping to bring those ideas into fruition by providing tools and resources to actually make them a reality. That is why I think those are the most helpful experiences, to actually have young people work on a day-to-day basis on changemaking.

Q: What qualities do you have that has empowered you to be a changemaker?

Victor: I think the first thing is to realize your true passion, to open up your mind to a global understanding, and to think globally and act locally. I think that is what a lot of people resonate with. To open up our broader mind-set to not only be involved in our own communities but to actually provide a safe space for everyone else, whether they're working in different key areas of impact from philanthropy to educational equity to humanitarian causes. Another thing that helped me develop those qualities was to, and this is a little bit counterintuitive, actually have those setbacks and adversities of adults who have told me "no" so many times and told me that "it's not possible for you" and that I "should stay focused on school." The very first catalyst opportunity like this was when I was in the history classroom—my sophomore year of high school—my teacher told me that because there were other adults working on problems that are solving crises around the world, all I needed to do was to focus on memorizing the textbook information and highlighting the textbook so that I could actually just work to be most prepared to answer multiple-choice questions on the test. Experiences like those led me to believe that there is so much more than I can do and providing worth to my own experiences, not just being a student, but as someone who is actively involved in every single part and segment of making my community a better place. That is where changemaking comes from. It is my fuel, my drive, and my passion, but it also comes from the people who continue to tell us "no" and who insist that we are not able to create opportunities for those who need them the most.

Q: What piece of advice would you give other young students with dreams of becoming changemakers but who may be hesitant to start their involvement in social entrepreneurship?

Victor: The first piece of advice I would give is that everyone starts from zero; no one is starting from any particular way or frame and picture. When I started, a key example is that I really had nothing, and what people sometimes overlook is that they see a lot of the impact, they see a lot of the measurements of the statistics or the number of people who were impacted, or the number of projects that come out of it, and see it's great success and impact. But, I also like to talk about the importance of having to see the first step of the process, which is the actual ideation, and the important realization that anyone can do something about a problem. When I tell my story, I honestly share that three years ago, I was just like everyone else studying in the classroom, listening, paying attention, and doing my work. However, when it comes to highlighting the true emphasis of everyone starting from a clean slate in the field anyone can do anything. The biggest takeaway should be that if you work hard enough,

Afterword: Schooling and the Development of Changemakers   253

and if you find the right allies, the support mentors, the team, the people, and the right framework and vision for what you are setting your goals to become, because in the end changemaking is a hard journey, because you are working against the status quo, to actually create positive change, otherwise the social impact will not be there in the first place. It is quite like an exponential function, where it is going to be super static in the very beginning, you won't see a lot of changes, but as soon as you get the traction you start to go at an increasing speed of not only validation but also an extension of your work. So everyone starts with a clean slate. Everyone is also going to be working just as hard as you are, so there's no need to worry if your work in the very beginning is not very effective because you're going to be testing and exploring different ways to communicate your mission.

Q: What is the reason that they were not able to discourage you when you had your first meeting? Is it still the same reason?

Victor: That's actually a really good question. The first thing that did not discourage me from continuing forward is I had always known that if I had the ability to change people's mind-sets that would be my first calling to continue going forward. I am not someone who really gives up after one or two tries, and I also see the possibility of realizing the result of what would happen if I actually proved the adults who doubted me wrong, how I would then be able to speak about my classroom experience to encourage others. So, from that example of having the first workshop of only seven people with my family and just two of my friends, to the second workshop having over 150 people, I realized that if I am able to prove the doubters wrong about the work I am never going to give up. If people really see the true light at the end of the tunnel, they will be able to work hard and prove themselves, if they have the right tools and resources that can provide that same opportunity. For example, because the adults did not believe in me, I actually went back to my school and I gathered about fifty testimonies from different students. I then got twenty different testimonies from teachers to prove that what we were doing was actually worth something.

Q: I see on your website that the other members of InnovaYouth are young too . . . Can you talk about teamwork among youth?

Victor: I would like to say that this is not at all only my effort. I only provide the resources and the space for people, but everyone else is going to be actively contributing. Fifty percent of our initiatives are covered by the core team, so my job as changemaker is to provide spaces for others to become changemakers as well. Because that is the whole point to empower others to see the real light at the end of the tunnel and see where their own passion and interest lies. Most of my other teammates are going to be the driving forces around not only finding the conferences, finding speakers, rallying support and partnerships but also in terms of press and publications, and also communicating to various outlets. Our collaboration is very flexible in nature, there's no hierarchy, even though there are different titles, everyone works together in a team. The one thing that people learn in terms of social entrepreneurship when they are starting these social impact projects is to see that everyone really starts from not that much and when we are working on the process of not only the adversities and the challenges, but we continue to see that success growing, everyone feels the fuel and the passion that they see within themselves. Everyone is young, for example, Casey just turned seventeen or eighteen a few months ago. When he started in our work, he was around like thirteen or fourteen years old. It is very powerful to see young people who want to get involved and then to see them receive the same validation and the same results, it inspires other young people to do the work too.

Q: With such a large focus on youth, what, if anything, do you do to encourage multigenerational two-way learning? Can you give an example?

Victor: The first thing that we do is double mentoring, which is providing experiences to young people and the mentors as well. The way in which that happens is that during conferences, for example, there are sessions in which there are mentors and panels who talk about their experiences and their fields of work and also talk about ways in which they have been able to go from a journey of being a young person to someone who is truly influential or trailblazing in their own field and expertise, and afterward we have these small sessions of roundtable discussions where the adult is in the middle listening, but everyone around them are young person and they're the ones providing expertise of ways in which they can get involved or the adult is pitching questions like "how can I support you?" That is when young people start talking about particular problems of their schools or things that they are working on that they find trouble with, or may be funding outlets that they've not been able to find like small amounts of grants of USD 100 to really get them moving on with their projects. This two-way learning is crucial and important and happens already inside classrooms where teachers not only facilitate learning but also provide opportunities or spaces for young people to teach as well. That is where two-way learning comes into play. It is when teachers can provide outlets not only for their students to be engaged in the learning process but also by providing opportunities to teach other young people and create projects in which adults become team members instead of team leaders. That is where I see the most impact in that they are on the same kind of level for young people to not only work together but also to see that "oh wow teachers are also learning from me." This brings a great deal of motivation to continue going forward and helps support teachers with more insight on ways to drive social impact and change.

Q: You have talked a lot about older kids . . ., but how about younger children? What tips would you give elementary teachers to start helping develop changemakers very early in life?

Victor: At the very end, changemaking is about empathizing with people and realizing that there are always opportunities to make a difference. This can be done at the elementary school level like creating small teamwork projects for young citizens so that they can get the bigger picture. I would ask elementary teachers for ways in which to make learning more fun or maybe what is something that you would like for schools to improve and get students to start brainstorming even though they might go crazy. So students, of course, when they're five or six or seven think of crazy ideas that are where their juices are flowing and when you get to see their faces light up from all those small ideas. I think that is when you see that teachers can actually engage better with their students, that is when everyone is more proactive and ready to go into the classroom experience. For me, teachers can definitely provide more opportunities to get students who usually just think about ways of making a difference to get in front of the classroom and to start talking about their own ideas. If they see particular things that they're passionate about, then it should be cool for young elementary students to bring up their own role models as well and to get to imagine what they can do with the right kinds of support as well. For example, if a young student loves cars and finds Elon Musk to be a super amazing role model and inspiration, she or he might as well talk about it inside the classroom experience and in front of every student so peers get to see ways in which their role model is impacting other people. I think through that experience, young people realize that there's more than just learning, more than just earning money, there's more than just going through the school education, and that there's a lot that one can do with their educational and classroom experiences for years to come.

About the Contributors

CHAPTER 1

Mary E. Walsh is the Daniel E. Kearns Professor of Urban Education and Innovative Leadership at the Lynch School of Education, Boston College, and director of the Boston College Center for Optimized Student Support. Dr. Walsh is also the founder and executive director of City Connects, a school-based and evidence-based intervention that addresses the out-of-school factors that impact learning. Her expertise and interests include social-emotional and healthy development of children living in poverty, design and evaluation of systemic interventions that enhance students' development, and the impact of homelessness on children and families.

Amy Heberle's primary area of research focuses on the mental health functioning of pre-adolescent children (primarily in the preschool to early school age range) who are marginalized based on their economic, socioeconomic, or class status. She is interested in how children think about their own social class and in how children's expectations for themselves are impacted by growing up in poverty, particularly in societies like the United States that have high levels of economic inequality.

Kirsten Rene, PhD, is a post-doctoral fellow at Cambridge Health Alliance/Harvard Medical School where she works with high-risk youth across multiple, intersecting systems, including the juvenile court, police department, high-school teen health center, and hospital outpatient clinic. Her research interests include the impact of systemic interventions such as City Connects on student well-being, with a particular focus on social-emotional outcomes, as well as best practices for effective partnerships across sectors. Dr. Rene worked with the City Connects intervention for six years at Boston College where she obtained her doctoral degree.

CHAPTER 2

Lodewijk van Oord is head of College at UWC Maastricht, the second largest school within the United World College movement. He previously worked at the UWC schools in Wales, Swaziland, and Italy. He has written extensively on international education, educational leadership, cultural theory, and current affairs. He has published widely on global and values-based education, cultural theory, and current affairs. He holds MA degrees in Ancient History (Leiden), Bilingual and International Education (Utrecht), and Educational Management (Bath).

CHAPTER 3

Laura Hay works at the intersection of Education and Social Innovation from grassroots initiatives to systems change efforts. With an MA in Social Innovation from the University of Cambridge and a BA in Linguistics from Duke University, Laura is currently the Strategy and Partnerships Manager at the Edge Foundation. As part of the Edge Future Learning team, she collaborates with an international network of partners to deliver Community Connected Learning across the UK and align the latest education research, policy, and practice. Prior to this, Laura spent five years working with Ashoka on their Empathy Education and Young Changemakers initiatives aimed at transforming education systems for the twenty-first century.

CHAPTER 4

Amy McConnell Franklin (PhD, MPH, MEd) believes in educating educators. She has worked extensively with a broad range of learners, teaching students from pre-K to university, and developing and delivering teacher training courses in the United States and internationally. Through teaching, research, and program design, she guides communities to integrate transformative social and emotional learning and ethical emotional intelligence skills and concepts as a foundation for peace, sustainability, and justice. She is the author of "Choose to Change: a step-by-step teaching guide for fostering emotional intelligence in the classroom."

Kei Franklin is a writer, coach, facilitator, performance-maker, and musician, working at the intersection of culture and the environment. Concerned with questions of power, identity, race, and justice, she designs interventions that speak to the systemic, cultural, and psychological roots of our current moment. She believes deeply that our collective liberation depends on making education synonymous with conscientization. She is the editor-in-chief of Brack (brack.sg), a platform for socially engaged arts in Southeast Asia.

CHAPTER 5

Josefina Santa Cruz is an elementary education teacher with a master's degree in Education from Pontificia Universidad Católica de Chile (PUC). Since December 2014, she has been the dean at the Faculty of Education at Universidad del Desarrollo, Chile. She has been a subject matter expert and member of consulting commissions for the government in preschool and elementary education. Her research and publications have been related to the areas of teaching for understanding, teaching thinking skills in schools, deep learning, conceptual change, and self-regulation.

Kiomi Matsumoto is an early childhood education teacher and holds a master's degree in Education, with emphasis in evaluation from the Pontificia Universidad Católica de Chile (PUC). She is currently finishing her doctoral studies at the University of Salamanca, Spain. Since July 2015, she has been director of Practical Training at the Faculty of Education, Universidad del Desarrollo, Chile. As director, she has led innovation in teacher education programs to promote high practical training in the curriculum and the commitment of pre-service teachers to education in vulnerable sectors.

Josefina Valdivia is a elementary school teacher, with a Master's Degree in Management and Educational Quality. Since 2015 she has been the director of Early Childhood program at Universidad del Desarrollo, Chile. In 2019, she launched the first elementary grade outdoor learning program in Chile, an innovation that gives educators the opportunity to educate outside the walls of the classroom in connection with nature, and expanding students possibilities for movement and free play.

Trinidad Ríos is a high-school teacher of language with a master's degree in Curricular Innovation and Educational Evaluation from the Universidad del Desarrollo. Since 2011, she has been the director of the Elementary Education Program and currently Elementary Education with an English specialization at Universidad del Desarrollo. Her academic career has focused mainly on the management of processes that have an impact on the initial training of teachers and on the generation of innovation projects for the transformation and updating of pedagogical methodologies in university classrooms.

Paulina Guzmán is a primary school teacher with a master's degree in Educational Innovation. In 2018, she led the Enseña Sustentable Award for changemaker teachers, which highlighted innovative and inclusive educational practices. Her research and publications have been related to the areas of school climate, teacher well-being, and the role of the teacher as an agent of change. She is currently leading a longitudinal study on teacher well-being in Chile and Latin America.

CHAPTER 6

Catalina Cock Duque is an Ashoka fellow, accomplished social entrepreneur, civic leader, global weaver, and the cofounder and executive director of Fundación Mi Sangre. Fundación Mi Sangre facilitates systemic cultural change in Colombia by activating the ecosystems surrounding youth and engaging them as the primary contributors to personal, community, and societal transformation to impact sustainable peace.

Ariel Safdie is an associate director at Conexión Américas, an NGO dedicated to building a welcoming community and creating opportunities where Latino families can belong, contribute, and succeed. Previously, Ariel was the leader of Planning and Development at the Colombian NGO, La Fundación Mi Sangre. Ariel has over fifteen years of experience in international development working in NGOs in Colombia, the United Kingdom, and the United States leading programs committed to using education and social justice to build citizenship in children, youth, and migrant populations.

CHAPTER 7

Kate Dickinson-Villaseñor facilitates professional development, faculty training, and education initiatives related to social-emotional learning, cultural competency, antiracist pedagogy, community engagement, and social justice. Kate earned her EdD in Organizational Change Leadership from USC, her MEd in Special Education, and a BA in Diversified Liberal Arts and History. Kate has worked in k-12 and higher education settings as a classroom teacher, administrator, and teacher educator.

CHAPTER 8

Carmen Pellicer Iborra is the president of Fundación Trilema (Trilema Foundation https://www.fundaciontrilema.org/) where she leads numerous programs for teacher and administrators training from public and private schools across Spain. She is a theologist, teacher, writer, and an Ashoka fellow since 2016. Carmen is the director of seven educational centers that focus on models of innovation and change. Along the Fundación CEU Andalucía, she leads the "Learning Leaders" online master's degree for the preparation of leaders in educational innovation. In 2018, she became the director of the Journal *Cuadernos de Pedagogía (Pedagogical Journals)*. She is the author of books, didactic, and audiovisual materials in collaboration with well-known publishing companies. Carmen has also produced the short films "Profes" (Teachers) and "La Buena Educación" (The Good Education).

Martín Varela Dávila is a teacher and earned a degree in Psychopedagogy and a Diploma in Teaching in the specialty of foreign languages. He is a coach level-5 ILM and senior certified by AECOPE. He received his professional development under the mentorship of members of the Harvard Project Zero, the National Thinking Center of the United States, and the British consultant Independent Thinking in various fields of learning. Martin is responsible for the program and degrees for the Leadership and Educational Coaching and Evaluation of Teaching Performance by the University of Nebrija. He is the author of the book *Forgotten Virtues, Values with a Future* and various textbooks on Civic Values, Religion and Entrepreneurship Projects for high school at the ANAYA publishing house.

Rosa López Oliván is the director of R&D&I and Pastoral Care of Trilema Schools and doctor in Hispanic Philology in the specialty of Hispanic-American Literature. She currently coordinates the master's degree program for Learning Leaders offered by the Trilema Foundation with the San Pablo Andalucía CEU Foundation and the Cardenal Spínola CEU Center for University Studies. Rosa directs the Expert in Intelligence Executive Functions of the Trilema Foundation with the Nebrija University and is responsible for the Teaching Practicum II in this university carried out in the Trilema schools. She is part of the editorial board of the *Journal Cuadernos de Pedagogía* and coauthor of the KUMI Secondary School projects of the Edelvives publishing house. Rosa is a trainer for the Trilema Foundation, supporting management teams for educational transformation, evaluation, and tutorial and pastoral action.

Marta Monserrat Salcedo is the pedagogical coordinator in primary education for the Trilema schools. She also supports the practicum in the master's programs at the Nebrija University of Madrid, the CEU Cardenal Spínola of Seville, in the Trilema schools. Marta is pedagogical director of the Trilema school Safa and member of the school management team and coordinator of Infant and Primary Schools of the Trilema Schools. She is a coach and trainer of teachers in national and international schools, and she specializes in supporting management teams to carry out processes of school transformation and educational innovation. Marta has extensive experience in editing educational materials. She is a specialist in personalization and executive functions, as well as in evaluation as a key to learning.

Miguel Ignacio Garcia Morell studied English and Catalan Philology from the University of Valencia and graduated in Contemporary Studies from the University of Coventry in the United Kingdom. He obtained a master's degree in Teaching Secondary Education and Training Cycles, assistant professor of Spanish in the International Language Program Pathways (ILEP), in New Zealand. Miguel is also a DELE examiner and author of several publications with the Ministry of Education and Culture, in addition to collaborating in Bilingual Education programs. He is a trainer of faculty with the Trilema Foundation and the Pedagogical director of the Colégio Nuestra Señora del Pilar Trilema in Madrid. He coordinates the EQAp Network—with more than fifty Schools in Europe, Latin America, and Africa—supporting complex transformation processes in diverse contexts.

CHAPTER 9

Polly Akhurst is the cofounder and coexecutive director of Amala School (formerly Sky School). She is a passionate advocate of the power of change-maker education. Amala aims to open up access to learning that enables young refugees around the world to become agents of change. She has also acted as a working group leader of the OECD's Education 2030 project that aims to help education systems determine the knowledge, skills, attitudes, and values students need to thrive in and shape their future. Polly is an alumnus of UWC (United World Colleges) and is a member of the Education Committee of UWC Atlantic.

Stuart MacAlpine is the founding director of education for Amala and co-developed the educational model and programs with Polly Akhurst and Mia Eskelund Pedersen. Stuart is a learning designer. He currently works at The LEGO Foundation in Denmark and is the director of Hesscairn Learning Design

Studio. He has developed progressive and regenerative educational programs in a wide range of settings, including the Green School New Zealand High-School Diploma focused on regeneration and permaculture principles and the concept based curriculum for UWC South East Asia. Hesscairn Learning Design Studio focuses on bringing joy, elegance and simplicity to learning design.

Mia Eskelund Pedersen is the cofounder and coexecutive director of Amala (formerly Sky School. With a background in international education, international development and project management, Mia set up Amala four years ago alongside Polly Akhurst. With a desire to close the acute lack of secondary education for refugees, Amala has developed the first international high-school curriculum for refugees that not only gives young refugees access to vital secondary education, but also develop their sense of ethical agency and changemaker skills. She oversees Amala's program work as well as fundraising and finance.

CHAPTER 10

Maria Isabel Valente-Pires, PhD, is a retired professor of Escola Superior de Educação de Setúbal Headmistress of Colégio de S. José—International School in Coimbra. She is a consultant to the Portuguese Secretary of State for Education, coordinator of Gulbenkian's Knowledge Academy Educar para Voar, and the teacher training Projects Ensinar é Voar and Ensinar é Voar II.

Luiza Nora has a degree in German Philology (North-American Literature) and a post-graduation in "Modernism" (North-American Literature). She taught English as a foreign language in Colégio de S. Teotónio, Coimbra, Portugal from September 1977 to November 2012 for fifth-grade to twelfth-grade students. From 1999 until 2019, she organized and supervised English language summer courses all around the United Kingdom and in the United States (New York and Boston). Since October 2012, she belongs to the Board of Directors at CSJ, International School as the coordinator of International Projects.

CHAPTER 11

Asma Hussain has spent half a decade with children inside the classroom as an educator. Spending her time inside the classroom taught her to be patient, humble, curious, and a believer in persistence. She has completed her bachelors in Economics. She also has a bachelor's degree in Education. Before joining Design for Change as the global coordinator, she was a fellow at Teach for India.

Beatriz Alonso is a journalist with a PhD in Media and Communications Research. Passionate about international fieldwork using the framework of Communication for Development to analyze the political, economic, and social areas, especially educational innovation. She used to work with different newspapers in Spain and France, and in 2018 she became the Communications Manager at Design for Change España.

Elena Bretón studied a double degree in Translation and Interpreting and earned a bachelor degree in Global Communication in Universidad Pontificia Comillas. She collaborated in Design for Change España tasks such as Marketing campaigns creation, preparing content for the organization's social resources, writing sections of the DFC España blog, and designing press releases or scripts for possible entity podcasts. She is a translator who manages Spanish, English, and French.

CHAPTER 12

Patricia Limaverde is a biologist, educator, and researcher. She held a post-doctorate in Cultural Biology with Humberto Maturana, at Instituto Matriztica, Chile, researching the transformations of human social systems. She is an adjunct professor at the State University of Ceará, a researcher at Escola VILA, and a researcher at the Complexity Studies and Research Group of the Graduate Program in Education at the Federal University of Rio Grande do Norte. She systematized the Ecosystem Pedagogy and promotes training throughout Brazil.

CHAPTER 13

Seth Sampson is an assistant professor and program coordinator of the School Counseling Program at Texas A&M International University. He also serves on the Board of Directors for the Texas Association of Future Educators. Dr. Sampson has presented in national and state contexts on School Counselor Advocacy in Counselor Education and Supervision, School Counselors as Change Agents, Gaining Professional School Counseling Competencies through Supervision, The Screening, Brief Intervention, and Referral to Treatment.

Nancy Lewin is sr. director at ACT's Center for Equity in Learning. She was a former nonprofit executive director at The Association of Latino Administrators and Superintendents in Washington, DC. Her experience in k-12 education includes roles as bilingual teacher, school administrator, school district special education director, and the chief academic officer. She earned her undergraduate degree at Texas Southern University, a master's degree from the University of Houston-Victoria, and a doctoral degree in professional leadership at the University of Houston.

Paul Rogers is an associate professor of Writing Studies at the University of California, Santa Barbara. He is a cofounder and the immediate past chair of the International Society for the Advancement of Writing Research and a coeditor of seven edited collections of research. His research publications include articles and chapters on longitudinal writing research, writing development, and writing for social change. He has spent more than ten years working as a strategic advisor and change leader with Ashoka: Innovators for the Public.

CHAPTER 14

Viviana Alexandrowicz holds a PhD from the Claremont Graduate School/SDSU Joint Doctoral, MA from San Diego State University, and a bachelor's degree from the Universidad Católica de Chile.

About the Editors

Viviana Alexandrowicz, PhD, is an associate professor in the Department of Learning and Teaching and executive director of the Changemaking Center for K-12 Education at the University of San Diego which serves teachers across the globe by providing resources and professional activities. She is also the coordinator for the TESOL Master's Program which she created in 2003 and directs the K-6 Bilingual Authorization for the teaching credential and Master's Programs. Her areas of expertise and scholarship focus on the effectiveness of pre-service bilingual teacher education, theory and methodology for teaching English as a second language, language and academic language development, and changemaking. Professor Alexandrowicz has been involved in community service learning and engagement for over twenty years, mentoring faculty and guiding students in service and was nominated for the prestigious Tomas Ehrlich Civically Engaged Faculty Award. Over the years, Dr. Alexandrowicz has delivered a variety of workshops for immigrant Latino and Vietnamese families in communities in San Diego and has presented at over sixty professional conferences globally and has been a speaker at Dean meetings on the process and frameworks of transforming teacher preparation programs into changemaker teacher education. She has served on the board of directors for several organizations including Bayside Community Center and Doors of Change, a nonprofit that serves homeless youth in California , the United States. She is the cofounder of the Open University initiative that provided immigrant community members with free access to university courses. Dr. Alexandrowicz is a Global Change Leader for Ashoka U. Viviana's favorite activities are spending time with her husband and two sons, skiing, snorkeling, and traveling.

Paul Rogers is an associate professor of Writing Studies at the University of California, Santa Barbara, where he also earned his PhD in education (2008). He served as a senior scholar for the George Mason University, Center for the Advancement of Well-Being, and as the director of the Northern Virginia Writing Project. He is the cofounder and immediate past chair of the International Society for the Advancement of Writing Research. As an associate professor of English at George Mason University, Paul helped launch the Mason Center for Social Entrepreneurship where he served as academic director and developed an interdisciplinary masters degree in Social Innovation and Entrepreneurship. Paul also served as a strategic advisor to Ashoka: Innovators for the Public on their work in advancing the vision of Everyone a Changemaker. Paul's primary focus is on educational research and advancing transformation in policy and practice related to writing and literacy through data-informed decision making at all levels. He is a recipient of AAC&U's K, Patricia Cross Award for leadership in higher education, and NCTE's Janet Emig Award for research in English education. He is the editor of six coedited volumes and numerous other publications. His favorite activities are spending time with his family (the Seven Hearts Tribe), surfing, running, hiking, and reading.